D0811336

The British Labour Movement and Film, 1918–1939

Cinema and Society

General Editor

Jeffrey Richards
Department of History
University of Lancaster

The British Labour Movement and Film, 1918–1939

Stephen G. Jones

Routledge & Kegan Paul

London and New York

First published in 1987 by
Routledge & Kegan Paul Ltd
11 New Fetter Lane, London EC4P 4EE

Published in the USA by
Routledge & Kegan Paul Inc.
in association with Methuen Inc.
29 West 35th Street, New York, NY 10001

Set in Century 9/12pt.
by Columns of Reading
and printed in Great Britain
by T.J. Press (Padstow) Ltd
Padstow, Cornwall

Library of Congress Cataloging in Publication Data

Jones, Stephen G.
  The British Labour movement and film (1918–1939)

(Cinema and society)
Bibliography: p.
Includes index.
1. Socialism and motion pictures – Great Britain –
History.   2. Labour Party (Great Britain) – History.
3. Moving-pictures – Great Britain – History.   I. Title.
II. Series.
HX550.M65J65   1987   384'.8'0941   87–20497

British Library CIP Data also available
ISBN 0-7102-0973 8

For my grandmother,
Mrs Sarah Keegan

Contents

Illustrations

General Editor's Preface

The pre-eminent popular art form of the first half of the twentieth century has been the cinema. Both in Europe and America from the turn of the century to the 1950s cinema-going has been a regular habit and film-making a major industry. The cinema combined all the other art forms – painting, sculpture, music, the word, the dance – and added a new dimension – an illusion of life. Living, breathing people enacted dramas before the gaze of the audience and not, as in the theatre, bounded by the stage, but with the world as their backdrop. Success at the box office was to be obtained by giving the people something to which they could relate and which therefore reflected themselves. Like the other popular art forms, the cinema has much to tell us about people and their beliefs, their assumptions and their attitudes, their hopes and fears and dreams.

This series of books will examine the connection between films and the societies which produced them. Film as straight historical evidence; film as an unconscious reflection of national preoccupations; film as escapist entertainment; film as a weapon of propaganda – these are the aspects of the question that will concern us. We shall seek to examine and delineate individual film *genres*, the cinematic images of particular nations and the work of key directors who have mirrored national concerns and ideals. For we believe that the rich and multifarious products of the cinema constitute a still largely untapped source of knowledge about the ways in which our world and the people in it have changed since the first flickering images were projected on to the silver screen.

Jeffrey Richards

Acknowledgments

Acknowledgment is first of all due to those who allowed me to use illustrations: Miss M.E. Murphy: no. 4; Mr Jack Cosgrove: no. 12; Mr Arthur Donbavand: nos 13, 15–16; Mrs Dickinson: no. 14; Mrs Neatha Bottomley: no. 17; Mr Albert Findlow: no. 18; Mr Peter Higginbottom: nos 20–21; Mr Kenneth Sharp: no. 22; and Mr Reg Cordwell: no. 23. Illustrations 1–3, 6–11 and 24–32 appear by courtesy of the Stills Division of the National Film Archive. I have tried to trace the copyright owners of the remaining illustrations, but without success.

This study grew out of a wider project on the economic and social history of inter-war leisure. As such it is meant to supplement my more general and introductory book, *Workers At Play: A Social and Economic History of Leisure, 1918–1939* (Routledge & Kegan Paul, 1986). I have benefited from the help of many colleagues, friends and archivists. In particular, two colleagues at Manchester Polytechnic, Nev Kirk and Terry Wyke, read various chapters at a time when they were involved in their own writing and work, not least preparing for new arrivals to their respective families. Maryann Gomes and Marion Hewitt of the North West Film Archive, and Markku Salmi of the National Film Archive helped with photographs. I am also very grateful to Mike Rose, Tony Mason, A.E. Musson, Bert Hogenkamp and Ruth and Edmund Frow. Most of all, I would like to thank Jeffrey Richards for welcoming my initial proposal and for responding to my drafts with the greatest of speed and attention. Finally, Kathryn, Sam and Ben Jones have once again provided much needed support. Needless to say, I am responsible for any remaining errors of fact or interpretation.

Hyde, July 1986

Introduction

There can be few doubts that Labour history is now an important strand in the historical sciences. From its beginnings as an academic discipline taught in institutions of higher education, Labour history has expanded to cover a range of themes and debates. It is true that Labour historians have by and large focused on political and industrial struggles and the main areas of debate in the historiography have tended to reflect this. Yet, recent historical work has shown that the British Labour movement, encompassing the main Socialist parties, trade unions and co-operative societies, has a cultural as well as a political and industrial tradition. Fascinating accounts have appeared on the wider influences of work, community, and leisure. More specifically, it is now clear that there is more to the Labour movement than political and trade union organization – a balanced study would also have to consider cultural organization. Indeed, under the influence of the Marxist writer, Antonio Gramsci (1891–1937), scholars have started to examine the question of Socialist and working-class culture. As a result we now have important accounts of, for instance, Chartist cultural formation, and, as far as the twentieth century is concerned, contributions have appeared on the workers' sport, theatre and film movements.[1] It is the aim of this study to focus on the last of these, the workers' film movement, and to assess the wider Socialist approach to film in inter-war Britain.

The recently published work of Bert Hogenkamp and Trevor Ryan has shown that British Labour spawned a vibrant cinema movement in the 1920s and 1930s, which was involved in the production, distribution and exhibition of films.[2] The main aim of Labour activists concerned with film was of course political, to change the social and economic system. But it should be emphasized at the outset that because the film medium had recreational and aesthetic qualities, entertainment, pleasure and critical comment were always important concerns. Moreover, the Labour movement was dealing with one of the most important working-class leisure activities of the inter-war years. Consequently any study of organized Labour and film has to consider the nature of the relationship between Socialist culture – which workers' film was a part of – and working-class culture.

It is therefore imperative to distinguish between Socialist and working-class culture. Here we will draw upon Raymond Williams' conceptualization of oppositional and alternative forms of culture, between a culture which is different from the dominant society and aims to change that society, and a culture which is also different but wishes to be left alone to defend and improve its position within the given society.[3] Socialist or oppositional culture arises out of the struggles, concerns, ideas and institutions of the organized Socialist and Labour movement. Before the Second World War the Labour movement had a diversified network of theatre groups, sports clubs, social centres, temperance associations, a travel organization and many other groups reaching out into every conceivable leisure activity from chess to radio and film. Raymond Williams, in pressing the need for 'an autonomous politics of information, education and culture' provides a good overview:

> it was formerly recognised part of the business of the movement to build educational and cultural organisations, as necessary elements of the aspirations of working people. From adult classes to theatre groups, and from labour colleges to newspapers, magazines and bookclubs, these parts of the movement were seen as integral to its success.[4]

In essence inter-war Socialist culture was oppositional, in as much as it opposed the structures and organs of the dominant society. For Gramsci, Socialist culture was consciously mediated 'through a critique of capitalist civilization'.[5] More recently, two historians, in stressing the importance of cultural organization in working-class politics, have protested that if by Socialist culture 'we understand those ways in which the working class actively and consciously seeks to shape its own social activity as a class and, by so doing, differentiates itself from the values and principles underpinning the culture of the dominant class, then we arrive at a conception to which the notion of "explicit resistance", ie opposition to the dominant culture is fundamental'.[6] In this sense, then, the workers' film movement of the inter-war years was an integral aspect of Socialist culture, for it sought to challenge Capitalist culture and ideology. It should be stressed, however, that Socialist culture was neither uniform nor a continuous form of opposition. As the next chapter will show, there were contrasts between the Marxist and Labour Socialist cultural traditions.

For the most part working-class culture was not, and is not, oppositional. This does not mean, however, that working-class culture reflects the ideology of the ruling elite, for it is essentially an alternative. At root, the culture of the British working class has been shaped by the conditions of existence at work, particularly the wage nexus. It may well be the case that the working class has been 'docile', failing to challenge in any direct political way industrial Capitalism and the wage form. However, British working-class culture evolved as a form of protection and insulation from, and a means of advance in, an exploitative economic and social system.

One of the most durable features of an emerging and evolving factory proletariat has been its remarkable 'apartness' from other social classes. Out of the first industrial revolution came a class which was tough and resilient, with a 'collective self-consciousness' separate and distinct from the dominant society. There can be few doubts that the proletariat was, and is, a class in and for itself, having generated its own ideas, institutions and culture. Following on from E.P. Thompson, it has to be remembered, of course, that class is a process, not a thing but a happening. Accepting that class relationships and attitudes change over time, by the 1920s class consciousness permeated day-to-day existence in so many forms – at work and at leisure, and in dress, accent, manners, behaviour, attitudes, and in a profound sense of 'us and them'.

The inter-war culture of the people, with its roots in the workplace, the home and the local community was 'staunchly impervious' to bourgeois attempts at control. Despite changes in the wider political economy such as the increasing routinization of the work process and the spread of commercialized leisure, ruling groups found it difficult to penetrate or manipulate the cultural sphere of the working class. This was surely due to the inward-looking nature of proletarian culture. True, workers' institutions tended to be conservative rather than subversive, but they did act as a means of cultural and ideological defence. The institutional organs of the working class such as working men's clubs, neighbourhood sharing schemes and other systems of mutual aid were a sign of autonomy in the cultural sphere, but working-class culture was more than that. It was also about shared traditions and collective perceptions of the world. To understand the texture and feel of the workers' way of life, we have to penetrate attitudes, as well as the economic, political and cultural structures of society. Indeed, according to Williams, working-class culture is 'the basic collectivist idea and the institutions, manners, habits of thought and intentions which proceed from this'. He goes on to claim that working-class culture is a 'collective democratic institution', a creative achievement which bourgeois culture, with its 'basic individualist idea', would do well to follow.[7] We are therefore left with a rich and variegated picture of inter-war working-class culture which looks to ideas, as well as way of life, institutions and the determining influences of economic and social relations.

It has to be added that there has never been a homogeneous working-class culture. In the first place, there are real divisions within the working class on occupational lines. From the early nineteenth century, the working class has been stratified with a distinctive hierarchy based on skill and status. It is only right and proper to acknowledge that the culture of craft workers may be different to that of labourers, the culture of clerks different to that of shop assistants. Likewise, regional divisions have meant that in different parts of the country the working class has developed with its own traditions, forms of work and leisure, modes of behaviour and, most conspicuous of all, accents. Obviously a more detailed discussion would have to turn to the peculiarities and idiosyncrasies of Cornish tin miners, Norfolk agricultural labourers, Welsh quarrymen, Lancashire cotton operatives, Clydeside shipbuilding workers, and the rest. There may be a number of other differences, but none can be more profound than ethnicity, gender or age. Though the details cannot be entered into here, it has to be stressed that in the inter-war years there were important distinctions between, say, Jewish, Irish and English workers. Similarly, it is a rather obvious point that the female sphere was, to say the least, distinguishable from male-dominated culture, whilst it is possible that the period saw the emergence of a youth culture with its own concerns, interests, mores and conventions, set apart from the adult world. Such fragmentation within the working class manifested itself in a variety of ways, though the historian cannot get away from the fact that it was an element in the reproduction of chauvinism and cultural conservatism. The way ideology was received by the working class has to be linked to the broader division of life-experience engendered by work, the sexual separation of labour, race, region and nationality.

Notwithstanding all of this, it was still the case that the biggest divisions were between classes rather than within them. Ruling and subordinate classes faced each other with separate interests and identities. Proletarian culture and ideology as mediated at work, in the home or in leisure were in essential respects alternatives to the dominant society. To express it another way, workers have been able to resist Capitalist ideological impositions, and indeed reshape messages from above by all manner of means to conform with their own class needs and priorities. Thus bourgeois values such as diligence, thrift and respectability were reformulated by sections of the working class as necessary safeguards against low wages, unemployment and poverty. However, inter-war working-class culture was not the same as Socialist or oppositional culture, in that it did not seek to overthrow Capitalism with a new economic and social order.

Writing as a historian and not as a sociologist or social theorist, it is apparent that there are problems of semantic interpretation in all of this. For instance, using Raymond Williams' terms it is possible to designate the culture of the Socialist movement as oppositional, the culture of everyday working-class life as alternative. Yet, there was a thin divide between oppositional and alternative cultures. There was certainly no such thing as a closed working-class culture. Socialist (and Capitalist) ideas and precepts could, and did, penetrate those sections of the working class without a formal commitment to the Socialist movement. Eric Hobsbawm has even noted that 'the world and culture of the working classes is incomprehensible without the labour movement, which for long periods was its core'.[8] None the less, in trying to be historically specific, there was an important, albeit a tenuous, dividing line in the inter-war period between the subculture of the organized Socialist and Labour movement, and the culture of everyday life not encompassed within that movement.

The problem as it emerges is to provide some kind of link between Socialist culture and the wider working-class experience. There is a need to examine the tensions and contradictions between the aims of Socialists and the realities of day-to-day life. In the case of German Labour history Richard Evans has stressed that there is a need to constitute 'the *working class* and its culture and values as objects of historical study, and of investigating the relationship between these and the institutions, culture and values of the *labour movement*'.[9] This is no less a pressing concern for British Labour history. In more specific terms, in order to understand the Socialist approach to film in inter-war Britain, it is necessary to investigate the Socialist movement's relationship with the cinema-going public and the wider developments in the political economy. This introductory chapter will therefore provide an overview of the main inter-war trends in the economy and society, and investigate the cultural, ideological and political aspects of the new film medium.

The British economy and society

The traditional picture of inter-war Britain is one of economic depression, mass unemployment, the rise of Fascism, and general gloom and pessimism. Britain has been viewed as being in the 'doldrums' and the 1930s in particular regarded as the 'devil's decade'. The story is a familiar one, stressing as it does regional economic and social disparities. The industrial base of the British economy experienced all manner of economic and financial problems, as the staple industries of coal, iron and steel, shipbuilding, and textiles contracted. No doubt these problems were linked to the disruption caused by the First World War, the decline of overseas markets, the overvaluation of sterling when the Gold Standard was restored in 1925, the government's orthodox deflationary policies, and the general lack of competitiveness due to technological backwardness, entrepreneurial conservatism and poor industrial relations. In any case, as the basic industries declined, whole communities in the Welsh mining valleys, the Lancashire cotton districts and the Scottish and North-East ports were devastated. Unemployment was very high, often over 50 per cent of the insured work force in some towns during the cyclical troughs, and poverty and deprivation commonplace. There were, however, compensations. In the south of England and the Midlands newer industries such as vehicle manufacture, electrical engineering, chemicals and even motion pictures expanded, bringing employment opportunities and the hope of a new start. In fact some unemployed coal miners left the Rhondda Valley to find work in Morris Motors, Oxford. Given this structural transformation and expansion in certain industrial sectors, some historians have advanced a more optimistic interpretation of the period, stressing economic growth. According to K.S. Lomax industrial growth in Britain was occurring at the rate of 3.1 per cent per annum over the years 1920 to 1937. The most far-reaching claims, however, have been made by Derek Aldcroft who sees the inter-war years as a dynamic time in British economic history, a time of much needed adjustment and adaptation to the new trading realities of the world economy.[10]

At the time of writing there are both pessimistic and optimistic interpretations of the British inter-war experience. Whilst the optimists believe that the inter-war growth record was good and the market mechanism efficient, the pessimists feel that on both counts there was failure.[11] A revisionist school of thought led by Chris Cook and John Stevenson also points to the social reforms of the period, the increased standard of living and even the 'dawn of affluence'. Though accepting that in some communities unemployment was high and poverty a fact of life, the revisionists point to the rise in real wages, the increasing use of consumer durables, better housing and health care, greater opportunities for amusement and so on. By the end of the 1930s, Cook and Stevenson insist that:

> Britain was on average better paid, better fed, better clothed and housed, and healthier than it had been in 1918. . . . Indeed, after 1933 when Britain moved out of the trough of the depression, British society began to display some of the characteristics of affluence which are more commonly associated with the 1950s and 1960s.[12]

There is some truth in this, but as a number of Socialist historians have countered, the social improvements had their class boundaries. Living standards have to be considered as a whole, meaning that historians have to explore not only rather bland figures of real wages and conspicuous consumption, but also class inequality, gender, access to housing and health schemes, political rights and, perhaps most important of all, the work experience. Simply having a job and even a higher wage did not necessarily ensure an improvement in the quality of life, particularly if this involved moving from one part of the country to another, leaving behind cultural traditions, or working under conditions where there was little scope for skill and independence, and where trade union organization was difficult.[13] After all, as a number of studies have revealed, the jobs created by the new industries required little craftsmanship or skill, and once mastered were extremely tedious.[14] Certainly this area of analysis is problematic. How, for instance, can one measure the social costs of unemployment against the social benefits of higher real wages? How can one compare improved material standards of living with less autonomy and greater monotony on the shop floor?

All of this may seem rather remote from the question of the Labour approach to film. However, the inter-war economy and the associated influences of wages, employment, the character of work and the quality of life had important implications for the development of film, and the way film was perceived by the working class. It is the history of the cinema and the working class to which we now turn.

The working class and film

Film-going was undoubtedly a deeply ingrained habit among the inter-war working class. In 1934, 80 per cent of cinema admissions were for seats not above one shilling, meaning that the market was mainly a working class one, a fact confirmed by a number of other surveys.[15] Most social histories of the period comment upon the almost addictive pull of the cinema. The data for British cinema attendance indicates that film was a central leisure occupation. In 1914, 364 million people were admitted to cinemas, rising to 903 million in 1934 and 1,027 million in 1940.[16] By the later 1930s admissions were running at 23 million each week. More detailed estimates for Liverpool show that in a given week 40 per cent of the population went to the cinema at least twice a week.[17] Following on from this there was an increase in the number of cinemas. E.H. Haywood found that there were 3,910 British cinemas in 1923 and by 1934 the number had grown to 4,305 containing 3,872,000 seats.[18] Yet, these figures disguise the fact that in the decade after 1923 there was a great deal of rebuilding and reconstruction of cinema sites: approximately 1,000 new cinemas were built between 1924–5 and 1931–2.[19] Although only two out of every seven cinemas in 1934 contained more than 1,000 seats, an important development had been the advent of super cinemas, and, with the coming of the talkies, the conversion of older cinemas to sound. It should be emphasized that these new plush cinemas were very different cultural artefacts than the smaller, less glamorous alternatives. By 1940 the number of cinemas had again increased to 4,671. The question still remains, however, why was the local picture house so popular?

In the first place, there were a number of favourable conditions operating on the demand side.[20] As already suggested, real wages increased and this freed resources for leisure consumption, though there were significant differentials according to job category, skill, gender, age, overtime and underemployment. At the same time, spare cash was released as the consumption of beer declined. In order to visit the cinema spare time was required, as well as spare cash. The unemployed and those workers on short-time had a surfeit of free time. But by the same token for those workers in full-time employment, the hours reductions of the immediate post-war period stimulated various leisure interests, including the cinema. In the cotton trade, for example, operatives benefited from an agreement of 1919 which reduced the basic working week from 55½ hours to 48 hours. Similar reductions were recorded in other industries. All in all, in 1919, 6.3 million workers experienced cuts in weekly hours totalling 40.7 million. Despite the fact that some groups of workers were unable to retain these reductions and increases were recorded – especially in 1926 – on the whole hours were further reduced, albeit marginally, down to 1938 when the average weekly hours in manufacturing were 46.3. Greater amounts of voluntary and involuntary spare time and cash therefore fed the picture-going craze. Yet this does not explain why films were more popular than other pastimes such as the theatre or the music hall.

The cinema was a cheap form of entertainment catering for working-class pockets, as well as tastes. At a time in 1931 when average weekly earnings for males were about 56 shillings and unemployment benefit was 17 shillings (plus dependents' allowances of 9 shillings and 2 shillings for each child), a cinema ticket of 6d or less was obtainable. As one investigation also discovered: 'There can be no doubt that in view of the extreme cheapness of the cinema, the pleasures of theatre-going are generally regarded by manual workers as too expensive.'[21] Many of the surveys of the period found that even the poorer sections of the community and the unemployed visited the local cinema: 'Social investigators found that whatever the theoretical components of their "poverty line", most families found the money to visit the cinema once or more each week.'[22] Evidence for textile Lancashire certainly confirms this. Despite the high levels of unemployment in Bolton, the number of cinemas increased from 18 in 1919 to 26 in 1939, and their doors were generally open afternoon (cheap rates for matinees of 3d to 4d) and evening, winter and summer.[23] As Leslie Halliwell has commented in his evocative book *Seats in all Parts*, the film *Lost Horizon* (Columbia, 1937) directed by the great Frank Capra, was embraced 'because half-employed people in a Lancashire mill-town had more need than most for a Shangri-la to turn to'.[24] Equally in other cotton towns the number of cinemas increased between 1919 and 1939; from 3 to 8 in Ashton-Under-Lyne, 3 to 15 in Blackburn, 5 to 17 in Burnley, 6 to 17 in Oldham, 8 to 21 in Preston, and most spectacular of all 4 to 25 in Stockport.[25] It is true, as Fenner Brockway ascertained in his travels, that money for the cinema often came out of the food, rent or rates budget of the unemployed, but out it came none the less.[26] The *Kine Weekly* even claimed that it was unemployment benefit which sustained cinema-going in Blackburn.[27] In the centre of the cotton districts, the marketing capital of Manchester had well over 100 cinemas in the 1930s, so it is hardly surprising that one study commented on the state of unfair competition in the leisure market:

> It is against this habit that Scouting and the other voluntary recreational organisations are competing, but the dice is loaded and the cinema is winning. When it is considered that the only means of combating the bright lights, blatant advertising and ever-changing attractions of the cinema are the inadequate and often remote recreational facilities which have developed in piecemeal fashion in the city, is it to be wondered at that the 'pictures' habit is growing?[28]

The main point is that the cinema was such a cheap diversion that all sections of society could afford a seat. It is interesting that the depressed cotton towns of 1934 thus had more cinemas per head of the population than the relatively more prosperous areas of London and the Midlands.[29] Perhaps this was because Lancashire folk had, in J.B. Priestley's phrase, 'a zest for pleasure, sheer gusto'.[30]

Studies of horse-racing and rugby union show that they had a strong link with the state of the economy.[31] Similarly, one survey carried out in Brighton, London, Reading and Sutton in the late 1930s discovered that people were most willing to give up cinema-going when times were hard.[32] Yet, as the foregoing discussion suggests, the experience of industrial Lancashire appears to have been different – patronage of the cinema may even have been counter-cyclical. The fact that unemployed youths of Cardiff, Glasgow and Liverpool also spent some of their enforced leisure at cinemas leads to a similar conclusion.[33] Surely, then, James Walvin is above all referring to the cinema when he claims that it is ironic that modern leisure 'should thrive and continue in the new, harsh conditions of the slumps of the 1920s and 1930s'.[34]

Employed and unemployed alike may have used the cinema as a means of escape from the privations of work, home and community. For those with a job, it may well have been the case that the cinema offered an essential retreat from the rigour and monotony of work. After all, the inter-war period witnessed the spread of scientific management and de-skilling on the one hand, and speed-up and greater work intensity on the other. In either case it can be argued that leisure provided the opportunity for creativity and expression, something now denied by a less autonomous and less independent working environment. As Keith Burgess has suggested, the phenomenon of withdrawal from the workplace 'was evident in an obsession with having "a good time", as the antithesis of work, that was strengthened by the reduction in working hours, the spread of night or shift-working, and the expansion of public entertainment during the inter-war period'.[35] Seebohm Rowntree in fact claimed that for little cost 'a factory worker oppressed by the monotony of his work, can be transplanted, as if on a magic carpet, into a completely new world; a world of romance or high adventure'.[36] Equally, in Barratt Brown's study of *The Machine and the Worker* he found that for some people films acted as an antidote to boredom at work.[37]

Yet the cinema was more than a simple antidote to changes in the mode of production. Cinemas also provided recreational and cultural spaces for women, especially important at a time when they were first benefiting from the vote and a new assertiveness at work and in the community. By the same token, proletarian youth were able to stake their claim on the new cultural products of the cinema. A wealth of material illustrates that the pictures were very popular with women and young people. In York, Rowntree discovered that about half of film audiences were youngsters, and that of the adults about 75 per cent were women.[38] Likewise, working-class children in Liverpool were likely to attend the cinema at least once a week, and married women were more frequent attenders than their husbands.[39] In a slightly different context, the London social survey of the mid-1930s contended that the influence of films was felt in women's fashion, whilst girls tended to imitate and admire the 'stars', principally through fan clubs.[40]

The pictures also provided an essential meeting place for courting couples. A visit to the cinema, as Eric Hobsbawm informs us, 'not only cost less and lasted longer than a drink or variety show, but could be – and was – more readily combined with the cheapest of all enjoyments, sex'.[41] The back row had its own sexual meaning, but equally important was the warmth, comfort, privacy and darkness of the cinema, together with the type of film billed. Interestingly, the love story and romance was the most popular film classification among Liverpool's adult population. In 1929–30, 45 per cent of the films exhibited were of this kind, compared to 22 per cent for thrillers, 11 per cent each for musicals and comedies and 7 per cent for Westerns.[42] On the other hand, youth tended to favour cartoons, comic, adventure, mystery, war and Western films.

By the 1930s, cinemas were arguably a pillar of the local community, as much a central social institution as the pub and the chapel, if not more so. Hobsbawm, in a memorable essay, has intimated that the cinema was an integral element in the enrichment of working-class culture. Cinemas and their products may sometimes have been cultural imports from the United States, but they were especially important in the context of inter-war British culture as 'palaces of temporary dreams in which to forget the years of depression and unemployment'.[43] The picture palace could never hide the privations of the economic and social system, though it did provide an opportunity to get away from the harsh realities of daily existence for a few hours a week.

In the last analysis, film-going was a common pastime which gave the working class shared interests and talking points. One prominent historian of film, Nicholas Pronay, has thus argued that the working class had a special relationship with the picture house, based on early conditioning, habitual attendance and, perhaps most important, communal participation.[44] It is difficult to gauge the attitudes and responses of proletarian audiences to silent movies, cheap 'quickies' or Hollywood epics. Even so, impressions of the past certainly imply that picture-going was a collective experience, an essential ingredient of that alternative working-class culture already alluded to.[45]

A trip to the cinema with friends and family often involved queuing and the purchase of 'Mally' toffee, and once inside a great deal of raucous activity went on from singing, whistling and shouting to the work of 'chuckerouts' and the spraying of perfumed disinfectant by the usherette. One aspect of this boisterousness was described by a member of the London Society of Compositors:

> In the picture theatres there is a system under which when all the seats are occupied additional people are put into a pen at the rear, and when one or more seats become vacant there is a rush from the pen to get the vacant seats, the men and women scrambling with each other to get there first.[46]

In the local dream palace or flea pit, workers laughed together, wept together, and were thrilled together. And after the film had ended there was always the possibility of a 'delicious supper' at the chip shop. Cinemas also provided the double advantage of serials and a healthy diet of new films, giving workers something to talk about and look forward to. Additionally, some cinemas were used for other forms of amusement: 'kine-variety' whereby live entertainment accompanied sound films, music, medium-sized dance halls, eating places; the Cinema House in Oxford even having a 'Gleneagles Tom Thumb Golf Course' in its basement.

It is therefore with considerable justification that the American historian, Stephen Shafer, draws attention to the collective nature of the cinema-going experience:

> Before the movies would begin, audience members took advantage of the opportunity to visit and meet with neighbours and friends under relaxed conditions; older people sometimes came early just so that they could chat with others. Along with the pubs, the cinema thus served as something of a community center, a place where all could go for amusement, and one of the few opportunities a working class family had for recreation together.[47]

He goes on to describe the attachment of workers to those cinemas with concessions for the unemployed or the aged, Saturday matinees, Christmas events, Mickey Mouse clubs and the like. Lastly here, many cinema managers had working-class origins and even banded together in a Cinema Managers' Association, formed under the auspices of the National

Federation of Professional Workers. During the coal stoppage of 1926, cinema managers at the Empire Hippodrome, the Pavilion and the Queens in Ashton-Under-Lyne thus permitted collections for miners' relief.[48]

Cinemas in working-class areas were therefore collective cultural institutions, bringing working people together and producing common identities and reference points. Even though it is difficult for historians to evaluate the sense of class identity which cinemas may have reinforced, their spatial segregation is suggestive of class distinctions. Broadly speaking, there was a hierarchy of picture houses catering for different income groups, the middle classes being attracted to the modern cinema with its higher admission price and standards of comfort and service. An examination of the *Kinematograph Year Book* shows that in Manchester in 1934 admission prices ranged from the 2½d charged at the Picturedrome in the poor district of Ancoats to the 3 shillings 6d charged at the Paramount Theatre with its attached cafe and Wurlitzer organ in the more salubrious surroundings of the city centre.[49] Certainly the super cinemas of the 1930s, with their numerous seats and glamorous decor, were built to satisfy the new spending power of the higher income groups. The same can be said for the well-appointed cinemas of the middle-class suburbs, the modernist Odeons being particularly good examples. Films were seen by all classes, yet there was still an intensity of class division. From a slightly different perspective, C. Delisle Burns commented that, although films were making 'for similarity of outlook and attitude among people of very different occupations, incomes or social classes. . . . This does not imply that they are making those who belong to different social classes more friendly.'[50] Clearly, this enmity was determined by inequality at work and in the wider civil and political society, though the fact that films were viewed in different cultural contexts was also influential.

There is a pressing need here for local studies of the spatial distribution of cinemas and their audiences. Yet, in conclusion it is interesting that even in the less class-constrained setting of the United States, one detailed study of leisure in Worcester, Massachussetts has shown that the cinema actually lessened divisions within the working class.[51] In Britain too, the cinema had such class dimensions. If working-class culture is basically about shared ideas, then surely the perceptions, events and experiences of film-going contributed to these ideas, precisely because they were an important part of a collective view of the world. Going to the pictures was a lived experience which provided contact within the working class and common means of sociability and understanding. At least in the 1920s and 1930s viewing films in working-class communities made little sense as an individualistic form of entertainment.

Business and State regulation

Cinema-going was an integral part of the making and re-making of working-class culture and the working-class cultural experience. In order to take the analysis one step further, there is a need to appreciate the supply of films by private enterprise and their regulation by the State. As this study will show, the Labour movement was concerned about the production, distribution and exhibition of the commercialized film product and in turn the intervention of the various apparatuses of the State. Even though workers' film was in many ways the antithesis of the commercialized product, organized Labour kept abreast of the salient developments in Hollywood and Wardour Street. Workers' film groups were critical of the commercial dream machine, as will be discussed in subsequent chapters, and sought to provide a product which was a form of opposition to the images of the silver screen.

The economics of the film industry between the wars have been well chronicled, first of all by the Communist writer, F.D. Klingender, and the documentary film-maker, Stuart Legg, in 1937.[52] This was followed by a Political and Economic Planning (PEP) study in the early 1950s, and more recently by the exhaustive and detailed work of Rachael Low.[53] Very briefly, after the Cinematograph Films Act of 1927, the British film industry began to expand. Although American influence was ubiquitous in all sections of the industry, particularly distribution, British finance capital began to support British exhibition and production. The City of London, in particular, working through a variety of financial institutions, most notably insurance firms like Eagle, Star and British Dominions Insurance, Equity and Law Life Assurance, and Prudential Assurance, held the main purse strings of the industry. The industry successfully adapted to the advent of the sound picture and the effects of rapid technical change in the late 1920s and early 1930s, though considerable losses were made on silent films. The first British talkies feature was *Blackmail* (British International Pictures, 1929), and by 1931, 3,537 cinemas had been wired for sound. This was followed by various experiments in colour productions, so that by the end of the 1930s Alexander Korda had made five and Herbert Wilcox two films in technicolour. Also, under the stimulus of low interest rates, the early part of the decade witnessed a considerable rebuilding programme as many new, often deluxe cinemas were constructed. At root, the presentation of film had been transformed with modern, well-equipped cinemas, the introduction of talkies and extension of programmes, often with two features, perhaps a cartoon, newsreel and trailers. Film was not the same commodity as seen before the Great War.

In the studios over the period 1925 to 1936 more than 640 film companies were registered, 395 of them between 1930 and 1935. No doubt production was encouraged by major successes like Korda's *Private Life of Henry VIII* (London Film Productions, 1933), for which Charles Laughton as the King won an Oscar. Certainly some major British films were produced in this period at such studios as Denham, Ealing and Pinewood. Another notable example is Michael Balcon's superb *The Thirty-Nine Steps* (Gaumont-British, 1935), directed by Alfred Hitchcock and starring two of the most popular British actors, Robert Donat and Madeleine Carroll. *The Economist* noted that this received critical acclaim and outstanding success, having completed a record run of five continuous months' business in London's West End, and an equally enthusiastic reception in New York.[54] Notwithstanding the sparkling ambiance of the Hollywood star system, the 1930s saw the rise of the British film star – not only Donat and Carroll, but also Jack Buchanan, Gracie Fields, George Formby, Jack Hulbert, Jessie Matthews and the rest.

By the mid-1930s increased profits were being recorded by the main film concerns. The profits of the Gaumont British Picture Corporation (GBPC) rose from £462,612 in 1933 to £692,214 in 1934 and £720,483 in 1935.[55] In the same years the profits of the Associated British Picture Corporation (ABPC) grew from £138,395 to £156,967 and £656,725.[56] Prosperity continued until 1937; studios were opened or extended, more British films produced and, as suggested, new cinemas built. All in all, the industry had experienced considerable growth and investment, and despite set-backs can be viewed as one of the expanding areas and modernizing influences of the inter-war economy. At this point, however, there is a need for one or two caveats.

Arguably, financial support for films made little long-run economic sense, being principally a way for US companies to satisfy their quota requirements and a form of short-term speculative investment. *The Economist* claimed that film production had 'been too undependable [sic], and its financial excesses too notorious, to provide any regular basis for long-term investment'.[57] The main problem was the method of finance. Rather than seeking an increase in working capital, film companies financed their ideas through bank overdrafts, capital from the film renters or short-term loans, often underwritten by insurance companies. This was a particularly risky way of raising money for it was clear that the industry faced a number of structural problems – overproduction as studios mushroomed, dependence on an increasingly closed US market and high costs. Even in 1935 one expert noted with some anguish the precarious state of British film shares and investment, quoting John Maxwell of ABPC that production was far from being a 'land flowing with easy money'.[58] Indeed, the problem was bad enough by 1937 for the Bank of England, working through the Securities Management Trust, to conduct an inquiry into the state of film finance. This inquiry came too late, however, to save the industry from collapse. The bubble burst in 1937, with a succession of losses and receiverships, best represented by the financial fiasco of Max Schach and the Aldgate Trustees. Also fascinating was the failure of Korda's magnificent Denham studios to live up to expectations, personified by the fate of Charles Laughton who is to be seen in the rushes of the unfinished *I Claudius* (1937) repeatedly fluffing his lines and falling apart in front of the camera. Moreover, the Moyne Committee complained that the methods of film finance had resulted in a poor investment record:

> The evidence given before us made it clear that the British film production industry has an insufficient supply of capital for its needs and that the cost of production of British films has been increased by the necessary money being obtainable only at a high rate of interest. The more prominent financial houses have, we understand, generally speaking been disinclined to come to its assistance. Lack of finance is a powerful factor in enabling foreign interests to obtain control and is certainly an impediment to the industry's continued and satisfactory expansion.[59]

Expansion there certainly was, but this was not without its problems and drawbacks.

From the late 1920s the financial and organizational basis of the industry led to an increasing concentration of economic power. As is well known, by the mid-1930s the vertically integrated company with interests in production, distribution and exhibition was well established. The three main concerns were GBPC, ABPC and Odeon Theatres. Their main interests were in exhibition, which they dominated through the acquisition of independent cinemas and chains, and the formation of huge circuits. By the autumn of 1936 the circuit strength of ABPC, GBPC and Odeon were 296, 305 and 142 cinemas respectively. They also had links with studios and renting companies. GBPC had interests in production through Gainsborough Pictures at Islington and Gaumont Pictures at Shepherd's Bush, extending into renting with Gaumont-British Distributors (which closed down in 1937) and finally into their extensive circuit, whilst ABPC had studios at Elstree under British International Pictures and Welwyn under British Instructional Films, the Wardour distribution network, and then again their own circuit. Likewise, by 1937 Odeon Cinema Holdings controlled a significant section of exhibition through the Odeon circuit, and had share holdings or cross-directorships in the US distribution company, United Artists, and in Korda's London Film Productions. Although Odeon did not have direct control over production – unlike GBPC and ABPC – they were able to secure a number of prestigious films for their cinemas. By the end of the 1930s, of course, the Rank Organization had emerged with a grip on all branches of the industry. Additionally, even the newsreel business was monopolized by five giants, Gaumont British News, Pathé Gazette, British Movietone, Paramount News and Universal News, all of which were associated with large British and American film corporations. In brief, the British film industry was more or less a form of oligopoly.

Given the economic and indeed political aspects of film, it is hardly surprising that the British State took an interest. After all, the State provides the necessary political and legal framework in which Capitalist industry can function efficiently. To be historically specific, as the Moyne Committee commented in 1936, 'The active interest of His Majesty's Government in the promotion of an increased supply of British films dates back to the middle of 1925, although prior to that date the Government had kept in close touch with the position of the film industry.'[60] In fact the first positive sign of government intervention dates back to the Cinematograph Films Act of 1909. Ostensibly, this piece of legislation dealt with safety regulations in cinemas and exhibition halls. Its aim was to provide local authorities with the right to implement measures to prevent cinema fires. Yet, it soon became apparent that the local State would also have the right to control film content through censorship. In order to forestall the precedent of State censorship the Liberal administration of 1912 sanctioned the creation of a trade body, the British Board of Film Censors (BBFC). The purpose of the Board was to recommend to local authorities whether a film should receive a licence for exhibition. As chapter four will show, the Board was to play a crucial role in the development of film in the inter-war years, directly impinging on the approach of organized Labour.

The most important piece of film legislation was the 1927 Cinematograph Films Act, passed to revive a failing British film industry. Broadly speaking, though Anthony Aldgate has questioned the extent of Hollywood colonization of the British cinema,[61] the British market had been penetrated by American films and film interests during the 1920s. As George Perry has observed: 'By 1926 the amount of screen time devoted to British films had dwindled to a mere five per cent.'[62] By the end of the decade the American film industry, comprising such giants as Paramount, Warner Brothers, and the Fox Film Corporation, was the fourth largest in the US. This provided a launching pad for a concerted attack on the British film market. Although few American companies had direct control over British cinemas, they were able to exert unfair influence over exhibition through their dominance in production and distribution. In the first place it must be stated that the poor quality of many indigenous films did not exactly aid the British case. Yet more significantly, because US companies were able to cover costs and make profits in their own market, they were able to penetrate overseas markets by selling their products more cheaply. Though this was not a form of dumping, it clearly was unfair competition. By the same token, US renters used block, advanced and blind booking. In essence, these discriminatory booking practices meant that if British cinemas were to capture a successful American film they often had to accept a block of other films in advance and even without viewing them or knowing their content. The 1927 Act therefore sought to stimulate British production by controlling booking practices, and most important of all by introducing quotas for British films of 7½ per cent for renters and 5 per cent for exhibitors both rising to 20 per cent by 1936. The Act was fairly successful, being extended for another ten years in 1938, albeit with certain modifications. Significantly, however, the Hollywood dream merchants did not disappear.

US interests such as Western Electric and RCA sold sound systems to British cinemas, whilst US distribution outlets remained dominant in the 1930s. More important still, Americans were able to circumvent the quota arrangement by controlling or sponsoring British production in studios turning out films of poor quality known as 'quota quickies' or 'pound-a-footers'. Fox and Warners, for instance, had varying degrees of control in studios at Wembley and Teddington, as did Paramount at Elstree. Also, there is evidence that American companies were even able to gain hold of some British cinemas. Geoffrey Mander, the Liberal MP for Wolverhampton and deeply embroiled in the films' question, made the following protest at a meeting of the Board of Trade Supply Committee in 1930:

> To show the Committee how far-reaching is the influence of the Americans on the film industry in this country, I would point out that they control, directly or indirectly, cinemas in the West End of London: the Tivoli, the New Gallery, the Marble Arch Pavilion, the Plaza, Carlton, Empire, Capitol and the Rialto. It is astonishing to find that all the principal cinemas in London are, directly or indirectly under American control, and the Americans are using all the power which they possess through this limited quota of deliberately getting British film a bad name.[63]

One Conservative MP therefore asserted in 1931 that ten US film-producing concerns remitted between £7 million and £8 million to the US each year.[64] It is also noteworthy that, taking into account the rise of a handful of British stars, it was still Hollywood performers – Astaire and Rogers, Gable, Cagney, Garbo, and Laurel and Hardy – who captured the public's imagination. There were other pieces of legislation in the 1930s dealing with film, notably the Sunday Entertainments Act of 1932 as will be discussed, yet it was protection which survived as the main policy approach of inter-war governments to the new medium.

Film and politics

By the early 1920s governments, policy-makers, political parties and pressure groups showed an awareness of the propaganda value of film. Throughout the inter-war years film was used by a range of interests at all levels. At the highest level, governments had first begun to appreciate the political advantages to be derived from the mass media during the First World War. By 1915 film had been recruited as a medium of propaganda, the War Office eventually forming a kinematograph committee from which Lloyd George invited Hall Caine to prepare a film for the National War Aims movement. Official propagandists sought to mobilize the nation's resources in support of the war effort and to win the hearts of domestic and international interests. For the rest of the inter-war period, film was utilized by official bodies like the Empire Marketing Board (EMB) to portray Britain as a fair and just society.[65]

The EMB was set up in 1926 and used film as a form of public relations, helping to sell images of Britain to the world. More practically, the Board under its secretary, Stephen Tallents, sought to stimulate overseas trade and sell Empire produce in Britain. As is well known, a leading light was John Grierson, the father and pioneer of the British non-fiction film, who coined the phrase 'documentary', when reviewing Robert Flaherty's *Moana* in 1926. The EMB's first production was *Drifters*, directed by Grierson in 1929. It was followed by a number of other films such as Arthur Elton's *Upstream* on salmon fishing in Scotland, Basil Wright's *Country Comes to Town* about London's market services, and the most impressive of all, Flaherty's *Industrial Britain*. Despite the fact that the EMB's film unit grew from two people at the very beginning of the 1930s to over 30 by mid-1933, no more than 2½ per cent of the Board's total budget was sanctioned for film in any one year. Indeed, due to the National government's economy campaign and desire for a balanced budget, the EMB was disbanded in 1933. Even so, the gap was filled by the newly created Central Post Office film unit and then General Post Office film unit; Tallents and Grierson again playing leading roles. Furthermore, as the Post Office film unit expanded, it stimulated the rise of the Strand, Realist and Shell film units.

At a different level, private companies such as Austin Motors, Cadbury's Chocolate and the London, Midland and Scottish Railway sponsored a variety of publicity and advertising films.[66] In the cotton industry, the Oldham Master Cotton Spinners' Association produced a film of spinning to be exhibited throughout the world, whilst the Belper branch of the English Sewing Cotton Company had talking pictures entertainment which included the advertising films of Wills' Tobacco, described as 'a success'. By the same token, there was a thriving independent documentary movement in the 1930s, helping to create 'a wholly new film form and established Britain's most permanent contribution to the development of world cinema'.[67] All in all, the main documentary film units in England produced about 300 films between 1928 and 1939.[68] In the context of this study, the documentary movement is an important theme, for it had such a potent influence on Labour's approach to film.

Political parties also used film as part of their political and electoral strategies. The work of Timothy Hollins has shown that the Conservative party appreciated the possibilities of film propaganda.[69] A cinema van toured parts of the country exhibiting films of the Empire or British industry, followed by short speeches on imperial or domestic subjects. In September 1924, for example, this novel form of electioneering was applied in a tour of Devon, and two years later in a tour of the Midlands.[70] By April 1926, *The Times* reported 'that the Conservative Party are now making use of the cinematograph regularly in propaganda work'.[71] As Joseph Ball of the Conservative Central Office explained: 'The enormous increase in the popularity of cinemas particularly among the working classes, pointed the way early in 1927 to the cinema film as a method of placing our propaganda before the electorate.'[72] The resources of the independent Conservative and Unionist Film Association, as the film section of the party became, had been extended by the early 1930s to include ten large cinema vans and a collection of silent and sound films.[73] Local reports also confirm that the Conservative cinema played a role in constituency politics, as was the case in Stalybridge in 1934 when 'just as the open-air market was closing down . . . a crowd of three or four hundred people attended to witness the "talkies" describing the work of the National Government'.[74] Also worthy of note is the fact that Alexander Korda had fairly close links with the Conservatives.

Film also fitted into the political culture of the British Union of Fascists. Reading through the *Blackshirt* for the years 1933–4 it is apparent that Oswald Mosley's party was catering for the recreational and cultural interests of its members. Along with sports, socials and community singing, Fascist films were presented. The first BUF film was shown at the national headquarters in May 1934 as a pictorial record of Fascist activities, including clips of a meeting at the Albert Hall and the work of the Milan branches.[75] Evidently, Fascist films were part of a wider 'kitsch kulture' aimed at healthy recreation, physical fitness and intellectual activity.[76] If the right of the political spectrum used film, then this was no less true of the left. As this study demonstrates, the British Labour movement was equally receptive to the importance of the cinema and film.

Film and ideology

There can be few doubts that film was, and is, a highly political medium. Karl Marx and Frederick Engels once said that 'The ruling ideas of each age have been the ideas of its ruling class.'[77] From a Marxist perspective, therefore, it may be thought that film in Capitalist society carries the ideological message of the ruling class to the masses. In other words, film can be regarded as a form of ideological conditioning, a way of forging class harmony and gaining acceptance for the status quo and the economic, social and political institutions of Capitalism. Certainly, those scholars interested in film have been influenced by the thought of the French Marxist philosopher Louis Althusser, and the Italian Marxist Antonio Gramsci.

According to Althusser, the Capitalist State gains consent and reproduces the relations of Capitalist production through repressive and ideological means. The 'repressive state apparatus', which is essentially coercive, exercises its power through the legal system, the police and the army. On the other hand, the 'ideological state apparatus' operates through the ideological work of a number of institutions – the arts, education, the family, literature, the mass media, religion, sport, the trade unions and so on. Film and the cinema are an integral part of all this, designed to teach the masses the contrasting virtues of 'modesty, resignation, submissiveness on the one hand, cynicism, contempt, arrogance, confidence, self-importance, even smooth talk and cunning on the other'. Whereas the repressive instruments have little independence from the State, the ideological instruments are said to be relatively autonomous. In Althusserian Marxism, film production and presentation have a degree of autonomy, yet in the final analysis the product is an agent of the system which supposedly functions to reproduce the values, ideas and economic power of the dominant class.[78]

For Gramsci, Capitalism is maintained on the ideological level, again in a relatively autonomous way, through hegemony. The notion of hegemony explains the way in which Capitalism is legitimized and made to appear 'natural'. Capitalist ideology, as mediated through the dominant or hegemonic culture of the family, schools, work and leisure saturates the consciousness of society. However, hegemony has the ability to adapt to external economic and social change and to accommodate alternative opinions and values. Essentially, hegemony is a historical process and is never finished or complete; hegemonic action shifts over time in line with economic and social conflict, the fluidity and interactive nature of society. As a result the subordinate class consents to the structures and indeed the contradictions of Capitalist society. Though the State still has to intervene in a repressive manner, cultural hegemony reduces the need for such intervention as the ruling ideas become the 'common sense' of the masses.[79] From this perspective, film can be viewed as a form of hegemony for it supposedly transmits certain beliefs and images of the world designed to generate agreement in the wider society. Interestingly, James Joll has asserted that this far-reaching Gramscian concept has been found useful by Marxists and non-Marxists alike: 'it is easier for the non-Marxist to conduct a dialogue with Gramsci than with any other Marxist writer of the twentieth century'.[80] Without entering into a critique of this Marxist tradition, this study will in fact be informed by the premise that inter-war working-class culture was fairly resistant to formal incorporation in the hegemonic culture or, for that matter, the ideological apparatuses of the State.

Recent historical contributions have focused on the ideological and cultural role of film and cinema. With one or two exceptions the broad view has been that the inter-war film industry gave rise to greater levels of confidence in the system. Jeffrey Richards has therefore claimed in his thoughtful account of cinema and British society in the 1930s that films supported the aims and objectives of the rulers. It is appropriate to quote his conclusion at some length:

> There can be little doubt that, although its influence for both good and ill was considerably overrated, the cinema in the 1930s played an important part in the maintenance of the hegemony of the ruling class. The film industry was run by men who desired to be seen as part of the Establishment themselves and who were anxious to maintain the continued goodwill of the government to ensure the legislative protection the industry needed in order to compete with the Americans. Even without these factors, film-makers operated under a detailed and strictly enforced code of censorship which aimed to eliminate anything inimical to the *status quo*. . . . The actual fims were used either to distract or to direct the audience's views into approved channels, by validating key institutions of hegemony, such as monarchy and Empire, the police and the Law, and the armed forces, and promoting those qualities useful to society as presently constituted: hard work, mono-gamy, cheerfulness, deference, patriotism.[81]

In a similar vein, Anthony Aldgate has pointed out that the cinema led to consensus, harmony and social integration: 'It reflected and reinforced the dominant consensus and sought to generate adherence to the idea that society should continue to remain stable and cohesive as it changed over time.'[82] Likewise, Nicholas Pronay suggests that censorship encouraged the working class 'to take joy and pride in the institutions, historic and "fair" of their country', and to believe in the 'harmony and hope of better days, arising from the innate strength and justice of the system in which they lived'; and finally, Stephen Shafer has concluded that 'the content of the British cinema in its portrayal of the class structure can be seen as a medium for maintaining the status quo'.[83] There is much validity in these statements. After all, censorship and the preferences of big business ensured that very few British films challenged the system.

It is necessary, however, to make an analytical distinction between the purpose and function of film provision. A purposive analysis seeks to examine the reasons for provision, whilst functional analysis attempts to delineate the objective functions which film appears to fulfil in the wider way of life. Thus it may have been the case that among the motives of film-makers and Censors alike was one of strengthening dominant ideas and institutions. But it is another matter to say that the cinema actually fulfilled such motives and functioned as a means of ideological conditioning. In other words, we have to analyse both the purpose and function or effect of film in Capitalist society. There are three further detailed points to be made.

The first point is that the primary purpose of film was commercial and not ideological, that is to make a profit. From a strictly Marxist perspective, Capitalists invest in the film industry not to secure some kind of ideological effect, but rather to extract surplus value or profit. Furthermore, given the distinction in Marxist theory between exchange-value and use-value, it is not possible to predict that films function 'in the ideological interests of those who secure the economic benefit'.[84] Indeed, in analysing cultural agencies like the cinema, it is essential to consider the economic determinants framing production and presentation, and to locate film within its materialist base; there is a need to investigate the economic development of the industry – investment and the role played by finance capital, profit levels, technical change, monopolization, legislation, labour relations – as raised in this study.

To enter into particulars, for films to be a commercial success they had to be receptive to working-class tastes and demands. In fact, Jeffrey Richards and Anthony Aldgate in their book, *Best of British: Cinema and Society 1930–1970*, have claimed that one of the ways cinema operates is 'to reflect and highlight popular attitudes, ideas and preoccupations', adding that films have 'an organic relationship with the rest of popular culture'.[85] If films fail in this task then they are likely to flop, as many British films did in the 1930s. It was no mere coincidence that the British public responded more enthusiastically to Hollywood films, as Peter Stead has shown, for they often portrayed life in a more challenging light: 'At the very least one could say that Hollywood took its myths, its pace, its idioms from the nation as a whole and its actors were recognisably men and women who had come directly from the streets.'[86] The gangster movies of James Cagney were of this genre. It is true that some British films tended to reflect middle-class society and 'refined' culture, in which the characters with their 'posh' accents were little more than wooden stereotypes divorced from working-class culture. But, needless to say, this was less true of the comedies of Gracie Fields, George Formby, Will Hay and Arthur Lucan (Old Mother Riley), who all had their origins in the proletarian milieu of the music hall. It was they who often focused in a light-hearted manner on the day-to-day concerns, worries and preoccupations of the poorer sections of society. And it was they who were particularly popular with the industrial working class.

In fact, the accepted view that the British cinema in the 1930s failed to portray the working class has recently been questioned by Shafer. He shows quite convincingly that there was a 'prevalence of working class characters, environments, and situations in the movies being produced. . . . In spite of the generally held belief that British films avoided the working classes, a close examination of the content of British features during the decade shows that working class characters and situations appeared with considerable regularity in British movies.'[87] Between 1929 and 1939 the working class figured in roughly two out of every five films produced in Britain, and about one in three films were set in proletarian environments: factories, mines, shipyards, pubs or slums. Moreover as Shafer again claims, 'attempts were being made for more accurate depictions of the working people on every level of production from the performers to the studio executives'.[88] More likely than not this had something to do with the search for profit, as Elizabeth Coxhead acknowledged:

> Is the commercial film growing class-conscious? Is it beginning to take the social background into account? Is it veering, ever so slightly and tentatively, towards the left? One or two outstanding productions suggest that it is; and then, when one considers the vast majority of pretty-pretty films, quite without social roots, these few seem mere accidents, or at least stunts, desperate efforts by producers who don't really like handling fire, but are forced into a course so contrary to their own interests by the increasing difficulty of holding an audience's attention.[89]

Indeed, by the end of the 1930s social dramas like *The Edge of the World* (Joe Rock, 1937), *South Riding* (Victor Saville Productions – London Film Productions, 1938), *The Citadel* (MGM British Studios, 1938) and *The Stars Look Down* (Grafton, 1939) were being made.

True, the working class was often depicted in a rather stilted and unrealistic way, but to some extent audiences craved escapism, romance and comedy. One film-goer thus posed a rhetorical question in a letter to the *Film Pictorial* in July 1933:

> Why do we spend our pocket money and our leisure hours at the cinema?. . . . To see our ordinary everyday lives portrayed on the screen over and over again? Emphatically not! What we want is to be carried

right away from our own sphere of life – we see and hear enough about
that! – and be taken to realms which have hitherto existed only in our
imagination.[90]

Evidence culled from letters reproduced in 'fan' magazines seems to
suggest that this was a somewhat typical view, though as just commented
there also appears to have been a rising demand for more 'true-to-life'
films. Either way, film capital had to respond to such views and demands.
Certainly, the trade could spot the preferences of audiences by consulting
the polls held by film papers, the largest of which was *Picturegoer* with a
circulation of 100,000. Moreover, Sidney Bernstein's Granada cinemas
conducted surveys of their patrons' likes and dislikes. This is not to argue,
however, that there was no advertising. Most significantly, it was Oscar
Deutsch, a Birmingham scrap-metal dealer, who created a trade mark in
the cinema itself when he launched his Odeon circuit in 1933.

The second point is that some films carried messages which were in a
variety of ways antagonistic to the social order. In the scenario and
production departments, studios engaged a number of radical, even
Socialist, playwrights, authors and cultural luminaries: Walter Greenwood – that 'champion of the underdog' – wrote the screen stories for *The
Hope of His Side* (British and Dominion, 1935) and *No Limit* (Associated
Talking Pictures, 1935); Miles Malleson, who had been the guiding light
behind the Independent Labour Party's Arts Guild, wrote the scripts for a
number of films, including *Action for Slander* (London Film Productions,
1937), *The Blue Danube* (British and Dominion, 1932), *Money Means
Nothing* (British and Dominion – Paramount/British, 1932), *Nell Gwyn*
(British and Dominion, 1934) and others; Ivor Montagu, the Communist
aristocrat who played a leading role in the workers' film movement, was
associate producer on such Hitchcock films as *The Man Who Knew Too
Much* (Gaumont British, 1934), *Sabotage* (Gaumont British, 1936), and
Secret Agent (Gaumont British, 1936), as well as writing scripts for
productions like *King of the Ritz* (Gainsborough – British Lion, 1933); and
of course the works of George Bernard Shaw, J.B. Priestley and H.G. Wells
were the basis for a range of pictures. It is also noteworthy that the
Christian Scientist, John Baxter, directed a number of films like *Doss
House* (Sound City, 1933), *Flood Tide* (Real Art, 1934), *Lest We Forget*
(Sound City, 1934) and *A Real Bloke* (Baxter and Barter, 1935) which
depicted some of the realities of working-class life, the spectre of
unemployment, poverty and the like. And perhaps most fascinating of all,
the Marxist composer, Hanns Eisler and dramatist Bertold Brecht, were
involved in the making of Max Schach's musical, *Pagliacci* (Trafalgar Film
Productions, 1936), whilst the young Socialist MP, Aneurin Bevan, was
enlisted as a technical adviser on Parliamentary procedure by Michael
Balcon for the political thriller, *The Four Just Men* (Ealing Studios, 1939).

Thus there were spaces for creative decision-making in film production.

Interestingly, James Robertson has recently argued that by the end of the 1930s films depicting social strife were beginning to appear on the screen:

> although supine in its approach to British working class characteris-ation, Labour ideology and industrial relations prior to 1939, film was by no means as intransigent as a simple investigation of scenarios and of British light entertainment film suggests.[91]

By the same token, he argues that 'in reality anti-imperialist material was also let through'.[92] The Empire was shown in a critical light in some of the Tarzan films of Johnny Weissmuller, in the disaster movie set on a South Sea Island, *The Hurricane* (Sam Goldwyn, 1937), in the comedy starring Will Hay, *Old Bones of the River* (Gainsborough, 1938), and in *Song of Freedom* (Hammer Production – British Lion, 1936), a vehicle for the vocal talents of Paul Robeson, the black actor/singer and, incidentally, promoter of the Socialist Unity Theatre. All of these, in various ways and degrees, portrayed imperial administration as exploitative, corrupt and inefficient. It must be added, however, that pro-imperialist epics, most notably London Film Productions' *Sanders of the River* (1935), *The Drum* (1938) and *The Four Feathers* (1939), remained the mainstream, dominant genre with their racism, chauvinism, class privilege and hierarchical values.

Of course, radical thought played only a minor part in film production. However, radical directors, writers and the like were not the only counter-balance to capital at the level of production. The studio trade unions were also able to fight for concessions, undoubtedly modifying the position of film capital, as chapter three of this study will show. Furthermore, even though the industry was dominated by an odd assortment of refugee Capitalists, aristocrats, Conservative MPs, self-made men and aesthetes – backed by finance capital – it is very difficult to show how the industry as a whole produced the required ideological effect. According to George Orwell, the governing class did not have the intelligence to use the movies and other cheap luxuries 'to hold the unemployed down' or avert a revolution.[93] That apart, there is a more serious point to make. Fundamentally, there were fractions of film capital; that is to say, differences of interest and identity between producers, distributors and exhibitors. Equally, there were economic and ideological conflicts between domestic and international, old and new, and competitive and monopolistic film capital. At another level, there were also disagreements between the industry, with its desire for profit, and the BBFC with its concern for moral and, perhaps, political conformity. The ideology surrounding film was therefore constructed by individual capitals in a highly volatile and conflictual way. A minority of individual capitals, like the Ostrer brothers, Michael Balcon or the head of the Granada chain, Sidney Bernstein (who was an enthusiast for Soviet films and actually purchased a copy of *The*

Soviet Five Year Plan), were even sympathetic to progressive ideas. Having said this, it is not doubted that sections of capital sometimes sought to use film to convey images of social harmony and an essentially stable and fair Capitalist order. But even then it is questionable that working-class audiences accepted such images or swallowed ruling-class ideas. To stress again, ideological indoctrination may have been intended, but this did not necessarily bring with it the desired effects. This is worth developing further in our third point.

Third and finally then, there is a need to focus on the objective function of film. Critics, grouped around the film journal, *Screen*, have tended to do this by combining Marxism with aspects of semiology and psychoanalysis. This is hardly possible in the present study, though it can be argued that the working classes were not passive consumers of the film product. Vincent Porter has recently maintained 'that people draw from the films those elements which seem most relevant to their own situation and their own attitudes':

> Film stories are frequently more complex than propagandists allow, however, and audiences are often able to take from the story those pleasures that suit them, ignoring those that do not. Some apparently non-political films are read as potent critiques of capitalism and its urban culture. One such genre is the private eye film which draws on the novels of Dashiell Hammett and Raymond Chandler, portraying big city life as corrupt, greedy, dishonest and immoral. In these films the private eye, driven only by a dedication to honesty, his own integrity, and the need to get to the bottom of the mystery, acts as and for the conscience of the audience. In his search, he exposes the evil and corruption that permeates big business, city politics and frequently even the police force and the judiciary.[94]

There is of course a need to be historically specific, and in the 1930s it was again the Hollywood film which tended to convey such radical sentiments. Moreover, ideological signals contained in films can be reappropriated by the audience and reshaped into alternative meanings and values. Even if the film product aims to create political consensus, it does not necessarily function in that way. As Alun Howkins has rightly pointed out, the working class is not 'a kind of empty bottle into which you pour culture, or a blank wall upon which you paint things' – workers are able to resist and contest cultural production.[95] To be fair, Anthony Aldgate has also acknowledged that it is difficult 'to demonstrate conclusively that [ruling] ideology was necessarily received in the manner that was intended . . . one cannot presume that [workers] were the passive recipients of the politics and values of the dominant classes'.[96] In an interesting book of childhood memories, Ted Willis, sometime member of the Young Communist League, author of the popular television series *Dixon of Dock Green* and more recently peer of the realm, has recalled the moral and political lessons he drew from watching 'Tom Mix, Buck Jones, Douglas Fairbanks and other hard fighting, hard riding stars of the films we queued to see at the fourpenny Saturday matinees in the Premier Picture Palace or the Coliseum Cinema':

> The simple morality of those silent Westerns and other dramas made a deep impression on me. As I left the cinema I would resolve to make myself as bold and selfless as the stars I had seen, to protect the weak and defend the innocent at no matter what cost in personal sacrifice.[97]

Even though these Westerns often had ideologically saturated messages, such as their shameful depiction of American Indians as villains, seemingly Willis chose his lessons selectively.

It is also worthwhile recalling in this final point that film-going in working-class districts was a part of a collective working-class culture. Thus the ideological impact of film cannot be judged by a simple reading of plot, dialogue and the visual image. In order to understand the meanings of the film experience, and what working people took from that experience, there is a need to look beyond the images of the screen. Going to the pictures was, in brief, more than just watching a film. Like other cultural institutions, notably the pub, the cinema was a meeting place bringing the local community together to share their leisure. Though there is a paucity of evidence, historians of film have to place their subject in a wider social and cultural context to take account of the cultural differences between, say, working-class and middle-class audiences. The notion that films had the function or effect of sustaining the dominant ideology is, to say the least, problematic. In the 1920s and 1930s the wider working-class culture was still under working-class control and linked to the community experience, though the significance of economic and in turn cultural domination and subordination should not be underrated. True, the cinema industry was controlled by capital, but this alternative culture of shared ideas, solidarity and co-operation helped to insulate the working class from vulgar attempts at ideological manipulation. Though not seeking to overthrow existing practice, working-class people used the cinema in their own ways and on their own terms, making them less vulnerable to cultural and ideological penetration from above. The argument that ideology acts independently of human agency and is structured so as to maintain confidence in the economic and social system thus fails to acknowledge the power and resonance of the working-class spirit. The view of McDonnell and Robins that 'the working class does not find it impossible to unmask the ideological mystifications of capitalist society', is clearly important here.[98] Arguably, the film medium, as a possible form of hegemony, was a site of ideological contestation between opposing social classes. As this study will show, the Labour movement was continually

1 (left) One of the biggest box-office successes was Gracie Fields. Here, crowds queue for the European premiere of *Queen of Hearts* (1936), outside the Gaumont, Manchester

2 (below left) One of Gracie's best loved films was Basil Dean's *Sing As We Go* (1934), shot in Ealing and on location in Blackpool

3 (below) Two very popular stars of the period were Robert Donat and Madeleine Carroll, seen here in Hitchcock's excellent *The 39 Steps* (1935)

4 (above left) The 1930s saw the rise of special cinema clubs, such as this one at the Plaza, Widnes, run by the manager Harold Cookson ('Uncle Harold')

5 (left) There was a construction boom in the 1930s and many new cinemas appeared; 350 tons of steel were used in the Plaza Super Cinema, Stockport, opened in 1932

6 (above) As well as new cinemas, new production facilities were established. The Gaumont British studio at Shepherd's Bush was built at a cost of £75,000, and described as 'Possibly the most perfectly equipped and best run studios in Europe.'

7 Craftsmen and technicians prepare for filming at the Shepherd's Bush studios

8/9 Even bigger than the Shepherd's Bush studios was the Denham complex,
opened in 1936 by Alexander Korda's London Film Productions

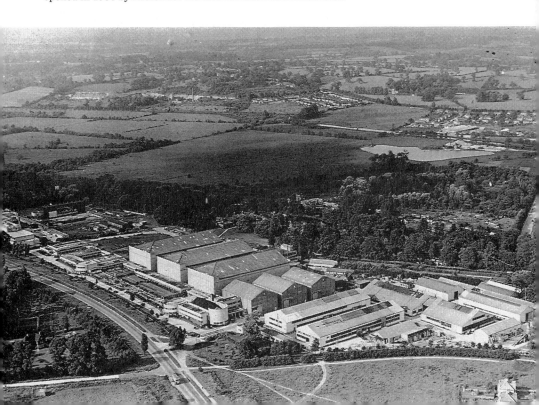

10/11 (above and above right) Denham studios catered for all aspects of film work from shooting to processing

12 (right) Another important studio was found at Elstree under the control of British International Pictures. Here, a film is being made about the techniques of film production

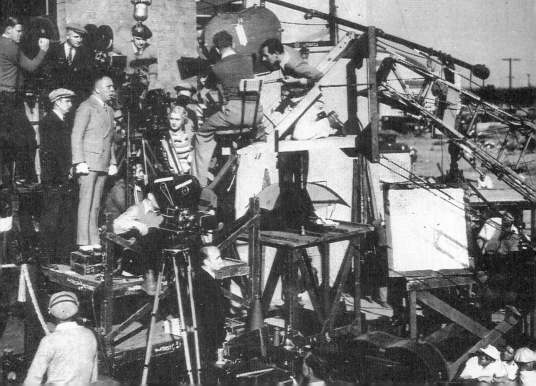

questioning and probing the Capitalist film industry, and posing the need for alternatives.

The aim of this opening chapter has been a rather limited one, of providing a conspectus of the political economy of film and the working class in the inter-war years. Hopefully the chapter will help the reader to situate the Labour movement's approach to film in the determining economic, social and political structures. In chapter two the ideological and organizational base of the Labour movement is explored: from this certain features of Labour's approach to cinema and film are drawn. Chapter three examines trade union organization and policy in the film industry. In chapter four the relationship between the State and the Labour approach is investigated. Here, the emphasis is on two particular aspects of State intervention, namely protective legislation and censorship. Chapter five provides a detailed study of the Sunday cinema question by focusing on the policies and attitudes of organized Labour to exhibiting films on the Sabbath. The final chapters, six and seven, provide detailed accounts of the development of the workers' film movement. Chapter six focuses on the Labour party, TUC and film, and chapter seven on the Communist party and film.

The Labour Movement, Ideology and Film

Cinema-going was undoubtedly a central leisure occupation of the inter-war working class. By 1939 about half of the British population of 46 million visited the cinema at least once a week. The cinema was also big business involving much commercial activity and State regulation. In addition, for those groups interested in the political system film became an important medium of propaganda. Indeed, as early as 1918 the Labour party was investigating the uses of the medium.[1] Before proceeding to our task of analysing the Labour movement's policy approach to film, let us outline the salient points of inter-war Labour history. This is necessary for, as Trevor Ryan has remarked, discussion of film and organized Labour:

> needs to be situated within the contradictions inherent in the labour
> movement generally; and the specific relations between film groups and
> the various political and campaign organisations need to be traced as
> the requirements and strategies of these latter bodies evolved,
> contingent upon a series of conjunctural factors which need to be
> analysed.[2]

From this we can then identify the key ideological factors and traditions which informed Labour's approach to film.

The inter-war Labour movement

By the 1920s the organized Labour movement in Britain was a broad chapel consisting of political, industrial and cultural organizations. On the political front the main organization was the Labour party, together with associated bodies such as the Fabian Society, the Independent Labour Party (ILP) and the Co-operative party. The Communist Party of Great Britain (CP), newly formed in 1920, and small Marxist sects like the Socialist Party of Great Britain, offered an alternative force. On the industrial front, the trade unions and the co-operative societies were the leading actors. And finally on the cultural front, the movement catered for a range of leisure interests, including film, within its own structures. Clearly, the Labour movement was a rich diversity of institutions, but the question remains, how did the movement develop in the 1920s and 1930s and what factors held it together or divided it?

There have been numerous studies of inter-war Labour at both the local and national level. Of these, a number of articles and monographs have suggested that the General Strike acted as a watershed in Labour's development. The period between 1918 and 1926 was apparently characterized by 'aggressive labour insurgency' and 'unprecedented militancy', a time when Socialist forces were on the offensive and unions used mass industrial action of a political character. With the defeat of the General Strike and declining membership, trade unionism is said to have become more 'responsible', rejecting industrial action for political ends, whilst accepting the need for class collaboration in the performance of a conciliatory and consultative role with employers and government. In short, the General Strike is regarded as a 'turning point' in the history of the Labour movement.[3]

This is not to argue that all historians agree with such an interpretation. In fact, another school of thought stresses the continuity of inter-war trade union and Labour history, and refutes the view that the General Strike was in any way a historical watershed.[4] In the aftermath of the strike the unions and political activists faced a number of difficulties – restrictive legislation, the defeat of the Labour government in 1931 and rising unemployment – but it was not long before membership began to recover and the movement began to rebuild its authority on more enduring foundations.[5] It is also clear that the unions were not under constant attack for there was little undercutting of standard wage rates through mass blacklegging or the use of unemployed labour, and few attempts by employers' organizations to 'undermine either the unions or their rights in collective bargaining'.[6] Moreover, industrial disputes were still commonplace in the years after the strike, and there was a great deal of labour unrest, particularly in the cotton and mining industries. Indeed, militant rank and file activity remained a feature of British industrial relations: the Communist-inspired National Minority Movement did not break up until 1933 and this was soon replaced by an effective shop stewards' movement. Despite an unfavourable economic and political environment, the unions continued to make improvements in rates of pay and conditions of employment, and various gains were made.

In political terms too, the 1930s witnessed some remarkable developments, most notably the rise of a more radical Socialist rhetoric associated with groups like the CP, ILP (which disaffiliated from the Labour party in 1932), Socialist League and sections of the Labour party, and in turn the emergence of an anti-Fascist movement. The Labour party was in a state of convalescence and increasingly influenced by the major trade unions, but it recovered to develop a clear perception of the policies it would introduce once elected to office. At the same time, there was a thriving Socialist cultural formation which challenged some of the mores and conventions of the dominant culture. In sum, the years after 1926 were not as dismal for the Labour movement as was once thought. The view taken here, therefore, is that the Labour movement was far from dormant in the years after the General Strike.

There was disunity in the Labour ranks, however. The major distinction was between Labour Socialism and Marxism. Labour Socialists dominated the Labour party, trade unions, co-operative societies and affiliated organizations, whilst Marxists were mainly found in the CP, the National Minority Movement and like-minded bodies. Significantly, the divide extended into the cultural field. In sport, for example, the Labour party and the TUC sponsored the National Workers' Sports Association, whilst the CP supported the British Workers' Sports Federation. Likewise, the Labour party's film organization, the Workers' Film Association, was a very different animal to the various Communist-influenced workers' film societies. In ideological terms, as the excellent work of Stuart Macintyre has shown, there were a number of co-ordinates which differentiated the Labour Socialist and Marxist traditions. Both Labour Socialism and Marxism were about political perspectives and the understanding of the economic and social processes which informed and supported those perspectives. Most importantly, Labour Socialists tended to criticize the Capitalist order from a moral or ethical standpoint, drawing upon a political and constructive view of the world based on experience. In contrast, Marxists provided a scientific critique of Capitalism taken from a comprehensive and systematic theory of society: they 'emphasised the methodological unity of their doctrine: historical materialism, the dialectic, class analysis, economics and so on comprised a complete and indissoluble system so that it was impossible for historical materialism, for example, to be understood separately from Marxist economics'.[7]

Following on from this, there were differences in political methods and strategy. Very simply put, Labour Socialists sought to reform the existing Capitalist system in piecemeal Parliamentary fashion, whereas Marxists sought to overthrow it by revolutionary means. One final point, these doctrines adapted to the changing economic and political circumstances of the inter-war years, and were elastic and fluid enough to accommodate a breadth of views from Labourism to militant trade unionism. This summary, whilst not doing justice to Macintyre's refined and tight analysis, is sufficient to show that the Labour movement was diffused with alternative ideological and political perspectives. It is now possible to proceed with an examination of the Labour movement's attitude to film.

Labour and film

The Labour movement's concern for leisure dates back to the Victorian age. Recent research has shown that some professional Labour leaders were eager to control the amusements of the poor. In their view, if the working class was intemperate and lacking in discipline then hopes of political and economic change would be stifled. With this in mind, Owenites, Chartists and Christian Socialists provided opportunities and amenities for rational recreation, so that leisure would not be wasted. Although it is important to stress the essential continuity and adaptability of popular leisure through industrialization and in turn the reluctance of Labour leaders to censor cultural practices, by the 1880s there were many Socialist rational recreationalists. In fact, despite the commercialization of leisure in the last quarter of the nineteenth century – the provision of music halls, seaside holidays, spectator sport for profit – the Labour movement failed to develop 'a new critique of the commercial leisure industry that transcended the moral homilies of rational recreation'. Chris Waters continues that 'the socialist attack on capitalism for its provision of frivolous pastimes, while new in that it was a specific assault on capitalism, developed from an ordering of amusements as useful or useless that would have again found numerous supporters in the movement for rational recreation'.[8] It was not really until the inter-war years and the commercial explosion of cheap diversions that Socialists began to systematize their views on leisure. Responses illustrated not only the continuing relevance of rational recreation, but also a distinctively Socialist interpretation of what actually constituted the rationality of leisure. Socialist versions of rational recreation were never free from Victorian notions of morality, though they did depend on clear perceptions of the Labour and Socialist interest.

In the inter-war years Socialists expressed a range of views about film and the cinema. It is therefore very difficult to categorize Socialist views and perceptions. Broadly speaking, however, this chapter will focus on three general perspectives. First, within the Labour Socialist tradition were the views of the rational recreationalist and Labour highbrow whose approach to the cinema was often puritanical, elitist and anti-populist in emphasis. Second, again within the Labour Socialist tradition, probably a majority of Socialists viewed the cinema from a libertarian perspective. Finally, there were the views of the Marxist who saw film in Capitalist society as an ideological lever of the ruling class. Before proceeding with the analysis, it is appropriate to stress that these three perspectives were never clearly defined or delineated.

The first perspective is that of the rational recreationalist or Labour highbrow. Stanley Pierson has suggested that the utopian versions of Socialism, which had emerged in the nineteenth century, had lost credence by the 1920s as organized Labour adapted to the political and industrial realities of power.[9] Nevertheless, a religious and ethical discourse survived. Even if those Socialists who had been nurtured on the principle of the Bible rather than Marx were incorporated into the political and industrial power structures, this did not mean that their spiritual values deserted them. Many Labour party members and trade unionists continued to play a part in religious life, and nonconformity in particular still exerted an influence.[10] It was from this ethical tradition that many of the puritanical attitudes to leisure arose. When this element of Socialism is grafted onto the self-improvement nature of trade unionism and co-operation, it is little wonder that there was a tendency to deprecate the hedonism of the workers. Not surprisingly, ethical Socialists were especially hostile to drinking and gambling, while maintaining that education was more edifying than other forms of relaxation. How does film fit into all of this?

The uses and nobility of leisure concerned many Socialists. In the immediate post-war period, a time of economic boom and cultural change, James A. Lovat-Fraser, a barrister and supporter of the ILP, asserted that for leisure 'to bring real happiness and to be really beneficial [it] must be well employed'. If it was not, the workers would apparently turn 'to means which are cheap and unworthy'.[11] What is important here was not the form of leisure but its social implications and manifestations. Lovat-Fraser was thus critical of the film precisely because he believed 'that a large amount of juvenile delinquency was due directly to the influence of the cinema'.[12] On another occasion, speaking during the passage of the Sunday Entertainments Bill, he made it clear that if films were allowed to run on the Lord's Day they would bring with them 'resulting evils'.[13] From a slightly different perspective, David Logan, Labour MP for the Scotland Road constituency of Liverpool – a heavily populated Catholic district – thought that the cinema was a poor alternative to outdoor recreation, including greyhound racing:

> I do not see any sport or anything to entice a man to look at a dead hare being chased by a dog, but other people do, and, if a place of that kind is properly conducted and properly regulated, it is surely better than spooning in cinemas and looking at some of the rotten pictures that are shown there.[14]

This underlying worry about sex was important for after all the cinema was bringing about a considerable change in courting customs. Logan in fact believed 'that the English mind demands clean and healthy films'.[15] The message that both Lovat-Fraser and Logan were presenting was that cinema-going, as then constituted, was an unsound use of leisure, if not prejudicial to social reform. In fact, at a more fundamental level, one contributor to the *New Leader*, the ILP weekly, claimed that the Socialist State of the future would provide more 'profound' interests than the cinema.[16]

Though Labour activists were reluctant to criticize cinema-going, it is interesting that films were rarely regarded as rational entertainment. A series of editorials on leisure in *The Post*, the organ of the Union of Post Office Workers, fails to mention the cinema. In recommending 'useful' ways to occupy spare time, the union refers to all manner of sports, arts and crafts, reading, photography, and gardening, but not the cinema. The implicit recommendation is that leisure should be active rather than passive.[17] More than this, a number of Socialists believed that for leisure to be used effectively it must take the form of education and self-improvement. One trade unionist thus argued that with proper training in childhood the working class would use their leisure fruitfully rather than in the escapism of the cinema.[18]

On the other hand, ethical Socialists like Philip Snowden, who were embroiled in the drink question and aimed to spread the temperance gospel, saw in cinema a much needed counter to the evils of the public house. It is true that Snowden believed that 'The cinema may not be quite perfect as an elevating institution, from the point of view of high art'.[19] However, writing in the British number of the *Bioscope*, he painted a slightly different picture: 'The Labour Party must be keenly interested in a great enterprise which is becoming more and more a part of the life of the masses of the people.' But most importantly he wrote that the cinema was 'a means of healthy recreation and enjoyment. It is an antidote to harmful pastimes and injurious habits.' Apparently, a future Labour government was to assist the industry by all the means at its disposal.[20] In fact, steps had already been taken: Snowden's first budget as Labour Chancellor of the Exchequer in 1924 reduced entertainments duty on cheap cinema seats.

An editorial of November 1929 in the Lancashire cotton operatives' weekly, the *Cotton Factory Times*, was equally positive that the cinema was a cure for the drinking habit. Surely, the paper asked, were the cinemas 'not better in their influence than mere beer-swilling houses?'[21] In other words, it appears that there was a hierarchy of rational amusements. For those Socialists concerned about the rationality of leisure, it is probable that drink, gambling and illicit sex were most despised, with cinema-going less appealing than outdoor hobbies, the arts and crafts, literature, and education.

In a similar vein, some commentators argued that there was nothing intrinsically wrong with the cinema, the problem was in the quality of the films shown. Chris Massie, for instance, was critical of the comedy picture:

> In happier days it was said of Englishmen that they took their pleasures sadly. Without much exaggeration it could be said now that we do not take any pleasures at all. We have become the easiest possible victims to Charlie Chaplin and Mary Pickford because life is not fine enough or funny enough. We pay thousands of pounds a year to a young man with

sad eyes and silly boots for curing us of incipient lunacy with the old-fashioned remedy of laughter.

However, he did believe that the cinema could be beneficial if used for the right purposes: 'Such fine scope as the cinematograph offers could be used to entertain and instruct in science, literature and art'. His answer to the problem was the establishment of State cinemas![22]

A section of the Labour cultural elite was critical of the cinema because of its Americanizing influences, in much the same way as those independent film-makers grouped around the journal *Cinema Quarterly* (1932–5) were. Along with other American imports like dancing and music, the movies were seen as undermining traditional forms of working-class culture, as well as 'high' culture. American cultural forms were viewed as morally bad, giving rise to standardized entertainment and mass society. As C.W.E. Bigsby has written, this came to a head in the inter-war years:

> The 1930s were remarkably conscious of the implications of mass society, for though the nineteenth century had felt the first impact of industrialization, it was the early decades of the present century, with the birth of the movies, radio and television, which really began to recognize profound social changes . . . which were threatening to change the profile of existence.[23]

For many Socialists, America with its search for profit and hence cultural conformity was an homogenizing agent which threatened to corrupt the British 'way of life'. As late as 1937, Reginald Sorensen, the Labour MP for Leyton West and also significantly a minister of the church, dreaded cinema-going on the grounds of 'having to spend an hour or two suffering from a mixture of glucose, chewing gum, leaden bullets and nasal noises', including American cinema jargon – '"O.K. Chief," "Sez you" and phrases of that kind'. As he commented: 'Personally, I do not like to feel that Britannia has constantly to appear on the screen speaking with the accents of Chicago, Oregon and Massachusetts.' In complaining that America had advanced far towards the cultural annexation of Britain, he went on to advocate British 'pictures of high merit . . . that conform to a real standard of artistry, both in the world of humour and in the world of tragedy'.[24] In fact, a number of Socialists seemed to be suggesting that the British arts should counteract the American cultural product.

The arts were seen by many Labour supporters, especially middle-class intellectuals grouped around the ILP and Fabian Society, as a *rational* leisure activity which could elevate and educate the workers above the proclivities of Hollywood. It was argued that the arts, as rigidly defined in terms of 'high culture' – literature, painting, drama, music, architecture – had the necessary mental and spiritual properties to enlighten those workers who had no conception of how to use their leisure profitably. Arthur Bourchier, a middle-class member of the ILP, a theatre owner and one of the first actors to be heard on the airwaves in a BBC transmission of September 1922, therefore contrasted the Hollywood product with the 'arts of painting and literature, as well as the arts of music and the theatre':

> to the majority of us the word 'pictures' means nothing more or less than American films. And these, on the whole, are inane, vulgar, and disappointingly trashy. Up to the present, they have made no contribution at all to the development of art and culture.[25]

Although Bourchier declared that films possessed 'immense educational possibilities', this was not so in the case where they were 'produced by vulgar minded money-grubbers'. With his educational background – he had been to Eton and Christ Church, Oxford University – it is hardly surprising that he advocated the promotion of libraries, theatres, concert halls and picture galleries. Yet for him, the working class would never achieve cultural emancipation until Capitalism was abolished:

> When we have succeeded, art and culture will at last be common property; we shall be a race of happy, cultured people . . . with full accessibility to art and culture, and benefits and joys of which at present we have but the slightest glimmerings.[26]

What Bourchier failed to appreciate of course was that American films were truly popular among the British working class because they enjoyed them. Workers simply preferred a Clark Gable or Greta Garbo movie to classical ballet or the promenade performances of Sir Henry Wood and company.

Interestingly, Bourchier was also antagonistic to 'crude, savage, cacophonous jazz', and in this was voicing the sentiment of many Socialists. In the ILP, for example, US jazz music was often portrayed as culturally moribund. As A. Williams-Ellis noted: 'Mention Paul Whiteman's Jazz Band to some leader of musical thought in an ILP branch, and he will probably as a matter of course begin to characterize it as vulgar.'[27] Similarly, some members of the CP, in praising revolutionary melodies, were critical of the necessity 'to descend to the level of the American jazz exploiters'; it was the task of the Marxist 'to raise the standard of that with which workers are familiar'.[28] Certainly, many British Socialists would have supported the view advanced by the German Marxist composer, Hanns Eisler, that popular art was both decadent and dangerous to the Socialist cause: 'commercial jazz and plagiarized entertainment music is the daily method of blunting the ears and sensibilities of the listeners'.[29]

The notion of a Labour Socialist approach to working-class culture which was ascetic and anti-hedonistic in tone, as represented by Sidney and Beatrice Webb, though recently challenged in the work of Ian Britain, is clearly relevant here. Britain has shown in a highly original and novel way that Fabianism was more than a utilitarian philosophy with a philistine outlook. Fabian Socialism did not have a uniform approach to art and culture; rather, it was ambiguous, flexible, non-dogmatic and heterogeneous. In essence, the Fabian Society had a balanced perspective in which 'there was a basic agreement on the importance of avoiding the real extremes of luxury and licence on the one hand, and of asceticism on the other'.[30] However, it is apparent that Beatrice Webb, in sounding out the possibilities of social organization for Labour women, displayed more than a grain of elitist aspiration:

> I am aiming at bringing into the workaday Labour world an element of
> intellectual distinction. We have to remodel official society on the basis
> of the simple hard-working life tempered by fastidiously chosen
> recreation and the good manners inherent in equality between man and
> man.[31]

The rather condescending approach of the leading Fabians to popular culture was reflected in one particular plan, endorsed by Sidney Webb, 'by which working-class luxuries, which yield little in subsistence or refinement would be made the vehicle of any necessary taxation'.[32] One can only speculate about the meaning of the phrase 'working-class luxuries', but presumably the burden of such a tax would have fallen most heavily on drinking and betting, and other activities considered extravagant such as unproductive cinema-going. This is not to say that the Webbs dismissed the cinema out of hand. As chairman of the Labour party sub-committee on film in 1919, Sidney was presumably enthusiastic about harnessing the medium as a means of Labour propaganda. When elevated to the peerage as Lord Passfield and serving as secretary for the colonies in the second Labour government, he also made it clear 'that the rise of the kinematograph film as an instrument of culture and education merits the closest attention'.[33] Yet, here was the basis of the Webb's philosophy: film was important not as mere entertainment, but as a cultural and educational form.

It is also possible that Labour 'highbrows' of the inter-war period were influenced by the Arnoldian cultural critique as then represented by F.R. Leavis and T.S. Eliot. Iain Wright has found that Socialists were aware of Leavis' Scrutiny movement:

> On their side, the left seemed for a time to be eager for an alliance,
> understanding the importance of Scrutiny's campaign against the
> growing power of the advertising industry, the commercialization of the

press, the cynically exploitative machinery of the new mass entertainments industry.[34]

Leavis was certainly desperate to preserve 'high' culture against the 'cheapest emotional appeals' emanating from the standardized cultural commodities of America. For Leavis the perversity of mass produced leisure was invading all areas of life as never before.[35] It was therefore the role of the educated elite to protect the integrity of the English cultural tradition as they defined it.

In much the same tone, Socialist intellectuals, like the historian J.L. Hammond, were critical of 'mass pleasures'. Hammond suggested that the working classes should be educated to choose their films judiciously:

A young man or woman who gets to the pictures two or three times a week, goes for enjoyment, but he or she is affected by that enjoyment just as the audiences that listened to a Greek play in ancient Athens or to a play of Shakespeare's in Elizabethan England were affected by that experience. If then the kind of art that we are going to develop in the cinema, the kind of culture that we are going to spread by the wireless, depends on popular demand, it is immensely important whether the minds and emotions submitted to this entertainment are raw and untrained, or whether these audiences have some quality of taste and judgement by which they test that entertainment. A man or woman who sees nothing but bad films, and enjoys them so much that he or she continues to see them, will not acquire in the process the capacity for enjoying good films.[36]

Likewise, Arthur Ponsonby, a Labour MP for Sheffield Brightside who had been educated at Eton and Balliol College, Oxford University, and served as page of honour to Queen Victoria between 1882 and 1887, complained about the commercialism of the cinema, whilst the Oxford philosopher Cyril Joad, also educated at Balliol, disparaged the fact that money was spent 'in the dark of the cinemas'.[37] Indeed, some middle-class Socialists were critical of 'sexuality in our entertainments'. 'The Socialist will always dislike this musical type of show because of its obscenity', as Terence Greenidge expressed it.[38] In the editorial already cited, the *Cotton Factory Times* also acknowledged that there was 'a certain amount of truth' in the allegations that the cinema, together with the theatre and music hall, 'reek of sex and sex problems' and 'that the working classes are letting themselves "go" in a freer manner than was the case, say, fifty years ago'.[39] In a different context, it is interesting that in the mid-1930s Equity, the actors' union, organized a kind of 'purity' campaign against coarse jokes.[40]

Cultural luminaries therefore feared that the popular arts would encourage over-indulgence and undermine aesthetic pursuits. By taking such a negative approach to contemporary cultural developments, Socialists failed to understand the nature of popular leisure and the organic qualities of working-class culture in the home, the street or the cinema. The Socialist arbiters of cultural and recreational taste sought to refine the pattern of leisure activities in an elitist way, without any real feeling for or appreciation of working-class life. To be sure, sections of the Labour movement did not understand or accept the alternative character of much of working-class culture – its apartness and separation from the dominant culture, and its ability to transform and mediate the values of, say, Hollywood through its own institutions. Even when the condescending approach to the leisure of the 'lower orders' was tempered and Socialists realized that people went to the cinema for positive reasons, films of social criticism which educated the viewer were still regarded as inherently superior to films of pure entertainment.

The reference to 'common' leisure activities as vulgar and unworthy was not, however, the sole prerogative of the intellectual: certain trade unionists, who had active links with the working class, also dismissed a number of popular pastimes in favour of traditional 'bourgeois' art forms. Charles Ammon of the Union of Post Office Workers and future Labour MP for North Camberwell, noting 'that the people followed the sloppiness and sensationalism of the cinema', emphasized the need for winter gardens, reading rooms, libraries, concert and lecture halls, and theatres.[41] The view of Ernest Bevin, probably the most powerful trade unionist of the period, also reveals a culturally didactic mentality: apparently the people did 'not want gramophones and the common records and the grinding tunes' to which they had been condemned, but rather the opportunity to learn about and appreciate opera.[42] By giving the working class access to the opera and the theatre, this also provided for rational recreation, 'for the right use of hours and days of leisure now coming within our reach'.[43]

Working class interests like the Electrical Trades Union also criticized the influence of America, even after the second world war:

> We hold the view that for private enterprise to control this medium of mass communication, exercising as it does such a potent influence on the adolescent minds of this country, is to abandon the youth of this country to an ever-increasing diet of American films obsessed with crimes of brutality and an unhealthy preoccupation with sex.[44]

Such fears were derived from the frequently expressed belief in an 'American conspiracy to cripple the British film industry' or the fact that 'the principal cinemas in Britain are about to pass under the control of foreign interests'.[45] The Labour Lord Mayor of Salford, Councillor J.W. Bloom even pronounced that 'a large part of adult picturegoers are sick of the Hollywood "sob-stuff" and want something with more "meat" in it'.[46] There was, however, little evidence to substantiate such a claim. The Socialist intellectual elite and the trade union highbrow had certain cultural prejudices – 'high' art was regarded as more valuable than popular art. Needless to say, such a perspective was in sharp contrast to the tastes of the vast majority of the working class.

Cultural elitism was not the only element in the Labour Socialist conception of the cinema. The Labour Socialist tradition was also informed by humanistic and naturalistic values. In contrast to the moral tone and elitism of some Socialists, there were groups which exuded a more thorough-going bohemianism. This could be labelled Libertarian Socialism – the set of beliefs that the working class should be emancipated from bourgeois moral dictates and have the liberty and opportunity to decide the course of their own lives.

The Labour journalist and writer of Clarion tracts on Socialism, Robert Bentley Suthers, expressed such beliefs in succinct fashion:

> The fundamental argument for Socialism is that in a co-operative commonwealth every citizen would enjoy a freedom of individual and personal liberty which the present system denies him. No phrase in the speeches and writings of Socialist propagandists is commoner than the expression 'a fuller and freer life.' That is what we promise under Socialism – a fuller and freer life. And we build our system of Socialism on the common ownership of the means of life, because without the means of life assured, no man can be mentally and spiritually free to develop his personality to the utmost.[47]

Emanating from this code was the idea that the individual should be free to choose the leisure pursuit he or she favoured, whether it be cinema-going, drinking or 'high' art. For the Libertarian Socialist an over zealous advocacy of rational or cultured amusement was anathema. It was the right of individuals to decide for themselves the ways in which to spend their spare time. In this regard the views of Frederick Montague are instructive.

Montague was in many ways the archetypal Libertarian Socialist. He was born in 1876 in Clerkenwell and joined the Marxist Social Democratic Federation (SDF) in 1894 and the ILP in the following year, serving on the first Metropolitan Council of the ILP. He became an organizer for the ILP and as a Clarion Vanner exuded a spirit of liberation from the conventional style of life. By the 1920s Montague was Labour MP for West Islington, serving under Lords Thomson and Amulree as Parliamentary under-secretary for Air in the 1929–31 Labour administration, though this did not compromise his essential independence. He remained on the National Executive of the SDF and, though a publicity copywriter by training, was also a performing magician. His views on leisure come out clearly in speeches delivered in the House of Commons. Speaking during the debate on the 1928 Dog Racing Bill he opposed interference in people's leisure.

> I wish to take this opportunity of objecting to some of the arguments which have been used in support of this Measure. I am a Socialist, and, therefore, I believe very profoundly in the principles of individualism. I do not think it is the business of elected authorities of any kind to interfere with the personal habits of the inhabitants of the country or any district.

Montague then spoke about leisure spending:

> I take the view that, from the standpoint of the economics of the question, this country is rich enough to enable every useful worker in it to waste 10s. a week. It is a question of expenditure. I have no use for those teetotal and anti-gambling economics, which are those of the old fashioned Victorian Liberal party – the idea that the workers must not have a halfpenny extra to spend, or even to throw away. I say that the workers work hard enough, and are useful enough, to be entitled to spend in any way they like a reasonable amount of their personal income. If they do not get enough to do that, that is a condemnation of the system of society under which we live. That is the point of view that I take with regard to the economics of the question.[48]

With little doubt, Montague was voicing the position of certain other Labour activists, as well as working people. Even the International Labour Organization had declared that, 'During spare time workers ought to be absolutely free to do as they please.'[49]

Equally, there were certain Socialist intellectuals who expressed similar thoughts. R.H. Tawney and J.J. Findlay, both educationalists as well as Socialists, protested that it was 'impertinent' to dictate to workers on the use of leisure hours. As Tawney put it: 'the first condition of any serious discussion of the use of leisure is to consider it in terms of the individuals concerned, and of the environment of their working lives. Anything else is unintelligent and impertinent'.[50] For Findlay it was improper for Socialists to regard those workers who spent their leisure 'staring at pictures' as lazy or aimless.[51] Significantly, Findlay became the TUC General Council's representative on the Advisory Council of the newly formed British Film Institute in December 1933.[52]

The Labour party's perception of film-going comes out most clearly from the debates on cinematograph legislation. As is well known, the Labour party opposed the 1927 Conservative government's Cinematograph Films Bill, designed to protect British film production from American competition. Labour's opposition will be examined in more detail in chapter four; here, the main point of interest is Labour's appraisal of the cinema-going habit. Simon Hartog has already made the point that in Labour's approach to the Bill 'there was an element of concern about Tory ministers telling the poor what they must watch at the pictures'.[53] More recently, Vincent Porter has concluded that the Bill was 'resisted by sections of the Labour Party who saw the cinema as the principal form of working-class entertainment and suspected the Tories of wanting to replace popular and classless Hollywood films with British films saturated with class snobbery and Tory values'.[54]

In the first place, it was pointed out that the British people had the right to watch the Hollywood product. At least implicitly Labour members were critical of those Conservatives who pronounced that American pictures 'are so cheap, so garish, so vulgar and their headlines and quotations are so bad'. After all, the American commodity was often superior to the British equivalent. Indeed, John Beckett, then Labour MP for Gateshead, felt that certain British films were of 'an even lower standard than some of the objectionable headings I have seen on the American films'.[55]

A crucial element in Labour's case was the right of working-class people to view films of their own choice, without undue interference by official arbiters of taste. This part of the Labour case was most eloquently articulated by Colonel Josiah Wedgwood, a late adherent to the Socialist cause in 1919, a former Chancellor of the Duchy of Lancaster in the first Labour government (1924) and serving member for the Newcastle-Under-Lyme constituency:

> I have listened for two days with a growing rage and anger to speech after speech from hon. and right hon. Gentlemen opposite. I have never in my life seen such a crowd of highbrows debating any question whatever. Really, I am a philistine; I admit it; I go to the pictures. I am, in the language of those shocking American captions, a 'film fan,' and I believe honestly that I have seen more of these 'second-grade American productions, don't you know,' than the whole of the rest of the present House put together. I have not been corrupted by them, but I do feel inclined to tell the House, that does not go to the pictures, something about this Bill from the point of view of those who do.[56]

As the self proclaimed representative of the ordinary film-goer Wedgwood presented quite a powerful case. In complaining that the five million weekly cinema attenders had not been considered in the provisions of the Bill, he stressed that the costs of establishing State machinery to oversee the film trade would be more or less automatically passed on to the consumer in the form of higher admission prices. But in the last analysis, Wedgwood was concerned that 'the most insolent piece of legislation that I ever heard of' would deprive citizens of hard-won rights and liberties. If the British people were 'thoroughly satisfied with what they are seeing to-day' and 'really know what they want to see best', it was a form of dictatorship to reduce consumer choice and impose on audiences films which they did not want. As he concluded, the public would not 'tamely put up with a Measure which dictates to them what they have to see, which compels them to a course which will strike every man who thinks as impertinent, as an interference by Government which no British Government has any right or ever will have any right to make'.[57] The test of time was of course consumer resistance to the legislation. But that is another story.

At this point a caveat is required, for even those Labour Socialists with a libertarian view of leisure were guided by certain hierarchical precepts. For instance, it was broadly agreed that the public should be free to spend their leisure watching American films, but at the same time Socialists acknowledged that there was a need to reform popular tastes. This position is well represented by Arthur Greenwood, the Labour MP for Nelson and Colne. There can be few doubts that Greenwood had a bohemian streak in his approach to life and leisure. Though rising to the post of Cabinet Minister in the first and second Labour governments, in the early 1920s he was secretary of the Labour Campaign for the Public Ownership and Control of the Liquor Trade, and significantly has been described by one historian as a 'heavy and near compulsive drinker'.[58] In matters relating to drink he was strongly opposed to the prohibition lobby, and such opposition to the circumscription of leisure extended into the cinema world. As he protested during the debate on the 1927 Bill: 'I do not believe that censorships can fashion the taste of the people.' Most crucially, however, he did consent to the view 'that many films shown to-day are of a deplorably low standard'. Unsurprisingly, he therefore suggested that the remedy was 'a matter of education of the film-seeing public who will learn in time to appreciate the better films that are now being produced'.[59] Again this was a strong, if less overt, manifestation of cultural elitism.

Lastly, however, it is appropriate to recall the views of Fred Montague. Speaking on the licensing of film renters, Montague made his position very clear:

I really am amazed to find how the Members of the Conservative party will strain at gnats and at the same time be willing to swallow camels. Constantly we are told that the object of the Labour party is to interfere with industry, is to extend the functions of the policemen, and of those people who are supposed to represent officialdom and bureaucracy over not only the industrial life, but the personal lives of the nation. That is a stock-in-trade argument against the Labour party. Here we have a Bill which interferes with the management of a particular industry – and it is indicative of the type of mind of the Conservative party when it suits their purpose – which interferes in a way that is more objectionable than any kind of Socialism could possibly be.

He proceeded to argue that intervention in industry was 'very necessary at times', but objected to the Bill's 'interference with individual liberty, the kind of interference which will not occur in Socialism'.[60]

The problem in dealing with Labour's perception of film is the paucity of evidence. Here the libertarian approach to film has been examined from the stance of a number of Labour MPs, who may of course be atypical of the Labour movement as a whole. Nevertheless, it is arguable that organized Labour had a liberal approach to and sympathetic view of the cinema. As the *Cotton Factory Times* commented, 'the films contribute far more good than evil in the world of entertainment'.[61] The majority of Labour activists up and down the country would surely have concurred with this view. Indeed, as chapter six will discuss, Labour groupings ranging from miners' institutes to co-operative societies embraced film, many of them exhibiting some of the Hollywood spectacles. Here there was surely some form of dialogue and correspondence between working-class culture and the sub-culture of the Labour movement.

Marxists had a more systematic view of the cinema than did Labour Socialists. Members of the CP were particularly critical of workers who squandered their leisure. They thought that workers who spent all their spare time in the pub, or concentrated their minds on Hollywood or London films, would be less likely to participate in revolutionary activity. Irrational leisure, for which from a Marxist perspective could be substituted the term Capitalist leisure, precluded the development of a class-conscious proletariat. It was not that working-class leisure activities like cinema-going were regarded as licentious, but rather that they were part of a bourgeois cultural manipulation which apparently had the effect of 'doping' the workers. In brief, the rationality of leisure was evaluated on the basis of the class struggle, a point which will be returned to in the final chapter.

In its crudest form, Marxism suggested to working-class activists, particularly those grouped around the Communist movement, that the Capitalist class who controlled the economy also controlled the organs of public opinion. As one of the founding members of the London Workers' Film Society, Emile Burns, put it: 'the class which owns the means of production . . . should strive to control every aspect of the life and thought of society, encouraging here, suppressing there, thus by direct and indirect means securing its privileged position'.[62] In other words, society's ideas and values were seen to mirror the mode of production and the social structure which prevailed at a particular stage in the development of Capitalism. Therefore for the Marxist, film and cinema tended to reflect the dominant ideology and culture of the ruling Capitalist class. The

Marxist Left asserted that films transmitted by commercial enterprise and regulated by agencies of the State were part of the dominant ideological cultural system. Capitalist films were regarded as, to use Herbert Marcuse's term, 'false' needs – 'those which are superimposed upon the individual by particular social interests' – which served the interests of the ruling class by assimilating the proletariat into the orthodox, consensual way of life.[63] Films in Capitalist society were situated in the political structures of civil life, where entertainment was said to reinforce the 'present system of society'.[64] 'Benn', the Marxist film critic of the *New Leader*, was particularly sensitive to cinemas as a medium of Capitalist ideology, serving to popularize imperialism with the people:

> Its special function is to develop in men and women a certain bias towards life, to give them a particular view-point, to crystallise in a certain definite way their attitude towards their fellows and towards their surrounding in general. . . . The cinema then is an efficient, an important, a universal statement of capitalist propaganda.

In brief, 'Benn' saw the cinema 'as an expression of class supremacy . . . throughout the capitalist and non-capitalist world'.[65]

Capitalist control of the cinema was thus interpreted as a form of incorporation into the dominant culture. Marxist intellectuals like Eden and Cedar Paul, no doubt placed films alongside 'pseudo-culture' as 'part of the dope whereby [workers'] attention is diverted from the class war and whereby their slave status is maintained'.[66] Equally, Edward Upward, the Marxist writer, claimed that the picture house and other amusements were 'but hypocritical decorations concealing danger and misery, fraudulent as vulgar icing on a celebration cake rotten inside with maggots, sugary poison to drug you into contentment'.[67]

At a time of mass unemployment and economic collapse Marxist critics looked to the cinema for an answer to the question, Why no revolution? That most perceptive of left-wing commentators, Allen Hutt, provided the following explanation:

> London affords excellent examples of the perversion of powerful cultural instruments by the bourgeoisie to its own class ends. Here the cinema, as everywhere, has undergone a meteoric expansion while the number of theatres and music halls has declined. And the whole purpose of the cinema under capitalism is expressed in the cynical comment of the *New Survey* on the report that unemployed men were seen visiting cinemas – 'there is no reason to regard the time or money as necessarily wasted or ill-spent. With all their defects the cinemas at least serve to divert the thoughts for a time from dark forebodings. As one of the London unemployed observed: "They make you think for a little while that life is all right." '[68]

In much the same way another Marxist critic, Dave Bennett, regarded the Capitalist newsreel as 'poison', asserting that they failed to show, and even suppressed, working-class demonstrations and marches, the Japanese war on China, and the Invergordon mutiny. On the other hand, he concluded that

> they do show our Smiling Prince, the Duchess of York, Sir Malcolm Campbell, Kaye Don . . . and so on, and so on. This is their news-reel. Poison for the workers. Trumpery tomfoolery to make them forget the stern, hard realities of daily life, the struggle to make ends meet, wage-cuts, speed-up, unemployment; and to make them think only in terms of royalty, sport, snobbery, romance and jingoism.[69]

It must be stated here that it is unlikely that celluloid functioned as a means of insulating workers from the stark realities of everyday existence struggles. Surely the cinema could not hide class inequality, the poverty of mass unemployment or the exploitative character of work and the wage form? Admittedly as some Marxists acknowledged, it was the sheer weight of economic, social and political deprivation (the creation of a reserve army of the unemployed, scientific management and speed-up, anti-union laws) which was the main means of social control; certainly not the cinema. Yet, for those Marxists interested in culture, commercial films or newsreels were seen as Capitalist 'dope' – soporifics to the working class.

To some extent this rather crude notion of ideology as 'dope' merely reflected the immaturity of British Marxism in the inter-war years. 'False consciousness' among the working class was simply explained away by reference to the bourgeoisie's control of the means of production and the media in general. There was a failure to appreciate that ideology and culture were sites of contestation between classes and not something simply transmitted by the ruling elite. In fact, as Eric Hobsbawm and others have explained, there are grounds for believing that working-class experiences at work, in the community, and maybe even in communal cinema-going, fused into a 'collective class consciousness', albeit one containing certain conservative, even reactionary, elements which it must be said inter-war Marxism did well to expose. Simply put, though in the 1930s university-educated intellectuals – who were beginning to replace working-class intellectuals in the positions of Marxist ideological leadership – began to recognize the significance of culture and ideology, the main concern of Marxist writings at the time was with the economic aspects of dialectical materialism and political change. After all, it was to be several more decades before Gramsci penetrated the left-wing publishing market. Since then a more sophisticated Marxist approach has developed which has undoubtedly contributed to our understanding of film and society.

Marxist views of the cinema in the inter-war years therefore display both a fundamental misunderstanding of collective working-class culture, of which film-going was a part, and in Stuart Macintyre's phrase 'contempt for the British Working Class'.[70] As outlined in the opening chapter, film-going in working-class districts was essentially a shared, co-operative experience, and when the social message of the silver screen was escapist this often reflected popular demand rather than being imposed from above. In commenting that Communists hated the cinema because it was 'a kind of dope, saving the workers from a discontent which they would fan into the flame of revolution', the *Cotton Factory Times* had a much greater grip on the realities of the day-to-day life of the unemployed: 'Life is short, and an hour of happiness to-day seems of more value than the problematic joys of some far-off Utopian commonwealth.'[71] In their teleological view of society and preoccupation with power certain Marxists failed to acknowledge that the deprivation of Capitalist society – poverty, unemployment, a more regimented work process – could be temporarily ameliorated through cinema-going. Rather than helping to create 'false consciousness', cinema was important because it allowed for a minor improvement in the quality of life and a means of much-needed enjoyment. Surely, at the very least, the working class was entitled to that.

At a slightly different level, Marxists were also critical of the commercial and financial organization of the film industry. Capitalist films were portrayed as a brake on the cultural development of the proletariat. In its various guises commercialism had supposedly negated the contributions of artist and consumer alike. In the opinion of Edgell Rickwood, that most radical of Marxist critics, Capitalism had artificially separated consumption from production, so lessening popular control over the cultural product.[72] Apparently, under the market economy, films were effectively controlled by uncultured speculators whose main consideration was the profit motive. Indeed, in Huntley Carter's classic leftist study, the cinema is described with some justification as 'a house of entertainment controlled by a box-office', where money was the 'over-lord', 'finance capital' the foundation and the profit motive the *raison d'être*.[73] Other leaders of advanced Marxist opinion, like Ivor Montagu and Ralph Bond, came to similar conclusions at the time of the trade slump in 1937–8. A short article by Montagu entitled 'Profit-Sharks Kill British Films', argued that British films would always face the possibility of collapse due to fluctuating levels of profitability – his answer was to run film production 'like the education system as a charge on the State for the State's benefit'.[74] For Bond, the industry's problems were simply a function of 'the expansionist needs of American finance capital', and 'the collapse of the speculative boom in British films, hastened by wild-cat financing and gross mismanagement and inefficiency'. If State control was not the answer, Bond concluded that progressive reorganization of the industry had to be placed on the agenda.[75]

Not surprisingly, Marxists were quite aware of the monopoly tendencies in the British film industry. There was little by way of oligopoly in the industry in the early 1920s, but this changed after the 1927 Cinematograph Films Bill received the Royal Assent. The most detailed early exposure of industrial concentration was provided by the Marxist-influenced Labour Research Department (LRD) in the early months of 1929. Interesting information was collected on the rise of the Gaumont British Picture Corporation and the way it had enveloped Denman Picture Houses, Provincial and Cinematograph Theatres and the General Theatre Corporation. Though it was conceded that there were many independent concerns, by focusing on the Gaumont group the LRD clearly anticipated the spread of monopoly in the 1930s:

> From the 'sex appeal' of their cinemas the British Theatre owners have reaped a rich financial harvest. The film industry, both on its productive and distributive side, is determined to stabilise that harvest by eliminating competition, and is steadily forming wide-spread combines and amalgamations as a basis for extensive rationalisation.[76]

Inevitably, these points were followed up in the 1930s by a range of Marxist critics. Even the moderate National Association of Theatrical Employees called upon the Prime Minister, Ramsay MacDonald, in 1932 to set up an official enquiry which would include 'ramification of the Combines and the general effect upon the employees and the national welfare'.[77] Though it was proposed to resume an enquiry first set up under the Labour government 'when circumstances permit', no such enquiry seems to have taken place.[78] Consequently, the Association carried out its own investigation into the organizational and financial base of the industry: 'The result was startling. There are coal combines, steel trusts, banks and investment houses, insurance companies, press lords, building trade combines, milling interests and many more all heavily involved in film finance.'[79]

Needless to say, Marxists pinned their hopes on the Soviet model. There was, after all, a great deal of enthusiasm for the Russian film classics of the period. In discussing 'The Film Achievements of the U.S.S.R.', Ivor Montagu wrote, 'The essential difference between the cinema in the USSR and the cinema as we know it in the world outside is that whereas under Capitalism it is used only for the crudest sort of frivolity yielding the greatest profit to its financial backers, under Socialism it is, of course, planned for service.'[80] Presumably, Montagu and his followers hoped for the time when a socialized film industry in Britain would emulate Russian films like *Mother, Battleship Potemkin, The General Line, Earth* or *Turksib.* Groups on the Marxist Left, such as the Friends of the Soviet Union, certainly enthused about the achievements of the Soviet cinema.[81] British Marxists were therefore extremely sympathetic to Soviet cultural production, though it must be added that such sympathy often bordered on blind acceptance of and unthinking loyalty to the Moscow line.

One last point, Labour party Socialists and supporters were influenced by Marxist sentiment. There was never a hermetically sealed Marxist tradition feeding the British Communist movement to the exclusion of other Socialist organizations. George Hicks, the left-wing general secretary of the Amalgamated Union of Building Trade Workers and member of the TUC General Council, was thus influenced by Marxist notions of a conscious and deliberate Capitalist attempt to 'dope' the working class. According to Hicks, the cinema was but one channel which saturated workers' spare time with Capitalist influences, and so subverted the claims and aspirations of the Labour movement.[82] Likewise, Peter Stead has shown that the Constituency Labour party in Llanelly was worried about the relationship between Capitalist interests and the rise of local picture palaces. Again, the concern was that 'the Pictures are being cleverly used to dope the workers'.[83] Significantly, even the Socialist highbrow agreed that the 'sordid, money-grubbing state of society' where people 'engaged in a frantic scramble for a livelihood' did not create candidates for an artistic and cultured way of life or stimulate 'originality and personal artistic development among the working masses'.[84] In the last resort, both Labour Socialists and Marxists believed that Capitalism, with its commercial, ideological and cultural instruments, had to be reformed or revolutionized in order to exploit the new film medium to the full.

Socialist perceptions of the cinema were linked to the ideological traditions of Labour Socialism and Marxism. Within the Labour Socialist tradition were found various attitudes to film, resting on notions of rational recreation, cultural elitism, and liberty. On the other hand, Marxism provided a more systematic overview of the role of cinema in Capitalist society. However, it needs to be stressed again that Labour's approach to the cinema was often informed by a mixed spectrum of ideas and opinions. Marxists provided a moral, as well as a scientific, critique of American forms, for example. By the same token, Ivor Montagu, the Marxist intellectual, though vehemently against State censorship of progressive films, had a condescending attitude to the more popular product.[85] In a similar way, some Labour Socialists were undoubtedly influenced by Marxism in their criticism of the commercial film industry. There was also much ambiguity and contradiction on the film question. In July 1931 the *Daily Herald* could talk about 'the bright quality of Hollywood', but only three months later under the headline 'Elstree Being Swamped' complain about the 'menace of American films'.[86] It is therefore difficult to draw a line as to where the Labour Socialist critique ended and the Communist critique began. This will be one of the tasks in chapters six and seven. Having outlined the ideological side of the Labour movement's approach to film it is now appropriate to turn to Labour organization and conditions in the cinema industry itself.

Trade Unionism in the Cinema Industry

The Labour movement certainly contributed to the debates about the British film world, expressing views and opinions on a range of questions from film content to industrial organization. This ideological input helped to shape the nation's perception and impression of the new medium, albeit in a marginal sense. Furthermore, the fact that Labour was embroiled in the film question made an impression on the policy-making process, be it within the Labour movement itself or in the wider political society. Yet, Labour's influence on the evolution of film had more than ideological substance. To understand the Labour movement's approach to film it is necessary to search beyond working-class ideology, culture and consumption into the broader economic and social formation; that is, to situate the movement's approach within a particular mode of Capitalist production. Indeed, at the point of production, the labour force, often organized in trade unions, had an important bearing on the texture and quality of the film product. It is therefore the purpose of this chapter to outline and discuss the salient trends in inter-war film trade unionism: the growth and spread of union organization, the nature of the relationship between labour and capital, and union representation on such issues as working conditions. But first it is appropriate to focus on the range and character of cinema employment.

Employment in the cinema industry

The employment structure of the British cinema industry consisted of many work categories. The obvious distinction to be made is between employment in production, distribution and exhibition. For our purposes, distribution will be omitted from the account, for the overwhelming majority of film trade unionists were engaged in production and exhibition. In production, men and women were employed as actors, artists, technicians, artisans, clerks and typists, labourers and the rest, whilst in exhibition as managers, electricians, projectionists, box-office staff, cleaners, commissionaires, usherettes and general 'dogs-bodies'. In addition, of course, building workers were engaged in the construction and modernization of studios and picture houses. The cinema workforce thus ranged from skilled to unskilled grades.

At the outset it is necessary to provide some approximation of the number of workers employed in the industry. This is no easy task, however. Needless to say, the historian is hindered by a paucity of data. Further, the fact that employment was of a temporary kind, makes it difficult to make comparisons over time. Rank and file film actors, for example, faced endemic casualization in the early 1930s: 'Engagements are usually from day to day at a recognised fee of one guinea per day. The artist has absolutely no security of tenure, and under present conditions is highly fortunate to pick up a couple of days' work a week.'[1] In the same vein, Charles Berry protested that 'crowd artistes consider themselves lucky to be given employment on two days a week, and in many cases they live very precariously and, indeed, dangerously near to what may be called the "hunger line" '.[2] Temporary contracts were a constant source of discontent among various grades of cinema workers. Even so, information gleaned from a number of sources (not always strictly comparable) indicate that there were quite high levels of employment in the inter-war industry.

According to the estimates of A.L. Chapman and R. Knight the average numbers employed in entertainment and sport rose from 101,700 in 1920 to 247,900 in 1938.[3] To be sure, leisure services in inter-war Britain underwent considerable expansion, an expansion which the cinema contributed to. To be more specific, it is apparent that both film exhibition and production recorded increases in employment. Though there are no precise figures for cinemas alone, the occupied workforce in England and Wales in theatres, music halls, picture palaces and concert halls rose by 29 per cent between 1921 and 1931, from 69,826 to 89,744. Given the increase in the number of cinemas and the decline in music halls and theatres, it is likely that most of this rise can be explained by cinema employment. For the same years, the number of manual and office workers engaged in film producing and film studios increased from 4,418 to 6,638, a rise of some 50 per cent and testimony to the resilience of the British industry to American competition. Of the 6,638 employees in 1931, 3,961 were male, 2,002 female and 675 temporarily unemployed. Interestingly, it may be added that the sum of persons professionally engaged as film producers and studio managers rose from 304 in 1921 to 520 in 1931.[4] All in all, Huntley Carter's estimate of 70,000 workers in the 1931 cinema industry seems to be acceptable.[5]

In the 1930s, under the stimulus of protective legislation and the popularity of the sound picture, there were further increases in cinema employment, though with the slump in production in 1937, unemployment began to raise its ugly head. To take a fairly small sector of the industry, the cinematograph film printing and developing trade, as an example, over the period 1924 to 1935 there was a marked expansion of employment, as Table 1 sets out. Of the 852 workers engaged in 1935 – at a total of 15 companies all in the London area – 612 were males and 240 females. Also interesting is the fact that net output per person increased from £294 in 1924 to £555 in 1935, a sure sign that methods of production were becoming more efficient. Obviously, this is only a small part of film production, yet it is again suggestive of more general growth. After all, the 1930s saw the rise of major studios employing literally thousands. Alexander Korda's studios at Denham, for example, recruited some 2,000 employees in the summer of 1936, whilst at the same time Julius Hagen's three studios employed about 1,000.

Table 1 Average numbers employed in the UK cinematograph film printing trade

Year	Operatives	Administrative, technical and clerical staff	Total
1924	520	80	600
1930	563	78	641
1934	650	71	721
1935	768	84	852

Source: *Census of Production*, 1935.

As far as picture houses are concerned, employment in the 1930s was again stimulated by further building and modernization programmes, particularly the arrival of the super cinema. For instance, in August 1930 Associated British Cinemas had a labour force of 3,000 employed at 120 cinemas, doubling to 6,000 at over 200 cinemas by July 1934.[6] As Michael Balcon, then general manager of production at GBPC, expressed it:

Up-to-date buildings, with accommodation for thousands, have sprung up all over the country, giving employment not only to a theatre staff, but with their combined restaurants, lounges and bands, to hundreds of other employees.[7]

Indeed, as one of the 'big two', GBPC employed many thousands of workers; actually over 14,000 in 1933 at its film printing works, two studios at Shepherd's Bush and Islington, and 300 or so cinemas.[8] Notwithstanding the lack of concrete data, the evidence seems incontrovertible – the inter-war years witnessed a marked increase in film and cinema employment. One trade unionist thus remarked that since the 'staple industries can never again be what they were' the film industry could help to fill the employment gap.[9]

Having outlined the industry's employment record, it is possible to move on and consider the hours and character of work. There can be few doubts that film workers experienced very long hours and low wages in the 1920s and 1930s. As we shall see, at a time when the majority of the British working class had achieved the basic forty eight hour week, the fact that film workers often had far greater work loads was a continual grievance and source of resentment. Again it is difficult to quantify the length of the average working week in the industry. Nevertheless, throughout the period in question some groups were spending up to, and sometimes over, seventy hours at the workplace each week.

It is well known that in some studios, filming took place round the clock, involving night and Sunday work, together with double shifts. With the coming of quota production and the talkies, hours were if anything further extended into the night and over the weekend. Michael Chanan has thus insisted that the 'effects of this were manifold. . . . Set dressers, for example, often had to spend the daytime scouring shops for the stuff they needed, and then work through the night to prepare the set for the next day's shooting'.[10] Similarly, the Association of Cine-Technicians (ACT), in their evidence to the 1937–8 departmental committee on holidays with pay, claimed that some technicians were working about a hundred hours on average each week, without overtime pay:

> Film technicians on production are often obliged to work excessive hours (12 to 15 hours a day is frequently worked on production), a seven-day week has been frequently worked, meal breaks are infrequent and often inadequate. . . . One reason for these conditions is that studios are engaged at a weekly rental by production companies and long hours and a seven-day week is, therefore, a form of economy to such producers. . . . That means that the whole time you are on the picture you are at it from eight o'clock in the morning till eleven o'clock at night.[11]

It is true that production was often intermittent and technicians were fortunate to find employment for half the year, yet the intensity of work obviously brought with it much strain and fatigue. Significantly, British Actors' Equity, supported by such 'stars' as George Arliss and Boris Karloff, were also complaining about the length of the working day.[12]

Even so, there were signs that producers were trying to reduce what little control labour had over work time. Julius Hagen, the head of Twickenham Films, no doubt apprehensive about the speculative expansion of 1935, lamented the union's regulation of Sunday work. He advocated the closing down of all British studios for three months to 'get sanity into the salary and wage schedule'.[13] At another level, that great actor and early Council member of Equity, Cedric Hardwicke, reckoned that 'our own film industry is, on the whole, overpaid and under-rehearsed', whilst Korda actually cut wages at Denham in the early part of 1937.[14] For the most part, however, workers of all grades engaged in production worked long hours on insecure contracts, though towards the end of the 1930s some engineers, electricians and other craft workers were enjoying a standardized forty eight hour week in the studios.

If anything the hours of cinema employees were higher than their studio counterparts. In the early 1920s the cinema proprietors conceded a forty eight hour week for electricians and projectionists in places like Birmingham, Bristol, Glasgow, London, and Manchester. However, this concession was eroded with the slump in trade and cinema workers returned to a sixty or seventy hour week. There is perhaps a need to distinguish between part-time employment in the smaller independent cinemas and full-time employment in the larger circuits, though in both cases long hours were the rule rather than the exception. To take but one example, at the time of the publication of the government's White Paper on film in 1937 – which incidentally ignored the question of the working week – the co-operative newspaper *Reynolds' News*, carried a report '70 Hours for 17s. 6d.':

Outside the catering trades and the licensed houses, no industrial workers are more sweated than those who serve the films.

Girls, attractively rigged out in uniform provided by the cinema houses, are working 60 and even 70 hours a week for wages averaging not more than 17s 6d.[15]

As a report of a committee under the chairmanship of Lord Elgin had already stated: 'The long hours during which cinema attendants and ice cream sellers are at the disposal of the employers is particularly noticeable.'[16] Though the International Labour Organization made a recommendation on hours of work in places of public amusement, this had no impact whatsoever on the length of the working week in cinemas. The stark reality was that of an industry which squeezed as much work out of its employees as was possible.

Turning to the character of work, it has been claimed by Michael Chanan, using a broadly-conceived Marxian framework, that work in the film world was, and is, qualitatively different to that in the main manufacturing and service sectors of the Capitalist economy. Very simply, Marx once claimed that under Capitalism workers are alienated or dehumanized in producing objects which are alien to them: the point being that production is not freely chosen but carried out for profit. Important here is the degree of workers' control over the labour or production process. Marxists have viewed this as declining with the rise of new patterns of machine production and work organization, and the transition from 'formal' to 'real' subordination of labour by capital. Notwithstanding the fact that workers have been able to obstruct capital's control of the labour process in a variety of ways, there are a number of reasons for believing that alienated labour is a real phenomenon of twentieth century Capitalism. The limited autonomy achieved by workers at the point of production has been gradually eroded with the introduction of new work systems and technological change, standardization, rationalization, de-skilling, the conveyor belt and a more intensive division of labour.[17] Here, the most fundamental change, so it is argued, has been the application of scientific management. The scientific management theories of the American managerial strategist, Frederick W. Taylor, have been inter-preted in a variety of ways, but generally speaking they have involved the separation of managerial and workers' functions, whereby control over the labour process has passed from the shop floor to the office. Hence it is claimed that new systems of work organization have driven a wedge between mental and manual labour. In the context of inter-war Britain, Craig Littler has asserted that there was a generalized diffusion of a more rational managerial approach to work organization, in the form of the Bedaux system.[18]

Stripped of control and independence, factory and office workers have thus been distinguished from film workers. Chanan explains:

> In all forms of cultural production, including the new technological media, aesthetic workers retain at least some degree of autonomy – if only that of individual style – of a kind which can be progressively denied to the factory worker as the capitalist reconstructs the labour process by introducing new technology, new means of production and new techniques of management ('scientific management'). This process, by which capital acquired real control over labour, depends on being able to quantify the labour process, establish fixed times which each part of the job is supposed to take, which the worker must keep up with. But there is no form of aesthetic production where, try ever so hard, this kind of 'time economy' can be properly imposed. You cannot pre-determine how long a composer should take to write a piece, or a painter to paint a picture. Nor exactly how long it should take to make a film.[19]

As Chanan has expressed it in a slightly different way: 'Ideally, then, a film or any artwork is the product of a particular form of non-alienated labour, which we ought not to reduce to the homogenised, average labour power which capitalism exploits in literally run-of-the-mill industrial production.'[20] In brief, film production is said to allow a creative role for all categories of 'aesthetic' workers from the technical expert, such as the cameraman on the studio floor, to the hairdresser in the make-up department, and the craftsman involved in painting scenery or making props. Chanan does acknowledge, however, that capital has attempted with some success to gain control over all facets of film production.

As the British film industry developed, becoming more sophisticated in the process, workers in the industry were at least partially reduced to the status of a factory proletariat. Aesthetic labour was forced in this direction under the dual influence of specialization and technical innovation. As already noted, there were various groups of workers in both studios and cinemas with their own hierarchies and internal labour markets. Essentially this division of labour between, say, electricians, scene painters, make-up girls, actors and directors was reinforced by technological change encompassing camera work, staging, lighting, music and sound, acoustics, new super cinemas and the like. Accepting the danger of exaggeration, it is arguable that by the 1920s sections of the cinema industry had more or less taken on the characteristics of factory organization. After all, the aim of the commercial cinema industry, at least in the last analysis, was to make profits, and to do this involved some form of managerial control over production, distribution and presentation.

In Hollywood between the wars a new division of labour emerged at studio level following 'the implementation of scientific management by the new vertically integrated corporations'. In Britain, however, Vincent Porter claims that 'production was a far less organized affair than in Hollywood, and films were made in a more artisanal manner'.[21] That is to say, British directors, actors, technicians and other 'aesthetic' workers retained a degree of autonomy and were able to express themselves creatively. There is certainly some truth in this. However, in the well-organized studios of the 1930s, as noted, there was a far more rigorous and systematic division of labour, together with technical adaptation.

Most crucially, it was the change-over to sound which heralded a new stage in the production process. As Rachael Low has pointed out: 'Studios, equipment and methods of work changed dramatically'.[22] Though it is true that the major British studios, particularly Denham and the concerns of Max Schach, were run with varying degrees of extravagance, there were clear signs that control was passing from workers actually engaged in day-to-day production to managers and producers. Since sound meant that cameras and projectors could no longer be turned by hand and had to be regulated by electrical means, artisans lost some of their control over and input into the final product. By the same token, when the talkies arrived, directors could no longer shout their instructions through those rather quaint megaphones, so evocative of the early motion picture industry. More generally, production became compartmentalized. The scenario department, cost and budget department, editing department, distribution department evolved under the general supervision of senior producers, and the studio head controlled the production process through daily viewing of the 'rushes'. Hardly surprising therefore is the theatrical and kine employees' comment that 'studio employment is analogous to a factory or workshop'.[23] Hagen's Twickenham studio has thus been variously described as 'a miniature mass production machine' and 'more or less a film factory'. At the same time, Warner Brothers' studio at Teddington was managed with much professionalism and expertise by the staff from downtown Burbank – 'Like a well run factory' – whilst Ealing under Michael Balcon was becoming 'one of the most consistent and worthwhile of all the British film factories'.[24] Equally, the biggest British studios of the 1930s, at Elstree, Shepherd's Bush, Islington, Denham and Pinewood with their surfeit of studio space, new technology, water tanks, automatic labs, permanent staff and the rest were indeed good examples of film factories, though this did not exclude individual creativity. At Islington, for instance, by 1936, Gainsborough Pictures were produced in the same vein as Hollywood, with production under the close supervision of Maurice Ostrer – the studio head.[25]

It can in fact be argued that finance capital failed to introduce adequate controls or safeguards over the cinema industry. As film companies went bust in the late 1930s, there were disputes between joint stock banks and insurance companies as to who was responsible for overseeing the day-to-day management of film finance. If the truth be known, financial interests failed to discharge this responsibility: speculation had run wild and created havoc.

Even so, on the ground, film work could be as arduous, monotonous, and alienating as other types of employment. This was particularly true as far as cinema employees were concerned, for they had little control over their working environment. In a recent book, *The Devil Makes Work*, John Clarke and Chas Critcher have made the point that in the 1920s girls and women found themselves 'employed in service and leisure industries, which were becoming the new sweated trades. The cinema usherette, working unsocial hours for low wages, suffering from boredom and sore feet was a symptomatic figure – the invisible support of the glittering world of the "dream palace".'[26] A similar claim was made at the time by Major Henry Procter, President of the trade union, the Film Artistes' Association:

> I would also like to call his [the Home Secretary's] attention to another section of this industry, and that is the girls who are employed in the cinemas. In many cases they are overworked and badly paid; they work tremendously long hours in order to give pleasure to the patrons of cinemas; they are working hours that are not decent and under conditions that in my opinion, are slave conditions.[27]

Interestingly enough, Procter was also a Conservative MP for Accrington (1931–45) and sometime director of Capitol Film Productions, British Cine Alliance, Trafalgar Film Productions and Buckingham Film Productions which in turn were all involved with the notorious Aldgate system of film finance.[28] With such a base in film production, Procter presumably had financial reasons, as well as purely trade union or humanitarian ones, for demanding improvements in the conditions of film exhibition.

It is possible to ruminate about the nature of the production process in the film industry, the division of labour and the scope for aesthetic labour to express individual talents. Yet what cannot be in serious doubt is that for some sections of the cinema labour force, work meant long hours and low wages, long stretches of monotonous yet demanding labour. Trade union organization followed in the wake of changes in the labour process and in many instances the deterioration of working conditions.

Trade union organization

The first stirrings of union organization in the entertainment industry can be traced back to the 1890s. In 1890–1 the UK Theatrical and Music Hall Operatives' Union was formed to organize backstage workers; this became the National Association of Theatrical Employees (NATE). The Amalgamated Musicians' Union followed in 1893 and the Variety Artists' Association (VAA) in 1902. With the rise of the itinerant cinema presenters in the early years of the twentieth century, a craft union named the National Association of Cinematograph Operators (NACO) was formed in 1906 as an affiliate of NATE. Despite NACO's base among skilled operators, it was soon forced to follow NATE's general line of recruiting workers from all sections of the cinema industry, both skilled and unskilled; though it should be added that still by 1925 the Association was demanding legislation to ensure that all operators had the appropriate training qualifications.[29] As the official historian of NATE shows, progress was made and a number of agreements were signed with individual cinemas.[30] Union recognition in the cinema was to prove, however, a long drawn-out affair – the site of much bitterness and contestation between employers and unions.

By the 1920s there was already a tradition of union organization in the industry. Even so, the inter-war years witnessed a proliferation of unions catering for cinema workers. Many of these unions, with their short membership lists and limited resources, were little more than nine-day wonders. The Kine Cameramen's Society was formed in 1918, but had only 61 members by 1925 and ceased to exist in the following year, whilst the British Association of Cinematographers lasted from 1928 to 1931 with probably little more than 160 members. The Coloured Film Artists' Association, formed in 1938 with 200 members, ceased to function in 1941 when it had about 18 members, whilst a similar organization, the Eastern and Indian Film Artistes' Association, formed in 1939 with an initial membership of 199 had disappeared a year later. At the same time, the British Film Make-Up Union had a brief history from 1937 to 1940, with approximately 38 workers on its rolls. The Actors' Association, Amalgamated Artistes' Association, Film Artistes' Guild, Film Workers' Union, Oriental Film Artistes' Union, Theatrical Artists' Film Society and Union of Women Musicians all had similar rather undistinguished histories.[31] This did not mean, of course, that all unions which catered for cinema employees were so transient. NATE survived the First World War and continued to organize in cinemas and film studios, and by the 1930s had been joined by the ACT, Electrical Trades Union (ETU), Equity, and the Film Artistes' Association (FAA). In addition some members of the Musicians' Union (MU) were drawn from the cinemas; perhaps over 50 per cent of the union's approximate membership of 20,000 by the mid-1920s.

It is true that unions in the cinema industry faced a number of problems, the most significant of which was the recruitment and retention of members. To some extent this was due to the cyclical patterns of the film trade and the temporary or part-time nature of work, though it must be added that cinema attendances and building seem to have held up even during the recession. As set out in Table 2, membership fell back in the 1920s and early 1930s, but recovered thereafter.

The membership of NATE, for example, stood at 15,000 in 1921 (no doubt benefiting from the boom of 1918–20) falling to 4,098 by 1933, but rising again to 13,408 in 1939. Whereas in 1928 the union's President, Robert Finnigan, complained that 'there is something lacking in the record of the membership', by the end of the 1930s the union congratulated itself on the success of a recruitment drive initiated in 1934.[32] Indeed, in 1938 there were 107 union branches compared with 28 in 1932. Obviously union strength tended to follow the general contours of the trade cycle, rising during a boom, falling in a slump. Also important of course was the level of union organization – the number of full-time organizers and the drive for recruitment.

Table 2 Membership of selected trade unions in the cinema industry

	NATE	MU	VAF[a]	FAA	ACT	Equity[b]
1918	6,000	12,000	3,000	—	—	—
1921	15,000	20,000	6,000	—	—	—
1925	6,000	19,753	3,000	—	—	—
1929	5,807	20,266	—	—	—	—
1933	4,098	10,677	—	380	98	2,190
1936	7,124	—	—	950	1,122	4,055
1939	13,408	—	—	790	1,212	3,469

Source: TUC, *Annual Reports.*
[a] Variety Artistes' Federation
[b] As at 1 January; figures taken from M. Sanderson, *From Irving to Olivier: A Social History of the Acting Profession in England 1880–1983,* London, Athlone Press, 1984, p. 249

Significantly, there was a fairly high incidence of female trade unionists. To take but a few random examples: in 1926 there were 2,082 women in the MU; in 1931, 2,000 in NATE; and in 1936, 370 in the FAA.[33] Locally, according to the *Amusement Workers' News*, there were 2,960 men and 1,078 women in the London branch of NATE in 1926.[34] Of course, not all members of these unions were employed in the cinema industry, some being found in music halls, some in theatres, others in dance halls. In the case of the ETU only a small proportion of union membership was working in film studios or picture houses. Yet, at a time when total membership rose from 34,000 in 1919 to 64,000 in 1939, despite the depression, the ETU gained recruits from the ranks of cinema projectionists and electricians. For instance, in 1937 the total membership of 48,000 included 1,500 projectionists.[35] Judging from the annual entries in the *Kinematograph Year Book*, the union had 'Branches confined solely to Kinema Operators' throughout Britain, including ones in Aberdeen, Belfast, Birmingham, Cardiff, Glasgow, London, Manchester, Newcastle, Southampton, and the rest.

Accepting that it is difficult to analyse the membership structure of entertainment unions, what type of worker was recruited from the cinema industry? Evidence suggests that NATE drew members from professional, craft, skilled and semi-skilled, and general grades: for example, make-up artists, managers and projectionists from the professions; electricians, carpenters, plasterers, painters and glaziers from the craft trades; property men, stage hands, scaffolders and riggers, and labourers from the skilled and semi-skilled trades; and cashiers, wardrobe staff, usherettes, and cleaners from a variety of general trades. NATE had members in both studios and cinemas. As far as ACT was concerned, membership covered the range of skills needed on the technical side of film production, from cameramen and photographers, to sound recordists, editors, directors, continuity girls (the director's secretary) and all those engaged in film processing and printing work. Whereas NATE was a general union, ACT took on the characteristics of a craft union. There were also a number of specialized unions like the FAA which catered almost exclusively for crowd artists. In any case, the entertainment and related unions certainly had to struggle for rudimentary organizational gains and for recognition by the respective employers' associations.

By the early 1920s, when NATE had twelve organizers,[36] it sought quite simply to gain recognition, increase membership and improve conditions of employment. In support of such objectives the union was affiliated to the TUC, Labour party and local trades councils, as well as being represented on the Entertainment National Industrial Council Joint Committee, which had emerged out of tripartite talks involving the unions, employers and the Ministry of Labour in October 1919. Yet, NATE still had to gain the recognition of the vast majority of cinema proprietors. Although the main employers' organization, the Cinematograph Exhibitors' Association (CEA, founded in 1912), announced towards the end of 1921 that NATE was the representative union in the industry, this did not amount to formal recognition. Indeed, the union was forced to fight on against a hostile tide of falling membership and employer intransigence. The union's general secretary, Hugh Roberts, even referred to the exhibitors as 'the most relentless and unscrupulous individuals the world has ever seen'.[37] Perhaps this was one reason why the union demanded statutory enforcement of wage agreements in a deputation received by the Home Secretary in 1935: 'the result was very satisfactory, and prospects are distinctly hopeful for a change in the regulations', as the NATE minutes optimistically put it.[38]

It would be otiose to detail NATE's organizational campaign, though to judge from the union's records, organizers travelled the length and breadth of the British Isles, from London to Aberdeen. Advances were certainly recorded. Notably, in 1932 the London and Home Counties branch of the CEA, NATE and other interested parties formed a Joint Conciliation Board consisting of five members each from the employers and unions, an independent chairman, Sir Henry Davenport (a City Sheriff), and Joint Secretaries, Arthur Taylor (CEA) and Alfred Wall (Entertainment Industries Federation) to explore the conditions of 'staffs employed at Cinema Houses'.[39] In 1935 the Board in fact agreed to a schedule of hours, pay and conditions covering members of NATE, the MU and the Guild of British Kinema Projectionists and Technicians; though it must be said that the ETU failed to sign due to the terms laid down for projectionists, namely a sixty hour week.[40]

However, the CEA only accorded national recognition to the National Association of Theatrical and Kine Employees (NATKE), as NATE was by then called, in 1937. As the official announcement stated:

The Cinematograph Exhibitors' Association and the National Association of Theatrical and Kine Employees, after two years of negotiation,
have arrived at an understanding whereby the national officers of the
CEA have agreed to recognise the NAT and KE as the trade union for
the purposes of the negotiations of wages and working conditions of the
employees of cinema exhibitors.[41]

Responses to the agreement varied from the *Daily Herald's* somewhat optimistic suggestion that it was an 'important step in promoting orderly negotiation of cinema conditions', to the *Daily Worker's* more realistic protest that, by failing to recognize the ETU and other entertainment-related unions, it would lead to inter-union strife and 'factional fights to the detriment of their employees' wages'.[42] For the most part, independent observers and those from the employers' side welcomed this rather belated recognition. The view expressed by S.G. Rayment was echoed elsewhere:

A new era in the relations between proprietor and employee has dawned and the last few weeks of 1937 revealed a far better understanding of labour conditions than would have been thought possible only a year ago. Much preliminary work was done, of course, before there was anything practical to show for it, but the Union making itself responsible for the representation of the staffs, the National Association of Theatrical and Kinema Employees, has handled its members with considerable skill and has kept on amicable terms with the CEA. The two bodies have agreed to discuss grievances – if any – at meetings held in the territories wherever their branches can get together, and both sides have given evidence of a sincere wish for peace and progress.[43]

Whether recognition actually led to 'peace and progress' is highly questionable, yet at least the long drawn-out struggle for fundamental union rights had ended in victory.

On the production side, studio agreements were reached between NATE and a number of companies, the first being concluded over carpenters' rates of pay with British International Pictures at Elstree in 1930. Another one was signed in 1935 with GBPC, covering electricians, plasterers, riggers and scaffolders, stage hands, and labourers at the Islington, Islip and Shepherd's Bush studios.[44] Later in the year, the former stage electrician Tom O'Brien, who as part of a change of control and administration had replaced Roberts as NATE secretary in 1932, claimed 'We now have agreements with most of the British firms in this rapidly-extending industry . . . and we are going forward to include all.'[45] Moreover, speaking at a mass meeting of film studio members in September, O'Brien insisted that 'Already this year . . . the union had secured over £100,000 in increased wages for its members.'[46] It may well have been the case that these claims were somewhat exaggerated, though it cannot be doubted that as the decade advanced and membership revived the union made considerable progress. In 1937 the Association had agreements with twenty two film producing companies. With seventy sections for projectionists by 1938, wage agreements had been arrived at with the ABC, GBPC, Odeon and County circuits, as well as a number of individual CEA branches and all the main studios. According to Rachael Low, by the summer of 1939 the union 'had 33 agreements covering 45,000 workers in 2,500 cinemas'.[47] This is testimony enough to the gains made by O'Brien and his colleagues.

A further notable development was the joint co-operation between the Film Producers' Group of the Federation of British Industries (FBI) and the TUC General Council. The FBI Film Group had been set up to represent the principal British film producers, to encourage film as a means of national and industrial publicity and promote the British export effort, though not to negotiate with Labour. The Group joined forces with the TUC in the early 1930s, as we shall see in the next chapter, in order to ensure that the British film industry received the necessary levels of protection. In furtherance of this objective, meetings were held, a sub-committee set up, film studios visited, and Parliamentary deputations organized. But what is important in the context of union recognition and agreements is that this provided opportunities for representatives of labour and capital to meet on common ground, presumably helping to temper feelings of hostility and combativity. However, this is not to say that consultation at the national level percolated through to the rank and file and to other sectors of the industry. As the *Kine Weekly* reported in 1936, unionists could still attack exhibitors for using 'the language of slave-owners of 150 years ago'.[48]

Elsewhere, the ETU achieved one or two notable landmarks, albeit less publicized than in the case of NATE. According to Frank Tilley, writing in the *Kinematograph Year Book*, the ETU signed wage and hours agreements with CEA branches in the immediate post-war period.[49] Later in the decade the union arrived at an agreement with British International Pictures for electricians working at the Elstree and Welwyn studios. And in 1935 electrical workers employed in the studios of GBPC secured further concessions. 'The discussions throughout were of a nature which signified that the relation between the companies and the ETU was of the happiest', remarked a pleased trade union official.[50] There is certainly some indication that as the union campaigned for a forty eight hour week it gained new recruits. George Humphreys, the union's London district secretary, was very much of this view: 'A considerable number of the projectionists – the "key" people of the industry – are now in member-ship with us.'[51] By 1938, according to the *Daily Herald*, there were more than 700 projectionists and cinema electricians in the London branches of the union.[52] Even so, like NATE, the ETU faced considerable resistance from the employers, as is clearly evidenced by the stance taken by the Bristol CEA who failed to even negotiate with the electricians until prompted by the Conciliation Department of the Ministry of Labour.[53]

At the same time, as a number of accounts have shown, ACT was beginning to thrive. Given the extent of American penetration of the British market and hence the poor state of production in the 1920s, studio workers found it difficult to organize. With the growth of production in the 1930s, however, ACT was formally launched. Originally formed in 1933 as the Association of Studio Workers at the Gaumont-British studio, Shepherd's Bush, the Association aimed to organize and promote the interests of all those technicians in studios and laboratories. The director, Maurice Elvey has recalled:

There were two or three of us who got very annoyed because the people who owned the films and financed them, they used to take them and hack them about and that sort of thing. So, the directors of the period got together . . . and formed an association which claimed the right to edit the first cut of their pictures. Out of this the Association of Cinematograph Technicians derived and I supported this for all I was worth. I was one of the people who insisted on being a member and I used to use the letters ACT after my name and that sort of thing. This used to make me very unpopular with most of the employers, but I was sufficiently in demand not to care a damn, and I didn't and still don't.[54]

Led by the rather eccentric figure of Captain Cope, the first year of the Association's life was eventful, albeit one of mixed fortunes. Helped by Tom O'Brien and Alfred Wall, a rule book was drawn up, a policy worked out and membership increased. By the end of 1933 there were said to be approximately 1,200 members, more likely sympathizers. However, to all intents and purposes the union was little more than a professional association, with a number of middle-class, university-educated members. In the view of R.J. Minney, 'regrettably, the trade union aspect was overlooked and the organisation . . . became a snob association of top film technicians'.[55] Moreover, the union found it difficult to negotiate with employers, financial problems surfaced, and membership began to drop – the official figure for 1933 is ninety eight.

The watershed in the union's early history was the appointment of George Elvin as general secretary in January 1934. A son of the secretary of the National Union of Clerks and brother of an employee in the art department of British and Dominion Studios, George Elvin was a Labour activist and functionary of the National Workers' Sports Association. Little did he realize then that he would spend over thirty years as union secretary. By the mid-1930s the union had been reorganized on a firmer basis: finance was brought under control, regular meetings arranged, a journal published, an employment agency opened, and in 1936 affiliation taken out with the TUC. In addition, there was a more radical edge to the union's personnel: Elvin was an active member of the Labour party, whilst Ralph Bond, Sidney Cole and Ivor Montagu were all Communists. A number of Labour followers, including the leading cinema Capitalists – the Ostrer Brothers of GBPC – also offered their support. Unlike the bourgeois credentials of the early Association, few could now doubt its Socialist identity. The foundations had been laid for a union offensive.

From 1935 the main problem faced by ACT was the lack of a formalized negotiating structure. Anthony Asquith, the director elected to the Presidency of the Association in 1937 and incidentally the son of the former prime minister Herbert Asquith later recalled,

There were no employers' federations with which to negotiate. Studios and production companies had to be tackled one by one and, remember, we were a small and highly suspect body. Before 1930 there was not a single trade union agreement negotiated with a film studio or producer apart from one held by the Electrical Trade Union for their membership at Elstree.[56]

In fact, the Association's first industrial agreement was signed with Gaumont British at Shepherd's Bush in 1936. The agreement which was perhaps predictable given the Ostrer link covered a range of employment conditions. Elsewhere, Elvin and his colleagues found studio heads like Julius Hagen to be quite intransigent, though by the end of 1936 the union had members in thirteen studios, three newsreel companies and various laboratories.[57]

At the same time the Association turned its attention to organization in printing and processing companies. In one sense, this presented an uphill struggle as many of the employers in the trade were fiercely anti-union. Kodak, the American-based conglomerate, with its British factory at Harrow on the north west outskirts of London, started to make motion picture film in the late 1920s. Kodak's management was hostile to the idea of workers' organization and like so many of the newer industries of inter-war Britain attempted to wean employees away from trade unionism through a paternalistic or industrial welfare approach. This benevolent form of Capitalism, by which workers were provided with a range of welfare benefits and privileges, undoubtedly obstructed the ACT unionization campaign and it was not until 1973 that recognition finally came.[58] In 1937, the laboratory members of the Association met the FBI Film Group over the recognition issue, but unsurprisingly were met with 'the unyielding attitude of some of the employers' and 'practically no progress was made'.[59] On the other hand, the fact that in comparison with film studios, laboratory production and conditions approximated more to the division of labour of factory organization with quality control, automatic processes and production line techniques, made it somewhat easier for the Association to attract members. Indeed, already by the summer of 1936 out of perhaps fifteen laboratories the Association had managed to unionize eight, some 100 per cent strong.[60] Significantly this provided the ACT with a much-needed base in the working class. After a long campaign, in 1939 the Association negotiated the first national agreement for laboratory workers with the Film Production Employers' Federation. It covered the wages, hours – a normal working week of forty four to forty seven hours – and conditions of about 1,000 workers in fourteen film printing and processing plants, and was to run for two years. Since its precarious start in 1933, the Association had made advances among both studio and laboratory workers.

Policy and strategy

The unions in the film industry drafted policies which more or less conformed to union norms. That is to say, their major aim was industrial, to raise the pay and improve the conditions of their members. In this the film unions were a good instance of what the Webbs called in one of their best-known passages, 'a continuous association of wage-earners for the purpose of maintaining or improving the conditions of their working lives'.[61] Inevitably, of course, policy was enmeshed with the general question of organization and recognition. But given the abysmal conditions of many cinemas, studios and laboratories, the film unions were preoccupied with demands for normative concessions on wages and hours of work.

The primary aim was to standardize wages and hours for similar categories of work through general collective agreements. Here, unions supposed there would be mutual benefits for both workers and employers. Hence, film technicians demanded 'standard conditions of employment', stressing that it was unjust for men in the highest grade to earn as much as £100 a week in one studio, yet only £9 a week in another.[62] As the *Daily Herald* reported in November 1936: 'The rapid growth of the industry, the Association claims, has resulted in irregular conditions and varied salaries which they now seek to put on a stabilised basis.'[63] In the following year the General Council threatened industrial action to obtain 'a reasonable standardisation of working conditions and salaries for technicians'.[64] In brief, they called for a 48 hour week for studio workers and a 44 hour week, £4 average wage for laboratory staff. As a footnote, the *Daily Telegraph* claimed that 'The object is to bring the British film industry into line with Hollywood.'[65]

By the same token, Tom O'Brien, speaking at a NATE recruitment meeting in July 1934, when average weekly male earnings in the country at large were approximately 56 shillings, protested about the inequity of the wages system in cinemas: in the larger circuits girls were working from 50 to 60 hours a week for 25 shillings, while in smaller cinemas the hours were 55 to 70 with wages ranging from 12 shillings 6d. to 18 shillings. Moreover, sexual discrimination at the workplace meant that men employed for similar hours earned from 40 shillings to 55 shillings in the larger circuits, and 30 shillings to 40 shillings in other concerns.[66] Significantly enough, ACT gained equal pay for women at an early stage. Grievances about the lack of standardization were also taken up by the FAA, who sought a 'Magna Carta' or standard daily contract for the film 'extra'. In advancing the claims of 'extras' or crowd artists in October 1937, the FAA placed its demands before Geoffrey Lloyd, the under-secretary for Home Affairs, albeit with little success.[67] For the ETU, of course, the primary demand was for a standardized 48 hour week for all projectionists.

A popular union objective of the 1930s was holidays with pay. At a time when the wider Labour movement was campaigning vigorously for a general paid holiday for all,[68] film workers also took up the question. In fact, certain categories of the cinema labour force had signed relevant district agreements in the 1920s. The *Ministry of Labour Gazette* for March 1925 lists holiday pay agreements for cinema operators in Coventry, Glasgow, Sheffield and the West Riding of Yorkshire.[69] By 1937 many of the large circuits had conceded one week's paid holiday, whilst studio and laboratory technicians in permanent employment received two weeks' holiday pay. According to the unions, holidays were a necessity given the long hours of work and, in the case of laboratories, the dangerous nature of work (darkroom environment, use of chemicals, hot and steamy printing rooms, etc), a necessity which the industry could seemingly well-afford. It is significant that the unions were demanding paid holidays for all grades, including free-lance and part-time staff. As NATKE put it: 'We submit that all employees in all cinemas should obtain an annual holiday with pay.'[70] In the end collective agreements were to satisfy the workers' demands.

Aside from wages, hours and paid holidays, the unions framed a number of more general policies dealing with such matters as public safety in cinemas, censorship, training, taxation, and, as we shall see in the following chapters, protection and Sunday entertainment. Most important was the fact that throughout the inter-war years the unions were apprehensive about labour replacement and technological unemployment. After all, in national terms unemployment was the most protracted problem of the inter-war economy, a view shared by all trade unions. In 1923, for example, Sir Montague Barlow, the Minister of Labour, received a deputation from the Joint Committee of the Actors' Association, MU, NATE, and the VAF on the question of 'Importation of Coloured Performers'. Though the deputation stressed that 'They were not taking exception to the colour line, as there were some coloured people in this Country who were of the best', they were clearly opposed to 'alien' artistes and musicians who 'add seriously to the ranks of our own Unemployed' and 'invariably evade the payment of Income Tax'.[71] It must be added, however, that the unions' view on this question was never fixed or unalterable – by 1931 NATE, together with the VAF, the Water Rats, West End Managers and other bodies, were protesting that restrictions on the immigration of foreign artists be lifted so as to attract the best talent from overseas and stimulate demand for entertainment.[72]

The ACT was also anxious about unemployment. Given the cyclical downturns in production and the fact that a number of studios employed foreign technicians – Alexander Korda was well known for his patronage of refugees from Hungary and Central Europe – the ACT claimed that employment opportunities were diminishing. In November 1935, the film correspondent of the *Daily Herald* reported that the ACT expressed '"grave alarm" . . . at the influx of those whose skill it is claimed is not superior to that of British technicians, many of whom are without regular employment'.[73] With the production recession of 1937 an ACT deputation to the Ministry of Labour again espoused the view 'that no further permits be given for the employment of foreign technicians for the film industry until unemployment among British technicians has been reduced to a minimum'.[74] To be sure, unemployment which was running at 80 per cent by 1938 was a recurring hardship for many technicians, forcing some to pawn their belongings or surrender their insurance policies, and others to turn their hands to new fields like the cameraman who began driving a coal cart.[75] Yet to concentrate the blame for unemployment on foreign technicians deflected debate from other causes, namely the very instability of the industry itself.

A less kind analysis might point to the chauvinism of the ACT, particularly at a time when continental refugees were fleeing from Fascist tyranny. Even Ralph Bond slipped into the fray: 'The technicians must no longer be the victims of that inverted form of snobbery which makes a virtue of a foreign name, relegating the native talent to the third rate stuff.'[76] Less surprising perhaps was the opinion expressed at the 1937 TUC conference by NATKE's Tom O'Brien, who in praising such 'British' productions as *Catherine the Great* (London Film Productions, 1934), *Tudor Rose* (Gainsborough, 1936), *Victoria the Great* (Imperator, 1937) and 'those wonderful films of Jessie Matthews', called for the protection of 'British cultural and educational standards from alien disparagement and infiltration'. In this he was seconded by George Elvin, who insisted that the Aliens Order should be used against foreign technicians. Though R.A. Bradfield of the Shop Assistants spoke up for the internationalization of art and culture, the rather nationalistic resolution was carried. The biggest irony perhaps was that the next item on the TUC agenda was a fraternal address by E. Kupers of the International Federation of Trade Unions.[77]

Somewhat differently, with the arrival of the talkies in the late 1920s, the musicians rightly feared job losses. After much debate and campaigning the MU moved a resolution successfully at the 1930 Scottish TUC:

> That in view of the serious unemployment being caused among
> Musicians by the introduction of American controlled and manufactured
> apparatus and the deliberate campaign to force British cinemas to adopt
> sound films against their will, this Congress request all those interested
> in the trade union movement, especially officials and shop stewards, to
> use their influence with their fellow-members to induce them to refrain
> from patronising those places where human orchestras have been
> displaced.[78]

Support for dismissed musicians was indeed forthcoming, and in an official letter to all trades councils, the General Council of the Scottish TUC urged workers to boycott all cinemas in which the sound picture had led to redundancies.[79] The position of the musicians was quite understandable at a time when the realities of technical change have to be seen against a general worsening of employment opportunities in other sectors of the Scottish economy.

Across the border in England, the Entertainments' Composite Committee, comprising NATE, MU, VAF and the Concert Artistes' Association, was pressing the Minister of Labour, Margaret Bondfield, on the very same question.[80] As A.V. Drewe, the general secretary of the VAF, claimed, 'the mechanical form of entertainment known as Talking or Sound Films . . . is, displacing the human element in these employment markets, and is rapidly leading along a line of practical extinction for those persons concerned'.[81] In fact, at a deputation received by Bondfield in February 1930, Fort Greenwood of the MU stated that about 10,000 musicians had lost their jobs due to the talkies.[82]

Unfortunately for the entertainment workers concerned, claims about unemployment did not seem to gain a particularly positive response from Bondfield. Maybe this was due to the popularity of the sound picture, a point stressed by the Board of Trade and trade unionists alike.[83] James Brownlie, the engineering union president, thus asserted that no amount of resolutions could stop the talkies if they were popular.[84] Obviously the talkies were more than a passing fad; they were indeed very popular, leading to redundant cinema orchestras with many cellists and violinists finding themselves without a job, though the cinema organ was often retained.[85]

It is important to place the union demands for higher pay scales, reduced hours, paid holidays, employment protection and the like in an organizational and indeed a cultural context. Unions were attempting to organize and improve the material conditions of workers within a more ordered collective bargaining framework of negotiations and agreements. The aim to standardize employment conditions undoubtedly had a cultural as well as an industrial impact. This point is sometimes missed by historians of film. Without knowing it, the trade unions were associated with the construction of a more homogeneous film product produced and packaged in similar ways and under similar conditions. In one sense, of course, union organization was a channel by which 'aesthetic' labour could preserve or reclaim its independence and control over the cultural commodity, yet the unions, in stressing the need for uniformity in industrial relations practices and in negotiating with capital, were accepting to some extent the wage form, the need for technical change and a range of other factors which underpinned the Capitalist mode of film production and presentation. In other words, in analysing the shape and character of film, it has to be economically and socially situated within the relations of production; not only the hours and nature of work, with which the first part of this chapter was concerned, but also the ways in which union organization impinged on these conditions. This is to say nothing, of course, about the way films were actually received and experienced by working-class cinema audiences. That is another story.[86]

The way unions promoted their strategy, that is, their policies and demands, also influenced the development of film. Michael Chanan has made a distinction between the militant strategy of the ETU and the conciliatory, even collaborationist, strategy of NATKE. He suggests that whereas the ETU was willing to use strike action, the theatrical and kine employees aimed to prevent strikes. In particular, Chanan provides a detailed account of the 1938 projectionists' strike.[87] Very briefly, the CEA's national recognition of NATKE in 1937 prejudiced the negotiating position of the ETU. Consequently, ETU branches in Hull, London and Manchester came out on strike in the Easter of 1938, ostensibly to preserve the principle of the forty eight hour week which NATKE agreements had eroded. On the first day of the dispute over seventy cinemas were closed down in London, together with a further 250 temporarily stopped. Despite the use of 'scab' labour, there were demonstrations, pickets, leafleting, support from the studios and even a call by Manchester Post Office girls and shop assistants to boycott cinemas. The strike was particularly strong at Hull where, according to the *Daily Worker*, the proprietors 'distributed thousands of free tickets in a vain attempt to make a show of trade'. In June, the London dispute ended in defeat, having affected about 700 projectionists and caused a loss of 11,500 working days.[88] In the case of Hull, 'after a magnificent struggle which lasted for 30 weeks [the strike] had finally to be abandoned due to blacklegging by non-members'.[89] Only in Manchester was the forty eight hour week retained.

It is apparent that Tom O'Brien, supported coincidentally in the Commons by the Conservative MP Alfred Denville, regarded the ETU action as 'sabotage'. Indeed, O'Brien had already declared that the ETU was 'manifestly Communist ridden'.[90] Trouble between the two unions can in fact be traced back to the immediate post-war period. In 1920–1 inter-union disputes involving NATE and the ETU were referred to the TUC Parliamentary Committees in England and Scotland.[91] It is indicative that whilst the MU was calling for 'Unity Among Entertainment Workers', NATE continued to attack the ETU as 'an organisation whose intervention has been provocative of disunity within the Industry'.[92] Hardly surprising is the ETU's counter-claim that NATE had broken three separate agreements with the electricians by the early 1930s.[93] The Ministry of Labour was certainly quite aware that 'there is a good deal of rivalry in regard to the question of representation'.[94] As the Ministry's

Conciliation Department put it on another occasion:

> The efforts of the ETU have been handicapped by the National
> Association of Theatrical Employees who are making strenuous efforts
> to organise the miscellaneous workers at cinemas and have been
> disposed to enter into agreements with employers on lines which are not
> satisfactory to the ETU.[95]

Moreover, it has even been claimed that NATKE's recruitment surge of
the later 1930s was successful because ETU members were poached or
replaced during strikes.[96]

However, it is important not to exaggerate the differences between the
two unions. True, both unions were engaged in 'poaching' members and
this naturally led to some inter-union disputes. Yet, such disputes were
fairly commonplace in the wider trade union movement, for instance
between the transport workers and the railwaymen. Moreover, there was
certainly some co-operation between NATE and the ETU. In October 1923
the *Daily News* reported that both bodies were acting together to improve
labour conditions.[97] Then again, there had been some co-operation on the
Home Counties Joint Conciliation Board, whilst in 1934 meetings were
held under the auspices of the two unions to promote cinema organization.[98] Towards the end of the 1930s NATKE and the ETU, together with
the ACT, FAA and the British Association of Film Directors, acted on a
broad front through the Film Industry Employees' Council. If there were
signs of conflict, there were also signs in a different direction of mutual
tolerance and in some cases joint activity.

It is also doubtful whether NATE was totally averse to militant action.
In the summer of 1935 the union emphasized that 'Complete freedom from
Industrial Disputes has been the Association's boast for the year.'[99] There
are many instances of NATE intervening in unofficial disputes and
resuming negotiations or bringing about a settlement, for example at
Denham in July 1936 and at Wembley and Shepperton a few months
later.[100] But equally, given the intransigence of some employers, the
union acknowledged that industrial disputes were inevitable and worthy
of support.

The NATE minute books demonstrate that strikes were by no means
unknown. In the second half of 1921, for instance, industrial action was
taken in such towns as Blackpool, Nelson and Portsmouth.[101] Furthermore, it is suggestive that in 1928 the union was critical of the movement
for co-operation between labour and capital, colloquially known as
'Mondism'.[102] Indeed, at this time the Sheffield branch was engaged in a
long dispute with the CEA which even led the City's Chief Constable to
complain about hooliganism.[103] The dispute involved a boycott of various
cinemas in Sheffield, and though management hoped that with 'the advent
of the dark evenings and the return to the winter weather, that their lost

patronage will be regained', a range of Labour groups supported NATE's line.[104] Despite the fact that a Labour meeting addressed by Dr Marion Phillips was held at the blacklisted Wickham Picture House, organized Labour showed considerable sympathy for the entertainment workers' cause.[105] In particular the local trades council seems to have provided the Association with every assistance, though the exhibitors remained hostile.

Interestingly, trades councils up and down the country were to support the Association in a number of disputes. As O'Brien put it to the 1937 TUC:

> Delegates, especially those actively associated with the trades councils, already know of the great struggle we have been making in regard to the organisation of cinema employees in recent months. We have been involved in quite a number of organising campaigns. I want to thank those delegates on the trade councils for the great support they have rendered us, especially in recent disputes. We had great support in organising what is, after all, a very difficult industry to organise.[106]

The Association's *Annual Report* of the same year also noted that 'record is particularly made of the Trades Councils of Nottingham, Leicester, Pontypridd, Oldham, Manchester, Newport, Llanelly, Aberdeen, Cardiff and Huddersfield, for their recent support in many directions'.[107] In brief, NATE may have followed a conciliatory strategy and preached the need for peaceful labour relations, yet this did not preclude the need for industrial action on certain occasions.

More generally, when circumstances dictated, other unions were also willing to follow a militant strategy. In the early post-war period, when on the back of an economic boom the trade union movement was on the offensive, cinema workers were involved in a number of disputes. G.A. Atkinson summed up the situation:

> It was impossible that the kinema Industry could escape the prevailing unrest, and trouble in one form and another has been apparent throughout the year amongst all grades of kinema workers, partly because these latter were themselves in the throes of organisation.[108]

From then on until the end of the 1930s there were many sporadic disputes. In 1929, for example, the MU was embroiled in an official dispute at Wembley studios over the union's labour price list, which halted the musical and sound synchronization of a film version of Edgar Wallace's story, *The Crimson Circle*.[109] The Cine-Technicians, though committed to 'Co-operation with Employers' in its objects, had a left-wing leadership which was prepared to take industrial action. Even workers in the smaller unions were called out on strike. In 1936, the FAA struck at Denham studios during the filming of *Troopship* (Pendennis Picture – London Film

Productions; the film was released in 1937 as *Farewell Again*), whilst in 1939 coloured extras belonging to the Oriental Film Artistes' Union picketed Denham over a contractual problem.[110]

It is true that unions preferred peaceful negotiation, hence their repeated claims for recognition and negotiating rights, and their occasional deputations to Whitehall. In an industry with fairly low union density levels, and thus low funds, there was good reason to avoid strikes. In the last resort, however, when employers continued to exploit the workforce, when hours were long and wages poor, and particularly when fellow workers were victimized, Labour organizations had little option but to take direct action. This was perfectly summed up by the London branch of NATE in 1928:

> In accordance with our declared policy, to avoid disputes and to pursue the channels of conciliation to the fullest extent we negotiated with Mr Sidney Bernstein to try and arrive at an amicable agreement covering his Circuit . . . we were denied the right of organising his places. . . . Again steps were taken to avoid a conflict but unsuccessful, and eventually decided on the only alternative 'Drastic Action' [sic]. This was taken in the form of Boycott, Parade of Sandwichboardmen, Bill Distributing, circularising Trade Union and Labour Branches in all areas where Mr Bernstein had a place of amusement. Undoubtedly our attack had a very great effect upon the patronage . . . we have no apology to make for embarking upon the move which is quite in compliance with our duty as a Trade Union.[111]

Again, strikes had some bearing on the production and presentation process, and thereby on the form and content of films.

This chapter has argued that in order to understand the British Labour movement's influence on film, it is essential to focus on the mode of production and presentation, and trade union organization therein. Evidence suggests that cinema workers of various grades experienced poor working conditions. Though labour on the production side of the industry is ideally aesthetic or creative, there were forces militating against this in the special conjuncture of inter-war Britain. In an industry which was especially prone to booms and slumps, studio and laboratory workers were adversely affected by wide pay differentials, long hours, technical and organizational innovations, and insecurity of employment. For workers employed in cinemas, the main bone of contention was the length of the working week and the poor rates of pay, leading some commentators to disparage this most modern of sweated trades. To be sure, trade union organization improved the conditions of employment, though producers and proprietors were often unwilling to negotiate with or recognize the unions. Even the miners' cinemas in South Wales failed to concede recognition to NATKE,

13 As new cinemas were opened, more and more workers were recruited. Staff are to be seen outside the Paramount, Manchester, on its opening day in 1929

14 Even smaller cinemas, such as Scholes Picture House, Wigan, on the day the talkies arrived in 1929, had to have managers, projectionists, cashiers and doormen

15 Arguably, usherettes were the most exploited group in the cinema workforce, though even they were usually attired in neat uniforms, as was the case at the Paramount, Manchester

16 Workers at the Paramount, Manchester, were expected to do a range of tasks, like operating the electrical control panel

17/18 Projectionists were often looked on as the 'aristocracy' of the cinema work-force. Here we have the projection room at the Savoy, Darwen (c.1920), and the Roxy, Hollinwood (c.1939)

19 Musicians, such as those at Manchester's Piccadilly, were often employed in cinemas, though employment fell in the 1930s with the advent of the talkies

20/21 Cinema managers had to keep a close eye on finance, especially wages, as at the Macclesfield Majestic in September 1924

The Macclesfield Majestic Picture House, Ltd.

WEEKLY SUMMARY.

Week Ending Sept 27th 1924

				Wages and Insurance	40		
Takings gross	396	19	7	Petty Expenses	3		
Less Stamps	47	14	11	349 4 8	Films:—			
				Covered Wagon	100	0	0
				Pathé	2	15	0
				Eve		13	6
				Comedy	2	0	0
					2	10	0
Safe and Chocolates				Pictorial		13	6
				Man v Beast	1	0	0
				Heating		10	
				Lighting		2	
				Newspaper Advertisements		2	
				Posters		5	
				Posting		4	
				Bills Art Posters, Slides, etc.		2	
				Programmes		1	
				Carriage on Films and Posters			
						2	
				Rent Rates Taxes		2	
					200		
Total Nett Receipts	349	4	8	Total Expenses	200 0		
	200	13	3				

	WAGES DETAILED. GROSS								
...aye.	Occupation	£		Health	...ploy				
...Hoxton	Manager	7	10	0					
...oth	Doorman	1	7	6	6	9			
...Wood	Boilerman	1	5	6	6	9			
...denshaw	Heater	3	5	6	6	9			
...gdon	Asstt. ofenter	1	4	0					
...od	Bass	2	4	6					
...nwood	Violin	4	10	0					
...ges	organ	2	16	0					
...gton	Cornet	2	10	0					
...dley	Piano	3	15	0	6	9		5	
...eatther	Flute	3	0	0	6	9		5	
...ailey	Clegner		15	0	4			5	
...ellman	"		15	0	4	7			
...ott	Barhia	1	0	0					
...Davis	"	1	10	0	4	7		5	8
...gdon	Checker		10	6					
...lton	"		12	0					
...arter	"		13	0	4	7		5	8
...lin	"		13	0					
...a Checker	Lat. Even		4	6					
		40	3	0	3/6	5/6		3/9	6/2

22 A controversial issue in the 1930s was the Sunday opening of cinemas. Here, the public sign a petition for Sunday films at the Pyramid, Sale

leading Tom O'Brien to take up the matter with Oliver Harris, the general secretary of the South Wales Miners' Federation.[112] Nevertheless, slowly but surely the likes of NATKE, the ETU and the ACT began to make advances, in terms of both rising membership and benefits for that membership. By the end of the 1930s, as S.G. Rayment wrote, the industry was 'shaking off the casual labour methods of its fairground ancestry, and its employees are, or can be, organised on lines similar to those of other established businesses'.[113]

All in all, this chapter has stressed that discussion of the working class and film must focus on production and presentation, as well as consumption, if it is not to be incomplete and inadequate. In the first place, the social relations of production and union influences on those relations obviously fed into the construction of the film product. Despite changes in the production process, the discussion must end by once again noting the element of control over film-making exercised by scriptwriters, directors, technicians and the rest – the ACT being particularly concerned about this. At another level, though working-class audiences undoubtedly responded favourably to the expansion of cinemas and to some of the Hollywood and British epics of the period, this rather cosy picture has to be qualified by reference to the exploitative conditions of employment. The obverse of consumption is production, and here, notwithstanding certain levels of creative autonomy and countervailing union pressures, sections of the cinema labour force were literally degraded by the realities of their working existence. For every satisfied cinema audience there was almost certainly a group of underpaid and overworked technicians, laboratory assistants and usherettes.

Labour, Film
and the State

From the late nineteenth century there had been an extension of State involvement in economy and society. The period of the Liberal Welfare Reforms (1906–14) and the First World War witnessed a growth in the ability of government and its supportive agencies to regulate all manner of economic and social questions. Notwithstanding the remarkable durability of *laissez faire* doctrines, by the 1920s the collectivist tide was sweeping all before it. True, after the armistice of November 1918 there was clamour for deregulation of the economy and a desire to return to free trade, the Gold Standard and the balanced budget – a world of minimal State intervention and Gladstonian financial orthodoxy – but attempts to halt the growth of the State were only partially successful. Indeed, on balance, the public sector expanded in the inter-war years, and there was a rise in central and local government expenditure: as a proportion of Gross National Product, government spending increased from 12.4 per cent in 1913 to 30 per cent in 1938. Moreover, despite a number of economic, political, administrative and technical constraints, the period witnessed a growth of the government's policy-making machinery. In recent years a number of historians have suggested that there were important changes in the role of the State in inter-war Britain, together with changing perceptions as to the place of the State in a modern industrial society.[1] With the abandonment of the Gold Standard in September 1931 and the implementation of policies dealing with trade (tariffs and quotas), rationalization of industry, investment, agricultural marketing, the depressed areas and the like, the government was beginning to make a contribution, albeit a minor one, to the rejuvenation of the British economy. Though the Keynesian revolution in economic thought and policy had to wait until after 1945, even in the more conservative 1930s the ideas of John Maynard Keynes were beginning to influence sections of all the main political parties, the business community and the trade unions, and to penetrate the inner sanctuaries of Whitehall.

The State's sphere of influence was more than just a move towards the managed economy, it also involved a greater emphasis on legislation, regulation and licensing. Aside from central and local government, the Civil Service, the police, judiciary and the various quasi-official bodies of the British State were performing a much wider role in economic and social life. More specifically, as I have argued elsewhere, the question of leisure was gradually taken up at all levels of the State.[2] Indeed, since completing *Workers At Play*, I have found further evidence in the annual reports of the Ministry of Health showing that there was a significant rise in State spending on leisure. The annual expenditure of local authorities in England and Wales on libraries and museums rose from £1,009,804 in 1920 to £1,768,711 in 1927 and £2,787,188 in 1937, whilst in the same years expenditure on parks, pleasure gardens and open spaces increased from £2,530,181 to £4,498,418 and finally to £6,294,269. Thus in terms of public spending, as well as legislative reform, taxation policy, and regulation by the administration, police and courts, the State impinged on a wide range of recreational and cultural questions. This was as true of cinema-going as it was of other leisure activities.

As stated in chapter one, the cinema industry was also under some form of central control before the Great War. The 1909 Cinematograph Films Act provided local authorities with the power to inspect cinemas to ensure that precautions had been made against fire. Further legislation was to follow in 1927 and 1938, providing the means of protecting the British industry from American competition. From 1912, local authorities also received the advice of the trade-financed British Board of Film Censors (BBFC) on the suitability of film content. Having considered such advice, the authorities then had the task of granting licences for exhibition purposes. It was to be this form of censorship which was to play such an important part in the cinema story of the inter-war years. Furthermore, at a time when the British Civil Service was mushrooming, so too was the official machinery concerned specifically with films. The fact that in 1932 the Board of Trade welcomed proposals for a British Film Institute with powers to advise 'all Government Departments concerned with the use and control of films', on the condition that this did not replace the Board's own Advisory Committee on films, is just one small clue to the administrative momentum of the period.[3]

The Labour movement was a crucial force in the debates about legislation and censorship. Organized Labour was embroiled in the policy-making process leading up to legislation, and moreover was directly affected by protection and censorship. More than this, Labour made further inputs into a range of other film-related questions. As noted in the previous chapter, the film trade unions lobbied MPs and sent deputations to various departments of State. Then again there was the work of the British Film Institute and the Cinematograph Films Advisory Council on which Labour was represented. At a slightly different level, the Labour governments of 1924 and 1929–31 had an official responsibility for film policy, be it through changes in entertainment tax, the overseeing of the film unit of the Empire Marketing Board, or the establishment of a specialist brains-trust such as the Colonial Films Committee of 1930. It is especially fascinating that in 1931 Isidore Ostrer offered the Labour government the voting shares in the Metropolis and Bradford Trust Company which had a controlling interest in the Gaumont British Picture Corporation. After discussion with Ostrer's solicitors the government did not accept the offer on the grounds that it amounted to a minority holding and 'actual control' could not be assured 'without the vote of the independent chairman'. No doubt the Board of Trade was also suspicious 'that the offer is in some way related to the rivalry between Gaumont British and British International Pictures'.[4] Evidence therefore suggests that there was an intimate relationship between the British cinema industry and the various organs of the State, and that the Labour movement was part of this relationship. This chapter will explore the nature of this relationship with special reference to protectionism and censorship. But first a brief discussion of entertainment tax.

Entertainment tax

At a time when State spending was rising there was a search for new forms of revenue. Given that the leisure industry was expanding in the inter-war years, generating high levels of consumer expenditure and in turn rising profits, entertainment was looked upon as a possible source. In fact, entertainment duty or tax (as it was more usually referred to) was first introduced in 1916 as a means of raising much-needed war finance; it was imposed on all payments for admission to 'any exhibition, performance, amusement, game or sport'. In some ways an emergency or temporary tax, it was easy to collect, politically acceptable as taxing a 'luxury', and thus survived the war. Possibly the cinema-goer had become a sheet-anchor of the British fiscal system. Up until June 1924 a common scale for all admissions was in force, but then the Finance Act removed the duty on all tickets not exceeding 6d, together with reductions on tickets less than one shilling 3d. During the government's economy campaign in 1931, however, the free limit was reduced to 2d, and other duties were raised. Consequently, between 1931 and 1932 the percentage of gross receipts paid out in tax by cinemas increased from 11 to 16.5 per cent. It is true that the 6d exemption was restored in 1935, but by this time the average price of admission was above 6d, meaning that about 16 per cent of cinema receipts were still paid out in tax. By 1939, cinema proprietors paid out 2d in tax on every one shilling ticket, rising to 4d on every one shilling 9d ticket, and even higher rates on the more expensive seats. Further, the cinema industry contributed about 70 per cent of the revenue derived from entertainment tax. Indeed, by the Finance Act of 1935 cinemas had been discriminated against, for whereas they had to pay the full tax, live entertainments benefited from a reduced tax.[5]

Unsurprisingly, the trade through the Cinematograph Exhibitors'

Association was opposed to the tax and made repeated attempts to get it abolished or at the very least reduced. From 1916 there were numerous protests, and even during the war claims were made that up to 700 cinemas had closed down because of it. The 1952 PEP study of film summed up the trade's case against the tax:

first, that the rate was too high to be borne and that it was forcing the industry into bankruptcy; second, that the incidence acted as a form of price-control which virtually prevented the industry from passing on its increased costs to the public; and third, that the discriminating rates gave rise to unfair anomalies.[6]

Certainly the tax was a burden on the finances of the industry, no doubt having implications for pricing, investment and wages policy. In 1931, for example, Gaumont British was said to have paid out over £1 million in entertainment tax. And, in overall terms, the industry paid out £6.8 million in 1934, though falling to £5.6 million by 1939–40.

The Labour movement supported the exhibitors in their campaign against the tax. Both the TUC and the Scottish TUC passed the same resolutions of condemnation in 1921:

Congress protests against the continuance of the Entertainment Tax on the grounds (1) that it was originally a war-time tax, and now that the war is over it should be removed; (2) its incidence is grossly unfair, as it places a much heavier burden on the lower-paid seats and penalises the working-class section of the community; (3) it prevents the economic readjustment of the business and tends to keep down the wages of the employees engaged in it.[7]

It was claimed by the musicians in particular that the tax was unfair as it fell heaviest on poorer people. This was a significant anomaly, so it was claimed, for the poor had as much right as any social group to the new forms of amusement. J.B. Williams of the Musicians' Union put it this way: 'Entertainments are part of the cost of living so far as the working classes are concerned. Amusements and entertainments are just as essential to the brain as food is to the body.' He went on to claim that the tax was affecting profits and so damaging employment prospects.[8] The campaign against the tax continued in the early 1920s, receiving the wholehearted support of the Scottish TUC and backing from three hundred MPs.[9] Interestingly enough, support was also enlisted at local level. Having been prompted by the National Association of Theatrical Employees (NATE), the South Shields Labour party and Trades Council thus pressed the local borough to modify the tax.[10] Further south, the Walthamstow Labour party was not happy about the fact that there was the possibility of imposing the tax on Labour social evenings.[11] It is therefore probable that this opposition was an important factor in the

Labour government's decision to revise the tax in 1924.

Even so, the problem had not been resolved by the time the second Labour government took office in 1929. More significantly, despite claims from NATE that they needed to be consulted over this issue,[12] entertainment tax was increased in 1931. For the rest of the decade Labour groups continued to protest against various aspects of this fiscal policy. The National Conference of Labour Women recommended the abolition of the duty on all entertainment where the price did not exceed 6d, whilst the Manchester and Salford Workers' Film Society lobbied the Home Office on the same question.[13] Such demands had not been a waste of time for, as we have seen, the tax was rescheduled on several occasions in the 1920s and 1930s. Yet, it must be added that it was not until 1960 that the entertainment tax was abolished altogether.

Protection

As this study has emphasized, the British film industry was finding it very difficult to ward off American competition in the 1920s. The point has already been made that by 1926 only 5 per cent of the films shown on British screens were of British origin. This was the nadir of British film production, stunted as it was by American booking practices. Something had to be, and indeed was, done to reverse the trend. It is our task here to outline the debates about British film production, the responses to protective legislation and the position taken by organized Labour.[14]

A range of interested parties claimed that film production in Britain could be strengthened through the imposition of a protective tariff or quota. Whatever the form of protectionism the aim was apparent: to discriminate against the Hollywood product. Appropriate legislation was drafted in 1927, the Cinematograph Films Bill, designed to introduce quota protection. What were the origins of this legislation? Interestingly, The Era claimed at the beginning of 1928 that the protectionist idea had been first mooted by a leading trade unionist:

> Curiously enough, the Secretary of the NATE, Mr Hugh Roberts, has the distinction of being the 'father' of the Bill, though it was due entirely to accident. As everyone knows, he is a member of the London County Council, a position which he acquired entirely in the interests of the theatrical business. At one of the meetings of the Council a debate arose on the Cinema [c. 1925], and he made certain suggestions which were picked up by the other side. An agitation supported by the British Federation of Industry was made, and as a result an investigation was ordered, and the re-opening of British studios is now only a matter of time.[15]

In fact, as the paper acknowledged, it was the Film Producers' Group of the Federation of British Industries (FBI) which was primarily responsible for the legislation. The evidence suggests that the voice of the unions was rather muted on this occasion.

Broadly speaking, the FBI was in favour of an imperial economic bloc behind a common tariff, though there was some dissent by a group of free traders. In the field of film, it was hoped that quota protection could both increase British production and further the interests of the Empire. It appears from the records in the Confederation of British Industries' Predecessor Archive that the FBI Film Producers' Group began to discuss the question actively in 1925. Between May and December an effective policy was thrashed out at a series of conferences about film production.[16] At the same time, the House of Lords was discussing British films, as was the Board of Trade. Indeed, by the end of the year the Board of Trade had consulted all sections of the trade – producers, renters and exhibitors. Whilst the producers were strongly in favour of a quota, the exhibitors were less happy as they benefited from the popularity of the Hollywood product. Even though a Joint Trade Committee consisting of representatives drawn from all sections of the industry worked out a voluntary plan establishing quotas and tighter controls over unfair booking practices, this was rejected by a referendum of exhibitors.

Furthermore, the President of the Board of Trade, Sir Philip Cunliffe-Lister, was still unconvinced about the need for protection. Though drawing attention to the fact that 'nearly every film shown represents American ideas, set out in an American atmosphere (and in American language) [with] American houses, American motor cars, American manufacture, and so forth', he refused 'to take immediate and drastic action':

> My conclusions are that the protective measure of compulsory quota would be, at present, a mistake, for the following reasons:–
>
> (1) We should not have the general goodwill of the exhibitors; and we ought not to compel them to do what they may be prepared to do voluntarily.
>
> (2) Public opinion is still growing, and if the exhibitors are allowed to try voluntary methods, and fail, we shall be in a far stronger position to enforce the compulsory system.
>
> (3) An immediate compulsory quota would encourage the inefficient or unscrupulous producers (who are numerous) to raise a little money in the old way and produce bad films to force upon the exhibitors – which might damn the whole scheme.
>
> (4) Parliamentary time would not admit of a contentious measure.[17]

Nevertheless, he did conclude by stressing that quota legislation would be introduced if a voluntary agreement was not drawn up by the trade. He also toyed with the idea of restriction against block booking, and perhaps most interesting of all the need for a national studio with financial assistance under the Trade Facilities Acts (1921–6) – these had provided the Treasury with the means to guarantee business loans for approved purposes.

As is well known, a voluntary agreement was not forthcoming and the Conservative government, under the protectionist influence of Stanley Baldwin, was forced to take action. Admittedly, their task was made that much easier as the 1926 Imperial Conference had given some support to the notion of an Imperial films quota, whilst sections of the British press like the *Daily Mail* had come out 'flat-footed in favour of a quota'. Cunliffe-Lister therefore announced his plans for film legislation to the Cabinet in January 1927.[18] Soon afterwards a Bill was published drawing upon the FBI's quota proposals and the Exhibitors' call for regulation of the distributors' unfair booking practices. Not surprisingly, the Bill received broad support from the ranks of the Conservative party. But what we need to investigate further is the policy stance of the Parliamentary Labour Party.

As discussed in chapter two, sections of the Labour party were suspicious that the Bill was designed to interfere with the leisure habits of the working class. It was feared that the Tories sought to inculcate into workers elevated modes of cultural behaviour by preventing them from watching films of their own choice. However, there were further elements in Labour's opposition to the Bill. Reading through the Parliamentary debates, it is possible to discern three main areas of contention.

First and foremost was the position taken up by those Labour advocates of free trade. Since the formation of the Labour party in 1900 free trade precepts, to some extent inherited from the Liberals, had been influential. After all, Labour's first Chancellor of the Exchequer in 1924 was none other than Philip Snowden, a free trader *par excellence*. Snowden brought to the office a set of orthodox financial beliefs and policies. He stressed the need for a balanced budget, a return to the Gold Standard, and, most of all, free trade. In short, he followed Gladstonian financial orthodoxy to the letter, and exuded a thorough-going moral condemnation of government extravagance. Hence when he rose from the opposition benches in March 1927 it was with little surprise that he attacked the Films Bill:

the most important provision in this Bill is that which deals with the quota, and I declare that this introduces a hitherto unthought-of restriction and limitation of trade. . . . This is only the first step. It is ridiculous legislation, and if the House of Commons endorses such a proposal as this, it will be an encouragement to the President of the Board of Trade and other Protectionists to carry the restriction still further.[19]

For him, protectionism brought with it the likelihood of retaliation or reprisals by American interests, which would create a whole series of new problems. Put simply, he believed that the best and most efficient way forward was for the British cinema trade to modernize its own structures and practices: 'Let it apply brains and business ability to the problem, and then, in spite of the national advantages which America possesses, there would soon be, under the influence of competition, a reasonable proportion of British films.' There was some justification in J.T.C. Moore Brabazon's comment that Snowden was 'a great Liberal who wants things left alone'. True, Snowden espoused economic liberalism on many occasions, and, true, he may have been rather naive in assuming that British capital had the means to compete with Hollywood, but it is important to remember that he had a charismatic appeal in Labour circles. As one of Labour's leading financial experts, Snowden was able to exert a strong personal influence on the Party's economic and social policy.

The wider Labour support for free trade was most amusingly expressed during the films' debate by Colonel Wedgwood:

is the world going to come to an end because we cannot build up a film industry in this country? Do we really depend upon developing a more or less parasitic trade of that kind here? Hon. Members might just as well say that we must have a banana industry in this country, that we must produce bananas, that we must make a banana quota in this country, and to eat them when they are grown. We have got on very well all these years without growing bananas in this country, and I presume we can still get on.[20]

More generally, Labour members spoke of the need for freedom of contract; there was disquiet that the legislation would be used to interfere with the right of cinemas to conduct their business as they thought fit. That is to say, certain Labour members such as Snowden, Wedgwood, Thurtle, Beckett and Day felt it wrong for the State to intervene in 'normal business transactions' or, more specifically, to prevent renters and exhibitors from continuing with blind and advance booking of films. Significantly, Colonel Harry Day, the Labour MP for Central Southwark and an exhibitor, probed governments for many years about the condition of the cinema industry. Ernest Thurtle also drew an amusing parallel with book commissioning in which he referred implicitly to Lloyd George's infamous sale of honours:

Suppose, for illustration, the right hon. Member for Carnarvon Boroughs (Mr Lloyd George) were to go to a publisher and offer to write a book on money as it affects party politics. I am sure the publisher would make a blind booking of that without insisting upon the details of the particular book.[21]

If publishers were allowed this freedom, Thurtle argued, then exhibitors should also be allowed to book films in advance. Rather curiously then, the party of Socialism was advocating free trade, free competition and freedom of contract.

Following on from this, the second area of contention related to the administration of the Act. A number of Labour members argued that the Act would inevitably spawn new forms of State control and administration. The point was most eloquently stated by Arthur Greenwood:

> The President of the Board of Trade is the greatest exponent in this House of the fantastic caricature of Socialism, which hon Members profess to believe is supported by Members on these benches. This Bill is a caricature Socialist Measure, with its licences, its registration, its records, its books, its inspections and its penalties. . . . To anybody who has read its provisions, the Bill is the wildest farrago of administrative nonsense that was ever contained in the pages of a Measure submitted to this House.[22]

Far from the Labour party cramping industry, Greenwood asserted that the Tory government was creating the instruments of a 'slave state', a 'kind of bastard bureaucracy'. Additionally, as A.V. Alexander and Colonel Wedgwood noted, the new machinery of government would undoubtedly increase State expenditure, and in turn the taxation of working-class consumers. Presumably, Labour members wished for government funds to be directed into more deserving areas. Anyway, it is again rather ironic that countervailing pressures to dirigiste measures were coming from the Labour and not the Conservative benches.

Third and finally here, the Parliamentary Labour Party was especially critical of the links between the Conservative government and the FBI. It was easily assumed that the association between Tory Cabinet Ministers and leading employers was undemocratic and fundamentally against the Labour interest. As Harry Day rightly announced: 'There can be no doubt that the only people in the trade who want this Bill and who are the driving force in connection with it are the producing group of the FBI.'[23] Snowden even went so far as to claim that Cunliffe-Lister was 'simply a tool in the hands of the Federation of British Industries'.[24] At its most extreme, this view suggested to Labour members that the producers sought to influence government down undemocratic channels, and that relations between the FBI, Board of Trade and other organs of the Establishment had been essentially conspiratorial. Moreover, there was a feeling that the measure would foster and enrich vertical cinema trusts, and so benefit the speculator whilst adversely affecting the working-class consumer. From a Marxist perspective it is possible to argue that the government of the day had been captured by the vested interests of capital; or, to express it another way, the agencies of the Capitalist State were helping to regenerate part of the profit-making film system. The problem with such a perspective is, of course, that film capital was split on this question – there were deep divisions between producers, renters and exhibitors, and between British and American interests.

In essence, Labour's economic case against the Films Bill was designed to protect the interests of the working-class cinema-goer. The Bill was perceived as a Draconian piece of legislation which sought to promote certain sectional business interests, namely the producers, against the more general interests of the industry as a whole and the ordinary consumer. None of this means, however, that Labour was opposed to State intervention as such. Indeed, some Labour MPs argued that the best way to reform and modernize the industry was through direct State help under the provisions of the Trade Facilities Acts. It is doubtful if Labour realized that Cunliffe-Lister himself had already proposed this solution in the privacy of Cabinet. Even so, it is likely that Labour would have welcomed a government measure which was genuinely concerned about the interests of consumers as well as producers.

In the end, Labour was left with no alternative but to delay legislation through filibustering. Simon Hartog explains:

> In committee, Labour adopted obstructive and delaying tactics, but, apart from making the Bill's committee phase one of the longest on record, the only apparently substantial concession that they obtained from the government was the imposition of a time limit, eventually ten years, on the duration of the Act.[25]

Thus the legislation succeeded in establishing quotas of 5 per cent for exhibitors and 7½ per cent for renters, both set to rise to a maximum of 20 per cent by the mid-1930s. In addition, restrictive booking practices were to be stamped out, and at least 75 per cent of wages were to be paid to British labour (the scenario writer also had to be British). One final point, it is apparent from the debates that Labour believed the legislation was not 'going to enforce the making of better pictures than are made at this moment', as it presented the opportunity for 'incompetents to make fortunes'. In other words, Labour speeches were anticipating the coming of quota quickies. Having outlined Labour's initial position on the issue of film quotas, it is now possible to evaluate how they responded to the experience of protection in the 1930s.

In fact the general policy of organized Labour on this issue was soon to change. At first, there were certain complaints about the administration of the legislation. The TUC thus protested that there was no Labour representation on the Board of Trade Advisory Committee on the Films Act which had been set up to oversee the workings of the legislation. This grievance was made more galling as certain sections of the trade were represented.[26] However, it was soon clear that the Act was a success, a fact acknowledged by most commentators. Margaret Dickinson and Sarah

Street believe that it attracted investment and encouraged the transition to sound; George Perry demonstrates that it 'was immensely successful', making available money for the industry and encouraging the growth of circuits; and Jeffrey Richards suggests that it 'was a major stimulus to the industry, and a definite strategy emerged to meet the new situation'.[27] Certainly very few people doubt that the British picture industry revived after the Act; there was greater investment, a move towards vertical integration and concentration, the transition to sound, and the production of more British films, though many of these were cheap and of poor quality. Even though American domination remained, there were few calls for a return to free trade. The previously hostile Parliamentary Labour Party thus failed to modify the Act when they formed the government between 1929–31, the new President of the Board of Trade, William Graham, and his Parliamentary secretary, W.R. Smith, claiming that it was assisting British production. Indeed, there developed an all-party consensus in favour of protection, particularly after the introduction of the Import Duties Act in 1932.

By the early 1930s the trade unions in the cinema industry were in fact calling for 'an amendment to the Cinematograph Films Act, to incorporate that at least 50 per cent of the performance shall be of British character'. Apparently, NATE and others were apprehensive that monopoly powers in the industry were seeking to exploit loopholes in the quota. Moreover, there was a genuine fear that American domination was creating unemployment, and denying the general public the opportunity 'to choose the character of their entertainment'.[28] There is something of a paradox here, of course, as the Labour party had previously stressed that the limitation of US films was infringing upon the liberty of working-class consumers. Anyway, the unions continued to press for a more effective quota system.

During 1931, NATE made several representations to the Board of Trade and the Ministry of Labour, at which their request for an increase in the quota 'was received very sympathetically'.[29] The union emphasized to Percy Ashley, the Principal Assistant Secretary of the Industries and Manufacturers Department of the Board of Trade, seemingly with little foundation in fact, that they were architects of the 1927 Act:

> I am duty bound to draw your attention, first and foremost to the fact
> that we, as an Association, were not only interested, but can be claimed
> to be, without any vanity, the pioneers of the Cinematograph Films Act
> (1927) and we certainly appreciated the placing of that Act upon the
> Statute Book, although not altogether satisfied, but despite the short-
> comings it must be recognised that it did give an opportunity of genuine
> British Studios being formed and to cut away to a certain degree
> the powerful grip that foreign monopoly had upon the British screen.[30]

Again, NATE claimed that American interests such as Fox, Paramount and RKO, with the backing of British exhibitors, were attempting 'to regain their monopoly over the British screen under a subterfuge'.[31] Though the TUC was not wholly convinced by the arguments of NATE, particularly the call for a 50 per cent quota, they too began to argue for more effective protection.

From the summer of 1931 a sub-committee of the TUC General Council, consisting of J. Bromley, W. Citrine, W. Milne-Bailey and J. Rowan, held a series of meetings on the quota issue with the Film Producers' Group of the FBI, represented by H. Bruce-Woolf, A. Dent, J. Maxwell, S. Rowson, and C.M. Woolf. The TUC and FBI were not in favour of increasing the quota, but they did wish to 'eliminate worthless films' by making sure that quota productions 'must have cost at least £150 per 100 feet to produce (with a maximum requirement of £10,000)'. In addition, it was claimed that the powers of the Board of Trade Advisory Committee should be enlarged with direct TUC and FBI representation. Once again there was a rather crude anti-Americanism behind the TUC recommendations. Trade unionists and producers alike drew attention to 'the menace of the Americanisation of the world by means of the film', seemingly boosting US products and undermining 'English speech, customs, and cultural stand-ards'.[32] This rabid form of chauvinism, as stated, was a feature of Labour's general approach to film at this time. The TUC and FBI visited British studios, sent deputations to the Board of Trade and generally campaigned for legislative reform. However, Walter Runciman, the President of the Board of Trade, though acknowledging the claims of business and Labour, would not promise any radical changes.[33] Even so, Board of Trade officials were soon to be drawing up memos setting out the record under the 1927 Act and observing the views of all sections of the industry.[34] In fact, by the mid-1930s fresh legislation had to be considered as the 1927 Act, given a ten year life, was coming up for renewal.

In order to consider the future of the British film industry on the expiry of the 1927 Act, the Board of Trade set up a departmental committee of Inquiry in 1936 under the chairmanship of Lord Moyne. Significantly, by this time, as Simon Hartog has asserted, 'The influence of the film trade unions . . . was much more noticeable and direct'.[35] The cinema unions with their rising membership, resources and campaigning strength were able to exert a not too insignificant influence on the deliberations of the so-called Moyne Committee. Already Robert Finnigan, NATE's president, had condemned those interests that were agitating for the repeal or modification of the quota.[36] Equally, the newly-formed Association of Cine Technicians (ACT) campaigned for the retention of a quota. Both NATE and ACT submitted evidence to the Moyne Committee in which they argued the case for protection. Without going into the details, it may be stated that the unions' main concern was to ensure that new film legislation should provide safeguards against foreign competition and so protect the employment prospects of British cinema workers. Interestingly enough, ACT also suggested that legislation should include a minimum cost test – so as to solve the problem of quota quickies – a fair wages clause, and restrictions on the number of foreign technicians allowed to work on quota films. What emerges from a reading of the relevant departmental file is that the ACT was particularly anxious to prevent all but the top foreign technicians from securing a job, a point already discussed in the previous chapter. Thorold Dickinson thus stressed that the union 'would always welcome the real expert, but was strongly adverse to the admission of the lesser qualified foreigner who could teach British technicians nothing'. It must be added, however, that the Ministry of Labour believed that since the industry often depended upon foreign specialists, such as trick cameramen, they had to be admitted into the country.[37]

The TUC General Council consulted and to a degree co-ordinated the policy of the main entertainment unions. In its memorandum to the Moyne Committee the TUC proposed that new legislation retain the principle of quotas to be fixed at 29 per cent rising to 54 per cent in the sixth year in the case of renters, and 25 per cent rising to 50 per cent in the case of exhibitors. A cost test was also sought, but in overall terms the aim was 'to ensure the maintenance and development of a strong and intelligently conducted British film producing industry and to assist progressively to improve the quality and to extend the influence of British films'.[38]

The Moyne Committee received voluminous evidence from Labour, business and other interested parties. Unfortunately from the unions' point of view, the Committee decided at an early stage not to 'make a detailed enquiry into the wages and other conditions of employment in the film production industry, as these are matters for which the Minister of Labour is primarily responsible'.[39] In essence, Moyne reported in favour of legislation designed to prevent foreign domination of the British film industry. In order to achieve this the Committee recommended quotas for both long and short films on a progressively rising basis, and, as a way to improve the standard of the British product, financial assistance, a strong Films Commission and a quality test.[40] As was the case in the 1920s, recommendations of this kind did not satisfy all interests, particularly Hollywood. The unions had certain reservations, whilst there were again divisions in the trade between exhibitors, renters and producers: whereas the Cinema Exhibitors' Association was opposed to a shorts quota, for example, the FBI was in favour. Moreover, soon after the report was published a slump in trade exposed the serious structural difficulties which the industry faced: US domination, overproduction, high costs, speculative finance and the rest. This made the debate about the future of the industry all the more contentious and fragile. Given such circumstances, rather than implement the recommendations of the Moyne Committee, the government again had to take the responsibility for legislative reform. The role of the State was as a broker of conflicting interests.

What is immediately clear in reading the main Parliamentary debate on the new Cinematograph Films Bill of 1937 is that the free trade question was now inapposite. As Tom Williams, the Labour member for Don Valley and advocate of the unions' case, put it: 'whatever our general views may be on the fiscal problem, I do not think we can import into this Debate questions of Free Trade or Protection, or any other of those ancient problems'.[41] Labour accepted the need for protection, unsurprisingly perhaps given the remarkable degree of consensus on this fundamental issue. In broad terms, Labour Parliamentarians voiced support for the trade unions, particularly when it came down to the need for fair working conditions, and the need to prevent legislative evasion through a strong Films Commission. It should also be remembered that during these debates the working-class movement, and other interests, outside Parliament were carrying out a concerted campaign, ably described by Rachael Low.[42] The minutes of NATKE for November 1937, for example, clarify that there had been a great deal of correspondence between the union and a variety of interests including the TUC, FBI, British Advancement Council and others. At the same time, a 'magnificent united demonstration held at the Victoria Palace on the 7th of all interests on the working side of the Film Studios was given', whilst meetings were taking place with a group of MPs, Isidore Ostrer, and Oliver Stanley, the new Board of Trade President.[43] Furthermore, in the early part of 1938, NATKE, ACT and the Film Artistes' Association participated in a mass lobby of those MPs on the Standing Committee considering the Films Bill. Their main aim was 'to amend the Films Bill to ensure Continuity of Employment, Fair Wages and Working Conditions to all engaged in the Industry'.[44] The channels of union influence were therefore fairly wide-ranging.

The Cinematograph Films Bill became law in 1938. The new Act provided for long film quotas of 15 per cent in the case of renters, 12½ per cent for exhibitors, rising in stages to 30 and 25 per cent respectively. It also seems that the unions had been fairly successful in their efforts, as the legislation included a minimum cost test, a fair wages clause, and the means to set up a Cinematograph Films Council on which two places were allocated to the employees – to be taken up by A.M. Crickett of the Film Artistes and George Elvin (Sir Walter Citrine, the ex-TUC secretary was to be an independent member). However, though there was a degree of self-congratulation, the unions still had a number of grievances. For instance, A.M. Crickett complained that the fair wages clause was being contravened by those production companies which represented American renting concerns, whilst others called for an increase in the quota.[45]

Somewhat earlier, Ralph Bond had rather amusingly referred to the legislation 'on the basis of the double personality of Oliver Stanley, President of the Board of Trade – one of the two being Oliver Hardy, the other Stanley Laurel. Certainly the destructive activities of the Laurel-Hardy team are well paralleled in the attitude of the Government towards an industry of considerable national importance.'[46]

Whatever the course of the 1938 Act, obviously the second world war intervened, and after 1945 the economic and social conditions in which film functioned were to be radically transformed. None the less, the quota protection of the late 1920s and 1930s was not without its successes, providing the means for a more dynamic British film industry. Though the Parliamentary Labour Party had at the time been against the main provisions of the 1927 Act, by the following decade policy had changed. Under the influence of the cinema unions and the TUC, and with a general turn to protection, the broad Labour movement accepted the need for film quotas. It is true that US domination continued and that quota quickies were a problem in the 1930s. Even so, the Labour movement, and the unions in particular, were able to participate in and perhaps influence the official policy-making process through their negotiations with employers and frequent dealings with the Board of Trade, Ministry of Labour and other organs of the State. At least the unions were able to ensure that governments, public servants and other policy-makers were informed of the interests and policy positions of organized Labour.

Censorship

To be sure, the British Labour movement played a part in the formulation and implementation of film policy, even at the highest levels. As such, Labour was incorporated into the structures of the State, having some bearing on its internal development. Notwithstanding a number of financial, administrative and technical obstacles, the State had greater controls over the British cinema industry by the end of the 1930s than it had ever had before. There was quota legislation, entertainment tax, safety regulations and a growing State bureaucracy which channelled powers and funds into such quasi-official bodies as the British Film Institute, General Post Office film unit, Cinematograph Films Council and the Cinematograph Section of the Stationery Office. Organized Labour participated in, or at the very least was aware of, such developments. We will now discuss the relationship between the Labour movement and a further quasi-agency of the State, the British Board of Film Censors.

The film legislation of the 1920s and 1930s undoubtedly had an ideological and cultural purpose; that is, to promote British values and institutions, and prevent the spread of American ones. This was also the case with the BBFC, which to a degree was an arbiter of tastes and conventions. It is important to appreciate at the outset that the BBFC was not a formal organ of the State. From its beginnings in 1912 the BBFC had an independent status, being financed by the trade and simply asked to make recommendations to local authorities on the suitability of films by issuing 'A' (adult) and 'U' (universal) certificates or by withholding certificates from 'improper' films, depicting such matters as horror, nudity and sex or miscegenation. It was the responsibility of the local authorities and not the BBFC to dispense licences. Thus, the BBFC was not part of the official State machinery, nor did it have any statutory powers, merely the right to advise. As one survey has suggested, 'To define censorship as intervention by the state is therefore misleading.'[47] Here, however, the activities of the BBFC are regarded as dependent on State patronage, and intimately linked to the needs of Parliament, the Home Office, local government, as well as private industry. After all, members of the Board acknowledged as early as 1921 that they had a close working relationship with government.[48] The BBFC often operated through official policy-making channels, and its hierarchy was in effect dependent on the State's appointment policy. The Home Office circularized local authorities on the need to abide by the recommendations of the BBFC, whilst the Board's President had to be 'acceptable' to the Home Secretary. Palpably, the major functionaries of the Board were of a politically and morally conservative disposition: successive presidents, T.P. O'Connor, Edward Shortt, and Lord Tyrrell of Avon, the secretary, J. Brooke Wilkinson, the senior script examiner, Colonel J.C. Hanna, and his assistant, Miss N. Shortt (Edward's daughter). In addition, by the early 1930s the Board was given extra powers – the right to vet scripts and the opportunity to liaise with local authorities through the Home Office's Film Censorship Consultative Committee. To be more precise in the context of this study, the BBFC, together with other more direct forms of State censorship, impinged on the activities of the workers' film movement. It is to this aspect of Labour's relationship with the State which the discussion must now turn.

In the late 1920s and early 1930s there was a great deal of controversy over the question of Soviet films. Although some of the Soviet classics were exhibited at the private shows of the bourgeois London Film Society from 1925 onwards, there was considerable disquiet in Establishment circles when it came down to presentation to proletarian audiences. Hence in 1927, questions were asked in the House of Commons about the 'subversive propaganda' of Russian films.[49] And from then on sections of the right-wing press began to attack Soviet films. Commenting on the performances of the London Film Society, A.W. McIntosh put it this way: 'The gutter Press has shrieked for the prohibition of such limited exhibition'.[50] Further, in 1930 Conservative party Central Office protested that seven films of 'Communist propaganda' had received a public presentation.[51] Not surprisingly, such protests were accompanied by calls for 'legislation giving powers to the Government to prevent the exhibition of films of a subversive nature'.[52] Actually, moves had already been made to curb the exhibition of Soviet films.

James Robertson, a historian of the BBFC, has shown that by 1924–5 the Censors were prepared to cut or ban films depicting 'Bolshevik propaganda'. Hence in 1926, the Censors in consultation with the Home Secretary, Sir William Joynson-Hicks, decided to ban Eisenstein's *Battleship Potemkin*. This was followed in 1928 by a ban imposed on Pudovkin's *Mother*.[53] By the end of the 1930s the Board had censored some eight early Soviet films. It was left, however, to the local authorities to implement such decisions. This in effect meant that Conservative councils were more likely to follow these recommendations of the BBFC, whilst Labour councils were less co-operative.

The Conservative-controlled London County Council began to intervene in the activities of the workers' film movement in 1929. In November of that year the Council banned a public film show organized by the London Workers' Film Society.[54] More significantly, in February of the following year, it refused permission for the ILP-influenced Masses Stage and Film Guild to show *Mother*, even though it had been presented by the London Film Society in 1928.[55] In the course of numerous protests, particularly from the Independent Labour Party who saw the ban as 'aimed at the working-class character of the Guild',[56] the Council codified its decision: films which had been censored by the BBFC, together with those that had as yet not been viewed by the Board, were not to be licensed for exhibition.[57] It does appear that there were political motivations behind the Council's position, no doubt apprehensive that Russian films were 'likely to cause a breach of the peace if shown'.[58] Even so, the Council did make a number of concessions, presumably due to the calls for a more liberal censorship regime. Privileges similar to those enjoyed by the London Film Society were extended to all film societies giving private shows, on the condition that those films rejected by the BBFC were not shown, that admission be by ticket only, and that programmes be communicated to the Council at least seven days before the day of exhibition.[59] In other words, films which had not been submitted to the BBFC could be shown in private. In some ways the London County Council had merely disguised its true intentions, which became more apparent towards the end of the year when they gave themselves powers to approve the rules of private film societies, and to prohibit films containing 'subversive propaganda'.[60]

Various local authorities outside London also sought to shackle the activities of the workers' film movement at birth. The Salford Watch Committee, for example, banned the local workers' film society's private exhibition of Pudovkin's *Storm Over Asia*, even though it had already been seen in Bristol, Cambridge, Edinburgh, Glasgow, Newport, Oxford, and West Ham. Despite protests from the *Manchester Guardian* in a leader entitled 'Storm Over Salford', and the Dean of Manchester, Dr Hewlett Johnson, who pointed out that 'there are fine things connected with Russia', the Watch Committee would not relent.[61] Eventually, permission was granted by the Manchester Watch Committee and the film was shown at the city's Futurist Cinema, 'a few yards from the Salford Border!'[62] Interestingly enough, by 1936 the film had been shown in Britain on 120 occasions within twelve months. Elsewhere, evidence suggests that local authorities in Birmingham, Cardiff, Glasgow, Liverpool and Sheffield were no more lenient, and again a range of Soviet films were banned. The emerging workers' film movement, which will be discussed at some length in the final chapters of this study, was indeed finding it difficult to operate.

Moreover, restrictive judgments by the local State were reinforced by the coercive action of the police and judiciary. Police intervention was commonplace. As Herbert Marshall has recalled: 'We found that in trying to show *Battleship Potemkin* . . . one was almost up against Scotland Yard and the Special Branch in those days.'[63] Further, it was claimed that the police attempted to stifle those workers' groups filming demonstrations, marches, and the like. Indeed, the Metropolitan Police kept a close watch over film and newsreel coverage of the 1932 May Day demonstration and 1934 Hunger March.[64]

At local level there is certainly evidence of police intervention; for example, in the affairs of the Manchester and Salford Workers' Film Society. According to the *Daily Worker*, the police were conspicuous at the performances of the Society, there was intimidation, and complaints about 'Communist propaganda'.[65] On this occasion, the *Daily Worker* was undoubtedly correct. Even the Home Office's Film Censorship Consultative Committee admitted that 'observation had been kept' on the activities of the Society.[66] Both Reg Cordwell and Alf Williams have also recalled that the police raided one show, leading to the proprietor of the cinema being fined and the Society being blacklisted by the Cinema Exhibitors' Association. In the view of Williams: 'they were always harrassing us . . . got us where they wanted us'.[67] The position faced by the Manchester Society must have been fairly intolerable, as its case was taken up by Ivor Montagu through the channels of the Parliamentary Film Committee. Even though the Manchester Watch Committee had a fairly liberal approach, and even though the Society adhered to the letter of the law, exhibiting only those films that had been passed by the BBFC and trade shown – 'everything had been done in accordance with the regulations' – the police and the licensing authorities still managed to impose fairly Draconian controls.[68] Equally, in Glasgow, as Douglas Allen has found, 'The socialist counter-culture's alternative film network had been struggling since 1930 to operate a regular workers' film society that could outlast the periodic police raids and magistrates' closure orders.'[69]

It is also as well to remember that the authorities tried to prevent the showing of non-inflammable films (sub-standard stock on 16 mm), in spite of the fact that they were outside the terms of the 1909 Films Act. This issue involved a range of State agencies and quasi-agencies from the Home Office, Board of Trade and Board of Education to the Treasury Solicitor, Tonbridge Fire Brigade Chief Officer, Warwickshire County Council Architect, Senior Electrical Inspector of Factories, Clerk to the Birmingham Justices and the rest.[70] Unsurprisingly, the Labour movement was dismayed by attempts to ban working-class films on sub-standard stock.[71] In 1934, the police prosecuted the trustees of the Miners' Hall at Bolden Colliery, near South Shields, for showing without licences *Battleship Potemkin* and a film about the British hunger marches. The courts judged, however, that since both films were non-inflammable the case should be dismissed.[72] At least the workers' movement had the freedom to exhibit acetate film without being compromised by the Censors, police and licensing authorities.

All in all, the various instruments of the State, whether the BBFC, Film Censorship Consultative Committee, local councils, police or licensing authorities, were hardly sympathetic to the working-class cinema movement. Somewhat inevitably, Labour activists pointed to the political character of film censorship, as seen to function against the Socialist interest. To put it in fairly crude terms, it was assumed that the BBFC would as a matter of course ban Soviet films or other films with a radical message, whilst providing certificates for those films of the status quo; and, even when films of a challenging nature got through the scrutinies of the Board, there was always the possibility of restrictive intervention by local watch committees, the police and judiciary.

Both Labour Socialists and Marxists pointed to the politics of censorship. The Labour MP and founding member of the all-Party Parliamentary Film Committee, Ellen Wilkinson, protested to successive Home Secretaries that the BBFC 'tends to conservatism and orthodoxy'.[73] If anything, her views became more militant:

> Apart from anything else, however good the British Board of Film Censors are – which they are not, for they are thoroughly bad – it still remains not the best way of acting. A Board that is paid by the Trade and depends on the Trade should not have the right to censor, because that means that the films of the big producers tend to get through in any case. You have this definite political censorship, and censorship of new ideas that are coming from the Continent, and which are much better for the public to see than some of the stuff that is being produced.[74]

Other Labour supporters interested in this question had a similar perspective, claiming that the censorship system needed to be overhauled and replaced by more democratic and accountable machinery.

On the Marxist left, censorship was hardly going to moderate their rather crude theories of ideological indoctrination by the Capitalist State. As chapter two pointed out, some Communist party members, for instance, viewed film simply as an ideological support of capital meant to win over working-class confidence to the system. The *Daily Worker* carried a number of reports and articles on the political aspects of censorship and even ran a column about banned Soviet films, 'Films Which Workers May Not See'. Outside the Communist party, certain left-wing commentators believed 'that censorship under present-day conditions is a political necessity' and 'one of the capitalist weapons that must be attacked'.[75]

On the face of it, there seems to be overwhelming proof that the censorship system was linked to the needs of the dominant groups in British society. Certainly there can be few doubts that the Censors were hostile to new ideas, especially those which were politically challenging. The National government's first Home Secretary and leader of the Liberal party, Sir Herbert Samuel, though imbued with a liberal approach and a reluctance to extend the powers of the State, conceded that censorship had a political role to play:

> This question of censorship is a very serious one. We do not want this country to close its eyes to things that are going on in the world and we do not want intelligent people to be refused the right of seeing films which are good in themselves merely because they may have some contentious elements in them of which most of us would disapprove. We do not want them to be limited to private societies like the Film Society for seeing those films. On the other hand, we do not want to have films exhibited which may give rise to great controversy and perhaps to breaches of the peace, and which would be distasteful to a great many people; so you have to steer a very careful line. The Board of Film Censors are well aware of that.[76]

It does not need too much imagination to realize that Samuel's comments were directed mainly against the Soviet film, even though a few months earlier, as a representative of the Parliamentary Film Committee, he had jumped to their defence. It is a peculiarity of the British policy-making process that permanent civil servants can moderate views in a fairly short space of time.

By the same token, the Home Office's Film Censorship Consultative Committee, representing the London County Council, County Councils Association and the Association of Municipal Corporations, 'agreed that, while they wished all reasonable steps to be taken to encourage the development of genuine film societies, they were unwilling to recommend the grant of unrestricted facilities to the other type of society which aimed at showing political propaganda films to as large a public as possible, and could not be trusted to restrict admission to genuine members of the society'.[77] On another occasion, the chairman of the committee, Sir Cecil Levita, recommended that newsreels 'be confined to description and that we should bar out propaganda or criticism'.[78] No doubt the decision of the authorities to censor parts of the American *March of Time* series can be related to the views of Levita and his colleagues.

Although the BBFC did not have the official right to review newsreels, as Anthony Aldgate's excellent monograph on the newsreels and the Spanish Civil War has shown, there were attempts at censorship over, for example, the depiction of the 1938 Munich crisis.[79] Furthermore, successive Home Secretaries seemed to be happy with the censorship system and were reluctant to accept the need for reform. Even the Labour Home Secretary, J.R. Clynes, 'was satisfied that on the whole the existing system of film censorship worked as well as any alternative which could be devised'. Hence his decision to turn down requests for an official enquiry into censorship made by both the Parliamentary Film Committee and the Birmingham Cinema Enquiry Committee.[80]

As discussed in the opening chapter, most historians believe that the purpose of censorship was to maintain the cultural and ideological status quo. The evidence compiled here seems to support such a view. However, there is a need for a number of caveats. First and most importantly, censorship may have had a politically conservative purpose, but it did not necessarily have such a function or effect. Producers of films had to respond to the demands of the cinema-going public and provide them with what they wanted. They could not afford simply to impose conservative views or standards of behaviour on audiences. And since the BBFC was trade-dominated, films in demand were invariably passed, albeit sometimes with minor alterations. Perhaps the Censors were able to ban Soviet films precisely because there was not such a buoyant demand to see them. Alternatively, producers were able to by-pass the strictures of Censors by employing a number of devices. Thus, to take but one example, though the BBFC was unhappy about films which were critical of Nazi Germany, Gaumont British was able to court their sympathy by producing an eighteenth century drama, *Jew Süss* (1934), which exposed the evils of anti-Semitism. Furthermore, even when films had 'bourgeois' messages it would be difficult to show that workers accepted them uncritically, or failed to readapt them to fit in with an essentially working-class culture.

Second, reading through some of the departmental files it does seem that the BBFC and outside interests were more concerned with films of a 'non-political' nature. From a Marxist perspective, of course, there is no such thing as a non-political film. After all, comedies, romance and adventure films all carry with them a particular view of the world, usually a middle-class one. Nevertheless, the Censors and others turned their attention increasingly to the moral and sexual content of films. In particular, there was some concern that young people were being corrupted by cinema-going. For example, some so-called experts maintained that there was a link between films and juvenile crime. Even King George V was concerned that the film, *The Blind Spot* (Warner Brothers – First National, 1932), would 'encourage bank raiders'.[81]

During the 1930s, pressure groups such as the Mothers' Union, National Council of Women, and the Public Morality Council made repeated demands for a more effective form of censorship. In 1934 the National Cinema Inquiry Committee, an alliance of forty six religious, social and educational organizations concerned with the cinema 'problem', thus suggested to the Prime Minister, Ramsay MacDonald, 'that the moral standard' of films was 'too low' and that there was a need for 'a substantial strengthening of the censorship of entertainment films'.[82] True, there was a certain degree of official concern. J. Brooke Wilkinson, the BBFC secretary, complained to British producers that he had evidence that some film companies refused to accept scenarios if they had 'insufficient sex appeal'.[83] However, on the whole, public officials refused to extend the censorship system. They too realized that the film industry would not be able to flourish unless it provided people with entertaining material, be this in the form of love scenes, bank robberies, or even social comment.

Finally, it has to be recalled that, notwithstanding the Home Office's wish for uniformity in the classification of films, the final decision on whether to allow a film to be shown rested with the local authorities. This gave Labour councils a good deal of room for manoeuvre. Most famous of all was the decision of the Labour-controlled West Ham Borough Council to permit the public exhibition of the banned *Storm Over Asia*. There were, of course, a number of protests from the media and voluntary organizations. Charles A. Loveless, the secretary of the Forest Gate Ratepayers' Association, urged the Home Office to veto the Borough Council's decision, fearing that West Ham was 'an area suffering from unemployment, depression and the prevailing economic stress and . . . a very fertile area for the dissemination of communistic propaganda'.[84] Characteristically, Clynes refused to intervene. Censorship there may have been, but this did not mean that Soviet or Socialist films were stamped out altogether – far from it. By the end of the 1930s the workers' film movement had recorded some considerable successes. Working-class audiences were given the opportunity to view workers' films, even if they did not always wish to do so.

One final point here. In private, the BBFC argued that they did not object to the two Russian films they had banned before 1930 on 'political grounds'.[85] Similarly, later in the decade the Censors argued that they had cut *Spanish Earth* not because it contained the 'suggestion that Germany and Italy were intervening in Spain', but rather 'exception was taken to gruesome details, including dead bodies etc'. At the same time, the BBFC stressed that there had been some delay in dealing with the left-wing *Peace Film*, not because it was controversial, but 'on the grounds of a possible infringement of copyright in connection with some of the photographic scenes'.[86] Perhaps such observations should be taken with a pinch of salt, particularly as officials of the BBFC were drawn from conservative sections of British society, though they do show that the Censors were eager to portray themselves to the Home Office as a disinterested group of individuals.

This chapter has shown that the State intervened in the cinema industry and that organized Labour played a role in this intervention. As far as the entertainment tax is concerned, there were protests that its incidence discriminated against working-class film-goers. More significantly, the Labour party and the trade unions were directly involved in the debate about the future of the British film industry. They contributed to policy-making at the official level, both within Parliament and outside it in the Board of Trade and Ministry of Labour. Indeed, it is possible that Labour was drawn into a kind of corporate policy-making structure, by which film policy evolved in the light of discussion between capital, labour and relevant agencies of the State. Certainly by the 1930s Labour was looking to influence official policy and indeed was consulted by governments on many occasions. It is apparent from the departmental files that union delegations dealing with film were received by the Board of Trade, Home Office and Ministry of Labour on numerous occasions in the 1930s. Labour was certainly able to extract concessions from the government – the 1938 Act, for instance, had clauses protecting the employment conditions of studio workers and promising the possibility of an apprenticeship scheme – and it is doubtful whether the State functioned simply as a mirror image of vested Capitalist interests. The State could hardly turn a blind eye to working-class interests, and this was equally true when it came to censorship policy.

Once again organized Labour contributed to the debate about censor-ship. This was particularly important as censorship was seen to be against the Labour interest, hindering the growth of the workers' film movement and supporting the status quo. Though a number of politicians and civil servants accepted the need to limit the public's exposure to new ideas, the issue of censorship was a good deal more complicated than is sometimes portrayed. Censorship of Soviet and other 'Socialist' films certainly took place, but this did not necessarily bring with it greater levels of consensus. Indeed, the controversy which bans of this kind created may well have attracted workers to the radical film. *Storm Over Asia* was shown to 'packed' audiences in Manchester precisely because its ban in nearby Salford had spawned so much interest. Equally important to note is the fact that there were both claims for more censorship and counter-claims for less censorship. In other words, the ability of the State to ban or cut films was never assured, it was a matter of debate and compromise. Needless to say, it was the Labour movement which acted as the representative and defender of working-class interests in its dealings with the State.

Labour and the Sunday Films' Question

The British Labour movement made crucial inputs into those film debates and issues which involved the organs of the State. The previous chapter has provided details concerning protectionism and censorship. To be sure, there were many other areas of debate which impinged on the State's official policy-making process, notably those concerning entertainment tax, conditions of employment in the cinema industry, and safety precautions in picture houses. Yet another area of contention, bringing organized Labour into contact with governments, Parliamentarians, civil servants and regulatory agents, was that of Sunday entertainment. The question of Sunday leisure, with its political, moral and religious overtones, created a great deal of discussion in Labour and other circles in the inter-war years. It is the purpose of this chapter to provide a detailed account of the Labour movement's approach to the question of Sunday cinema shows. In so doing, further light will be shed on Labour's attitudes to and policy on the cinema, the assumptions and ideological traditions which informed the Labour approach and the tensions and contradictions inherent in that approach. Further, the chapter will reveal some important changes in the use of leisure and the various responses to those changes.

Sunday entertainment

By the outbreak of the Great War in 1914 Sunday entertainment in Britain had been regulated by statute and by social and religious convention for a number of centuries. Indeed, one piece of legislation, the Weapons and Unlawful Games Act, which prohibited Sunday tennis and football dates back to 1388 in the reign of Richard II. From then on, Parliamentary Acts controlling a range of Sunday activities from trading to sports and religious services were passed. The problem of Sunday recreation began to command greater attention during the massive socio-economic, political and religious upheavals which followed the sixteenth century. Sabbatarianism emerged from both a particular Christian religious formation spreading from Anglicanism into Methodism which sought to observe Sunday strictly as the Lord's Day, and a new industrial society with its need for a regular weekly rest day to rejuvenate the workforce. Thus the rise of the Victorian Sunday, ably sketched by John Wigley, has to be placed in an overall historical context. But, for our purposes, the most important development was the Sunday Observance Act of 1780, which 'Declared places open for public entertainment on Sunday, to which admission was by money, tickets sold for money, refreshments sold at special prices or subscription to be deemed a disorderly house'.[1] It was this piece of legislation, basically making commercialized Sunday amusement illegal, which was to create so much political controversy in the early 1930s.

The Victorian Sunday came in many forms depending on social class and geographical region. However, the most potent influence on the character of Sunday came from the heart of the Sabbatarian lobby, namely organized religion and the Lord's Day Observance Society (LDOS). Very briefly, Sabbatarians campaigned for the performance of religious duties and where possible abstinence from Sunday labour and recreation. By all accounts, many 'respectable' English families, dressed in Sunday best, sought to observe the Sabbath in a rather ascetic way with strict attendance at Church and little pleasure-seeking. Having said that, sections of the working class continued to labour on Sunday and others to participate in quite lively and boisterous recreations from drinking to bicycle trips into the countryside. As John Lowerson has written in an excellent paper on Sunday sport:

> The Victorian or 'English' Sunday was never, in fact, anywhere near being the total reality that Dickens and Taine would have us believe, except in the most 'respectable' of households; as we shall see, the near-hysterical emphasis on it in the late Victorian period contained powerful elements of nostalgia.[2]

He goes on to provide evidence showing that the English middle classes were beginning to use their Sundays for recreational and cultural purposes. Of particular note was the expansion of golf, tennis, croquet, cycling and water sports during the last quarter of the nineteenth century. Significantly, organized religion was unable to build a united front against Sunday entertainment. Certain religious groups came out in favour of healthy recreations like cycling (which presumably fitted in with notions of 'Muscular Christianity'), particularly when they did not interfere with church and chapel-going.

It was into this milieu that cinemas arrived in the early twentieth century. Indeed, the supporters of the Imperial Sunday Alliance, founded in 1908 by Bickersteth Ottley, intervened in London County Council elections in their attempt to persuade local authorities to use the 1909 Cinematograph Films Act to outlaw Sunday film shows. Even so, by the Edwardian period many cinemas were opening on a Sunday. To take but one example: seaside resorts as centres of amusement found it commercially viable to sponsor leisure every day of the week, and it was in this sense that Blackpool became a pioneer of Sunday cinemas. In short, by 1914 cinema-going and other leisure activities had penetrated the more extreme versions of the Victorian Sunday.

After the war, organized religion continued to experience long-term decline. Ironically, the fact that religious services were broadcast each Sunday more than likely contributed to the fall in church attendance. Obviously, this had serious implications for the observation of Sunday in a Christian way. Though the LDOS and other organizations like the Imperial Alliance for the Defence of Sunday campaigned with much vigour, there can be few doubts that by 1939 Sunday had become increasingly secularized for the majority of the British population. It is true that the LDOS recorded some notable successes such as the Sunday closure of the Empire Exhibition, and of course Eric Liddell, the athlete and Presbyterian missionary, highlighted the Sabbatarian case when he refused to compete in the 1924 Paris Olympic sprints on a Sunday. Another fascinating glimpse of Sabbatarian ingenuity was that 'When the inhabitants of Clydeside presented the future George VI and the present Queen Mother with a clock on the occasion of their wedding in 1923, it was found to play marches on six days of the week, but on the Sabbath Day it was silent.'[3] Even so, Sabbatarianism was obviously fighting a losing battle.

The various social surveys of the inter-war period provide vital clues to the spread of Sunday entertainment. As far as music is concerned, a range of opportunities were provided for enthusiasts in the London area: concerts and organ recitals at the Alexandra Palace; the chamber music of the Toynbee Hall Musical Society performed at the Whitechapel art gallery; and the free concerts given by the Sunday Evening Concert Society at various venues. At the same time, working-class districts did not celebrate the Lord's Day in an overtly devout way. There was Sunday reading, wireless broadcasts, dancing (the London County Council granted Sunday music and dancing licences as early as 1889), cycling, boxing, drinking, football and even the occasional greyhound meeting.[4] In fact, the richness of working-class leisure in the London district of Bethnal Green has been vividly described by Constance Harris:

On Sunday mornings, from nine until one, part of the west of Bethnal Green is given over to a Dog Fair and Cycle show.

The Noise is incessant, and yearly it tends to become more like the old Fairs, with various side shows as part of the whole. The ice-cream man, the chocolate boy, the seller of tinned pineapple by the cube or slice from the opened tin, and the juggler balancing a cart-wheel on his head are now all part of the morning's entertainment, besides the many who come offering for sale patent medicines for dogs and men, and all the furnishings which go with the keeping of a dog or cycle. The seller of the motor-cycle gives trial trips in the quieter streets, and the whole neighbourhood is pandemonium until they have departed. It is hard to imagine anything less like Sunday.[5]

Elsewhere, the traditional Sunday was eroded, if not abandoned altogether. In his study of York, Seebohm Rowntree compared church attendances for two similar weeks in 1901 and 1935. He discovered that adult attendance fell by 25.1 per cent, even though the total number of places of worship had increased by 37 per cent and the adult population of the city by 50.5 per cent.[6] Presumably, more and more of the men and women of York were spending their Sundays in some kind of leisure activity. A survey of the leisure habits of some typical families suggests that only a minority attended a religious service. They spent a lot of time in bed, prepared the Sunday meal, read the Sunday newspaper or listened to the wireless, walked, played games, or, as one of the popular activities, went to the working men's club. Interestingly, none of the respondents mentioned Sunday film shows.[7] By and large, it seems fair to conclude that York, like other English cities, had witnessed the arrival of a more secular Sunday. Indeed, such bastions of the English Establishment as *The Times* welcomed the trend as providing an outlet for the 'abounding energies' of youth.[8] None the less, it is important not to exaggerate the degree of change. Writers such as Walter Greenwood, Richard Hoggart and Robert Roberts have noted the longevity of traditional working-class practices on a Sunday – best clothes and behaviour, Sunday dinner, Sunday schools – whilst J.B. Priestley in *English Journey* protested that the old-fashioned Sunday evening with pubs 'and nothing else' was still being imposed on people in the large urban sprawl of 1930s Bradford. But where does the cinema fit into all this?

As previously noted, Sunday films were spreading in the pre-war period. In 1916 the London County Council deemed that it would not enforce the provisions of the 1780 Act against Sunday cinemas. Additionally, by the late 1920s the Home Office pronounced that the legislation of 1780 was 'not in fact enforced either with regard to cinematograph, or other entertainments. . . . The opening or closing of cinemas on Sundays is therefore a matter of local choice'.[9] By 1931 Cecil B. Levita, who became chairman of the Home Office's Film Censorship Consultative Committee, claimed that over seven million people attended London cinemas on Sundays each year.[10] A number of local authorities up and down the country supported London's policy. Seemingly by the 1930s some ninety authorities had allowed the opening of cinemas on Sundays. The West Riding County Council, for example, sanctioned 123 single Sunday film exhibitions by cinema proprietors in 1929. In the same year, the *Bioscope* observed that many industrial areas were overthrowing the 'forces of reaction' to obtain Sunday opening.[11] Having said that, there were many towns which found the idea of Sunday cinemas anathema. In Manchester, for example, in a poll conducted in March 1927, by the *Evening News*, 30,078 people voted for Sunday cinemas, 205,643 against.[12] In the following year the Middlesex County Council decided by 64 votes to 7 to refuse permission for Sunday opening of cinemas. Clearly, the Council had thrown their lot in with the Middlesex United Committee for Sunday Defence rather than the local Cinematograph Exhibitors' Association.[13] In claiming that 'the peace and calm of the traditional day of rest has for centuries brought quietude and comfort to the hearts of men', the Liberal MP for Ross and Cromarty, Ian Macpherson, therefore claimed in April 1931 that 131 boroughs in England and Wales were 'dead against' Sunday cinemas.[14] This was obviously based on information culled from the LDOS, whose secretary, H.H. Martin, stressed that fewer than 200 cinemas outside London had regular Sunday performances.[15]

The issue of Sunday cinemas came to a head in the early 1930s. Under the stipulations of the 1780 Act which, as noted, banned revenue stimulating entertainment on a Sunday, a number of common informers brought legal cases against those local authorities allowing Sunday cinemas. Despite a great deal of legal activity, the High Court finally pronounced in January 1931 that Sunday cinema performances were illegal.[16] This created something of a storm in and around the streets of Westminster. Though postponing the enforcement of the law, various local authorities stressed that they could not keep cinemas open on Sundays unless some kind of Parliamentary action was forthcoming. Hence in April 1931, J.R. Clynes, the Labour Home Secretary, introduced a Sunday Performances (Regulation) Bill, designed to permit Sunday cinemas, concerts, lectures and debates where there was evidence of substantial local demand. Even though Labour was unable to proceed with its proposals, due to the defeat of the Labour government later in the year, there was much hostility to the Bill, hostility which swept across normal party demarcations. There were cross alliances of Labour, Liberal and Conservative members supporting the Bill, and similar alliances against.

The newly-formed National government faced the same problem, finding it politically expedient to leave the issue to a free vote. A Sunday Performances (Temporary Regulation) Act, enabling cinema managers to open their premises on Sundays, was passed in October 1931 as a means of conciliation, but this failed to resolve the issue because of· its temporary nature. Moreover, after the General Election of that year, a highly contentious Sunday Performances (Regulation) Bill was lost in Committee. As the Labour party clarified, opposition to the Bill was so strong that no further progress could be made.[17]

In the following summer, however, a less controversial Sunday Entertainments Bill received its second reading. As the Home Secretary,

Sir Herbert Samuel, rightly commented:

> We have now reached, I trust, what will prove to be the last chapter, at
> all events in our time, in the tangled history of Sunday cinemas. The
> question has cut across all the ordinary divisions that divide Parli-
> ament. It raises no issue such as those which separate Governments and
> Oppositions. Divergent views are held in every quarter, and we were
> told in our last debate by the Hon. Member for Gorbals [George
> Buchanan] that even the group of four Members of the Independent
> Labour Party were equally divided upon this subject.[18]

In fact the Bill received the Royal Assent in July 1932, this time with the
aid of party Whips. In essence, the Sunday Entertainments Act was a
compromise, legalizing Sunday cinemas in those areas where they were
already acknowledged practice, but subjecting them to local polls
elsewhere. This at least gave the Sabbatarian lobby the opportunity to
continue their campaign against Sunday entertainment.

Cinemas opened their doors to the Sunday public in a number of towns
and cities soon after the legislation had been passed. In Birmingham, for
example, 56 cinemas, including five in the city centre, opened on 5
February 1933. The experiment was a resounding success; the second
Sunday opening was attended by an estimated 40–50,000 people, and by
the close of the year 70 cinemas were open on Sundays.[19] In February
1933, Sir John Gilmour, the Secretary of State at the Home Office,
reported that 'Polls at which the majority voted in favour of the Sunday
opening of cinemas have been held in 14 areas; and in three further areas
a decision in favour of Sunday opening was reached without a poll being
required.'[20] All in all, according to the estimates of Simon Rowson, by
1934 Sunday opening prevailed in about 23 per cent of English and Welsh
cinemas, comprising between 850,000 and 900,000 seats.[21] In fact, George
Perry has written that in 'London nearly all cinemas opted for a seven-day
week, while at the other extreme, in sabbatarian Scotland and Wales, only
about seven per cent opened on Sundays'.[22]

By the legislation of 1932 an agreed percentage of the proceeds from
Sunday performances was handed to charity, 5 per cent of which was
passed on to a Sunday Cinematograph Fund to stimulate films as a means
of entertainment and instruction. Consequently, as A.J.P. Taylor has
stated, 'Most cinemas therefore put on inferior films when they opened at
all.'[23] There was also one rather perverse effect of the legislation for it
granted local authorities further powers of censorship – by October 1934,
Croydon had prevented 200 films from being shown in the previous two
years.[24]

The rise of Sunday film shows in the inter-war years was linked to the
decline of organized religion and the expansion of leisure on the wider
front. As we have seen, however, the Sunday films' question was not

without controversy. It is now our task to analyse the ways in which that controversy impinged on the deliberations of the Labour movement.

Labour and Sunday films

It needs to be stated at the outset that if the critical response of Sabbatarians and the church to the growth of Sunday entertainment was somewhat inevitable, the response of Labour was less easy to predict. In one sense, the fact that local councils and magistrates applied legal sanctions to restrict Socialist cultural events from being staged on Sundays was hardly beneficial to the Sabbatarians in their attempt to gain Labour support. In 1920, a local magisterial decision in the small Cheshire cotton town of Hyde banned the Sunday meetings of the Socialist Church from the Hippodrome cinema.[25] Likewise, across the Pennines in Sheffield, the police interfered with the Sunday meetings of the City's Federated Trades and Labour Council, held at the Firth Park Picture Palace.[26] By all accounts such interference continued into the next decade. The Independent Labour Party (ILP) paper, *Labour's Northern Voice*, thus carried a report in February 1930 under the headline 'Those Sunday Films', explaining that the Manchester City Council had refused permission to the local trades council to exhibit a film on a Sunday. Despite the protests of Labour activists, there was apparently 'still a large opposition in the Council to the idea of the workers being entertained or being allowed to play on Sunday'.[27] Indeed, the local Watch Committee rejected the application of the Manchester and Salford Workers' Film Society to exhibit films on a Sunday.[28]

Socialists in London faced similar problems. It is interesting to note that the objects of the London Workers' Film Society were 'to present on certain Sunday afternoons during the year film performances to the members of the society'.[29] Yet it was often prevented from doing this due to the Draconian stand of the Sabbatarian lobby and the restrictive rulings of the London County Council. Significantly, the LDOS lodged a protest with the County Council against the Sunday exhibition of *Storm Over Asia*, which they regarded as 'political propaganda'.[30] By the same token, as noted in the previous chapter, the Sunday film shows of the London-based Masses Stage and Film Guild were curtailed in 1931. There was obviously an element of class bias in such decisions as the more bourgeois London Film Society had gained licences from the Council for Sunday performances in successive years, 1925–30.[31]

Even after the 1932 Act had been passed the two workers' film bodies in Glasgow which met on Sunday evenings were suppressed by the ruling magistrates.[32] Fortunately towards the end of the decade the Scottish People's Film Association started to have regular 35 mm Sunday shows in city centre cinemas.[33] Elsewhere, the Manchester and Salford Society began to exhibit films on Sundays. As the prospectus for 1936–7 stated: 'The Society is the first organisation in Manchester to obtain the right to show films on Sunday; it intends to use the opportunity to maintain and improve the high standard of its performances.'[34] Even so, there can be few doubts, as the last chapter revealed, that the agencies of the State shackled the initiatives of Labour organizations to participate in political and cultural activities on Sundays.

In order to penetrate and evaluate the Labour approach to Sunday films, it is necessary to focus on the debates of the early 1930s. Generally speaking, there were three sides to the Labour approach. In the first place, the majority of Socialists believed that it was only fair and just that the working class had the right to visit the cinema and participate in other entertainments on Sundays. Second, there was the trade union view that Sunday films could bring with them a seven-day working week and a deterioration in labour conditions. The union perspective was not, however, opposed to Sunday film shows on moral grounds, and indeed welcomed general extensions to workers' leisure. Third, and perhaps most interestingly, there was a Sabbatarian sentiment in the Labour ranks which sought to preserve the Lord's Day and protect it from commercialized entertainment. These three perspectives will now be examined in greater detail.

Socialist demands for Sunday cinemas

For those Socialists who campaigned enthusiastically for Sunday leisure, there were a number of aspects to their case. Most fundamentally, it was argued that Sunday was the only day when the majority of workers were free from the demands of employment. In spite of the fact that the Saturday half-day holiday had been established in the nineteenth century, there were many groups in the working class who failed to benefit from the concession and, even if they did, physical exhaustion after a long working week was a perennial problem. To be sure, Saturday afternoon football matches or matinees were well-supported, yet for some workers Sunday offered the only time when workers in full employment could truly exploit their leisure. This point is particularly persuasive as far as women are concerned. As the Libertarian Socialist and Labour MP, Jack Jones pointed out: 'Sunday is becoming more and more the one day in the week when many workers get any leisure at all. It is absurd to talk of Saturday afternoon as the time for recreation. In many cases the mother is heavily engaged on Saturday.'[35] Unsurprisingly, he went on to advocate the Sunday opening of cinemas. The future Minister of Labour, Margaret

Bondfield, writing in 1923 as Chief Woman Officer of the National Union of General Workers, advanced a similar view in promoting the demands of the young working woman, commenting that 'Sunday is often the only day on which games are possible for the worker'.[36] Yet it must be added that the working-class mother was still responsible for family chores on Sundays, notably cooking the dinner. For the unemployed, of course, the weekly rest day must have been perceived as something of an irrelevance when every day seemed like Sunday. Notwithstanding such caveats, it is apparent that the vast number of Socialists were determined to transform Sunday into a time free for recreation and culture. This comes out clearly from some of the Labour contributions in Parliament.

According to George Lansbury, speaking as First Commissioner of Works and a keen advocate of the need for more recreational facilities, the Victorian Sunday had in fact changed its character by the 1930s. He wished the House to realize 'that the old days when you could keep the Sabbath rigorously and without work or amusement, have passed away'.[37] Returning to the same theme in 1932 as Labour party leader, he again stressed that times had changed and that it was fruitless to resurrect nineteenth century moral and religious precepts, explaining that the arguments against Sunday films had first been used in the debates between 1879 and 1886 opposing the Sunday opening of museums and art galleries. For Lansbury, protagonists should at least be 'realists' by acknowledging the spread of Sunday railways, tennis, cinemas and so on.[38] The evidence, as already outlined, certainly appears to support Lansbury's general evaluation. In truth, it is likely that he was in favour of Sunday amusements as a direct result of his own experiences. As a lapsed Anglican, he used Sunday to disseminate the Socialist, rather than the Christian, gospel. Indeed, he stressed that if people could preach Socialism on Sundays, they should also be able to go to the cinema.[39]

This rather pragmatic approach, albeit one based on an idealistic view of the world, was supplemented by a more systematic critique of leisure in Capitalist society. There were two main strands here; that the films issue was also a class issue, and that Sunday cinemas offered a respite from an inegalitarian society.

If local councils adhered to the Act of 1780 this meant that public places of entertainment were closed on Sundays. This did not matter to those with the resources to afford the annual subscription of the private club or society, for, in effect, money bought exemption from the terms of the legislation. Underlying this, for instance, was the late Victorian and Edwardian golf boom which continued apace during the 1920s and 1930s. The historian still lacks a comprehensive account of the development of golf in the modern age, though the excellent ongoing research of John Lowerson has advanced the boundaries of knowledge.[40] Gauging from the figures in the annual *Golfers' Handbook*, many English clubs allowed

Sunday play. A similar point could be made about the rather exclusive private film societies.

Quite legitimately, therefore, both Labour Socialists and Marxists questioned the justice of a system which provided for the rich yet deprived the poor. That most pugnacious of union leaders, Harry Gosling – president of the Transport and General Workers' Union, amongst many other positions – thus argued in his autobiography that if 'it was morally wrong to play games on a Sunday, then there must be no class differentiation: there must be no games for anyone at all'.[41] From a similar perspective, Ellen Wilkinson, the serving Labour member for Middlesbrough East, though of course immortalized later on as a Jarrow MP and Minister of Education, was 'strongly in favour' of the Sunday opening of cinemas. As with other Socialists, she based her arguments on notions of class inequity:

> I believe that the present position is one that differentiates unfairly against the working classes of this country. If you can afford to pay to belong to a private golf or tennis club, and to have a subscription to a film society, you can spend your whole Sunday playing golf or tennis and then go back and have your choice of film shows or a theatre society in one of those places which specialise in producing plays that the censor will never pass for public performance. But you are not allowed, if you can only afford a shilling for a game on a public court or half-a-crown for a seat in the cinema, to see a cinema performance. . . . The position seems to me to differentiate very seriously against the people who cannot afford the heavy subscriptions for Sunday amusements.[42]

Seemingly the spokesperson of the 'large mass of inarticulate people', Wilkinson like many of her colleagues argued that colour should be brought into 'the crowded conditions of town life'.

To the left of Gosling and Wilkinson, the Communist party made a similar point: 'It is noticeable that it is the pastimes of the workers that are attacked. The wealthy have their private golf clubs, their cars, etc. No hand is attempted to be laid on these.' In language which was typically extreme, the Communists were critical of the 'snivelling subsidiaries of the Church', and whilst 'not concerned with defending the interests of the rich cinema proprietors', they were anxious 'to defend the right of the worker to pass his Sunday in any way he pleases'.[43] Interestingly enough, this view conformed to the Libertarian Socialist perspective of leisure, outlined in chapter two, and was also given a Parliamentary hearing by Labour MPs such as Ernest Thurtle and Valentine McEntree.[44]

It should be noted at this point that the Sunday Entertainment Bills did not seek to legalize all forms of commercialized leisure. In the very first Parliamentary initiative on the Sunday films' question, J.R. Clynes stressed that 'we do not want, say, prize-fighting, boxing, football matches, gambling or horse-racing. We can go too far and this middle course is therefore suggested'.[45] For those Socialists who pointed to the inegalitarian character of Sunday entertainment, this 'middle course' was unsatisfactory. George Isaacs, Labour member for Southwark North and a printing trade unionist, simply maintained that the Bill 'does not go far enough'; he demanded Sunday theatre, music halls, boxing and ice rinks.[46] During the same debate, another London Labour MP, John Beckett of Peckham, claimed that the Bill should be enlarged to cover the whole of the entertainment industry. He went on to give his reasons:

> There is no compulsion on anybody to go to Sunday entertainments who does not wish to do so. What we ask is that those who want Sunday entertainments should have as much liberty to go to the form of entertainment they choose as the right hon. Gentleman [a reference to the Sabbatarian Sir Thomas Inskip] and his friends have to go to their chapels, or wherever it is they wish to go.[47]

Again, we hear the authentic voice of the Libertarian Socialist.

Some Labour supporters also felt that cinemas offered a temporary escape from an essentially drab and aimless urban existence. Most of all, the Labour MP for Glasgow Gorbals, George Buchanan, who must have known more than most about the reality of urban deprivation, articulated a persuasive case for Sunday cinemas:

> If I could see our people provided with good homes, with wireless sets, with gramophones, with good airy apartments where the family could mix and have a good song, I would not care about your Sunday cinemas. The people could then make their own entertainment. All that many people have nowadays, however, are single rooms or a room and a kitchen, with no gramophone, no wireless – nothing but shockingly drab surroundings. That is what drives the people to the cinema on Sundays. . . . Surely we ought not to prevent these poor people leaving their hovels on a Sunday and going to a cinema. . . . These entertainments make the poor people fancy for two or three hours that they are living in another kingdom, and that is a good thing. Anything that can give them pleasure for the few hours, so far from being an attack upon religion, is just the opposite. This question should be judged by the standard of how much joy it can import into life, and nothing can be wrong that imports joy into life. I welcome this Bill, because I think that on a Sabbath evening thousands of poor people enjoy these entertainments which bring joy where otherwise there is no joy.[48]

There seems to have been much justification behind Buchanan's statement. After all, the housing issue had been at the centre of local politics for many years, and still in the early 1930s about 200,000 or so Glaswegians lived more than three to a room. Moreover, recalling the regional dimension to Britain's inter-war economic history, the interlocked Clydeside economy with its heavy dependence on the working of metal, especially the production of ships and locomotives, was in decline by the 1920s, bringing high levels of unemployment, poverty and other social problems. Buchanan was so adamant that working people should be taken out of the slums that he even opposed the clause that aimed to impose a charity tax on Sunday films. As he wittily expressed it: 'I cannot see why we should place a levy on Sunday cinemas any more than upon hon. Members who play golf. We might put a levy on them for the improvement of British golf and to bring it up to the American standard.'[49] In this, the redoubtable Jack Jones added his support, explaining that the workpeople of Silvertown (London) regarded the cinema as a religion. Apparently, the new secular society had come full circle!

If the Socialist case for Sunday cinemas was based upon perceptions of class injustice and social deprivation, then the ILP's national speaker, Minnie Pallister, provided a useful synthesis:

> The reason why so much nonsense is written about cinemas is because the wrong people write about them. This can't be helped, because the only people who really know what cinemas are, are, as a rule, inarticulate. . . . To appreciate a cinema at its true value one must live in a mean house in a mean street; one must wear cheap clothing, and eat rough food; one must know the unutterable boredom and discomfort of evenings spent in stuffy rooms, rooms always too hot or too cold or too draughty or too crowded. One must know the misery of cold and damp faced with inadequate equipment, the fatigue of monotonous work, the absence of intellectual stimulus, the absence of grace, colour, romance, change, and travel.
>
> To the vast masses who live such lives the cinema is a fairy tale come true. It is not an entertainment only, it is a vicarious life. It is luxury, warmth, comfort, colour, travel; it is scent, romance, mystery, sunshine. It is escape.[50]

For Pallister, the facts of working-class life pointed to the need for Sunday cinemas. With few exceptions, the leadership of all the main Socialist organizations concurred with this line. The only Parliamentary party to give a majority vote in favour of the 1931 Sunday Performances (Regulation) Bill was Labour.[51] It is also interesting that many Labour supporters appear to have joined the National Sunday League, which had been set up as early as 1855 to fight for a Sunday free for recreations and amusements.

All sections of the Labour press, nationally, carried leaders and articles advocating Sunday film shows. One editorial in the *Daily Herald*, entitled 'Rational Sundays', provides a good example: 'On the grounds of liberty; of morality and of sane recreation and variety in life, the case for the Sunday opening of Cinemas is unassailable.'[52] Equally, writers such as Emrys Hughes, an editor of *Forward*, Herbert Tracey, the widely-read Labour journalist, and Hubert Griffith, the arts critic of the *New Leader*, all made positive contributions.[53] On the Marxist left, too, the *Daily Worker* reported that, despite the profit-making basis of the British film industry, 'to oppose the opening of cinemas on Sunday afternoons would merely amount to adopting the policy of cutting off one's nose to spite the Capitalists' face'. Sunday cinemas were regarded as a chief means of proletarian enjoyment and relaxation.[54] It is also appropriate to note that Marxist claims took on an overtly political form on occasions, as evidenced by the campaign of the Communist-inspired British Workers' Sports Federation for Sunday sport.[55]

The trade unions and Sunday cinemas

The second discernible perspective on Sunday cinemas emanated from the industrial wing of the Labour movement. As already discussed, there were a variety of unions in the cinema industry catering for workers engaged in production and exhibition. In addition, the TUC had a keen interest in the industry. Presumably, for those workers in production the Sunday opening of cinemas must have been looked upon with some relish, though this claim has not been substantiated. It is arguable that Sunday cinemas increased consumer demand and in turn stimulated production, with all the benefits this brought to studio workers in the guise of greater employment opportunities. Of course Sunday demand may have been met by the American product. Even so, the closing of all cinemas on Sundays may well have had serious implications for British productive workers.

On the other hand, what is not in doubt is the opposition of workers in exhibition to Sunday cinemas. For those employed in cinemas, box-office staff, commissionaires, usherettes, projectionists, cleaners and the like, the extension of the film-going habit to Sundays brought with it all kinds of fears and anxieties. At a time when cinema workers, with their low pay, long hours and general lack of protection, were perhaps one of the most exploited groups in the tertiary sector of the economy, an additional working day was bound to give rise to a fair degree of opposition. Obviously, the unions concerned were primarily against the seven-day working week. As they claimed, this could only bring a worsening of employment conditions, perhaps a reduction in hourly wages, and certainly greater strain and fatigue. After all, cinema workers were just as deserving of Sunday leisure as the rest of the community.

In fact, the unions' case against Sunday employment has to be situated within a broader historical and even international context. During the second half of the nineteenth century there were a number of important statutes, most notably the codifying Factory and Workshop Act of 1878 which forbade the Sunday employment of women, children and young persons in factories and workshops. Though the 1878 Act was repealed in 1901 – making it possible to employ females and other groups of workers in cinemas on Sundays – at least the principle that Sunday work should be avoided whenever possible had been established. Moreover, in the 1880s and 1890s trade union leaders like Henry Broadhurst, John Hodge and John Burns spoke out against Sunday labour. By the Great War the TUC had discussed the issue on a number of occasions, and in 1912 George Barnes, Will Crooks, Keir Hardie, George Lansbury and Will Thorne sponsored a Weekly Rest Day Bill designed to cover all workers.[56] In fact, before the War, the National Association of Cinematograph Operators had managed to preserve a six-day week, and in some cases the closing of Sunday cinemas.

It was this tradition of union opposition to Sunday work which the inter-war Labour movement and the cinema unions inherited. Also worthy of note is the fact that the International Labour Organization formulated a Weekly Rest (Industry) Convention in 1921, intended to make sure that all categories of industrial workers had at least one day's break from work each week. Seemingly, this had some impact on the deliberations of the British government, who introduced various pieces of legislation protecting women and children, hairdressers and barbers, and shopworkers from Sunday employment. Again, this policy and legislative environment shaped the cinema unions' attitudes to the spread of Sunday opening. In rather bland terms, cinema operatives (together with other members of the entertainment industry's labour force) resented being treated as a special case, when other industrial groups enjoyed a work-free Sunday.

As Sunday cinemas became increasingly commonplace during the 1920s, the unions began to articulate their case. Before the 'talkies' arrived in the late 1920s, musicians were employed in many picture houses to provide musical accompaniment to the silent picture. It is apparent that the Musicians' Union was apprehensive about the possibility of a seven-day working week. At the 1925 TUC conference, the union's general secretary, E.S. Teale, moved the following resolution which was carried unanimously:

> That this Congress supports the Musicians' Union in opposing licences for the Sunday opening of cinemas unless prior agreement has been reached between the representative organisations of musicians and proprietors to safeguard union conditions of employment and to prevent a seven days' working week. Further we recommend all Trades and Labour Councils to give this resolution support locally.[57]

In the same year, John Ratcliffe, the union's Scottish organizer and district secretary and also a member of the Glasgow trades council, spoke to a similar motion at the Scottish TUC's annual meeting at Dumfries.[58] In fact, Ratcliffe was one of the most vociferous advocates of the union case. In 1927 at both the TUC and Scottish TUC conferences, he returned to the now familiar arguments, urging that the union movement 'resist the introduction of Sunday opening of cinemas until such time as a six-day working week is guaranteed by legal enactment to the employees concerned, or other means acceptable to the unions, with definite penalties for infringement'.[59] The points raised by Ratcliffe are particularly interesting, as they were an amalgam of Labourist, quasi-Marxist, and social Sabbatarian principles.

In the first place, he desired proper safeguards for cinema employees; that is, a regulated six-day week as part of the conditions of licensing. In this he was supported by that union veteran and advocate of a weekly rest day, Will Thorne, who emphasized that cinemas opened in West Ham on Sundays, on the condition that all employees work no more than six days a week.[60] As a matter of fact, the Cinema Exhibitors' Association stressed that 'None of our employees work more than six days a week. . . . The London County Council and other Councils exercise the strictest supervision to see that no employees work more than six days in the week.'[61] With his union hat on, Ratcliffe's major responsibility was obviously to protect the interests of his membership and not to engage in political rhetoric and polemic. Nevertheless, there was a more politically systematic edge to his analysis. He referred to unscrupulous employers, the search for seven days' profit and the competitive environment in which cinemas functioned; and, at a slightly different level, to the Capitalist work process. For the musician, as with other groups of workers, labour was said to be an 'irksome duty', 'arduous' and monotonous. Whether this was intended as a rather clumsy exposition of the Marxist concept of alienation is doubtful, yet Ratcliffe was surely right in saying that music, though entertainment for most, was work for the musician. Lastly here, it is true that Ratcliffe and the Musicians' Union were not against Sunday films on religious grounds and, indeed, would have welcomed them if a statutory six-day week was guaranteed. However, the union's public position meant that they had much in common with the church. Despite the fact that Ratcliffe stressed that the musicians were not 'Sabbatarians or kill joys', he could still speak about a rational Sunday, and was not convinced, quite rightly, that there was public demand for cinemas in Scotland. Moreover, he quoted evidence frequently evoked by the church to reinforce the Sabbatarian case, specifically the *Manchester Evening News'* plebiscite of 1927. Additionally, the Sabbatarian lobby in the guise of the LDOS and the more moderate Christian Ministers on Social Questions both stressed to the Home Office the need for 'adequate statutory safeguards' to ensure cinema employees 'one day of rest in seven'.[62] There was, therefore, a certain amount of common ground between the

Musicians' Union and the Sabbatarians.

The National Association of Theatrical Employees (NATE) was also active on the Sunday films' question. Though they acknowledged that Sunday cinemas were already found in London and other urban centres, they displayed a feeling of some regret. As Hugh Roberts, NATE's general secretary, put it in 1931: 'we are not anxious for Sunday opening'.[63] Elsewhere, he also stated that the Sunday Entertainments Bill 'was a very dangerous one, and one that should be opposed from its inception'.[64] Judging from the records of the Association there had been considerable concern on this issue for some time. Indeed, the Association played a part in prosecuting the case against Sunday opening in the High Court. NATE also lamented the fact that the movement to legalize Sunday entertainment contained members of the Labour party and the Labour government. Given the fact that the Association represented a range of entertainment workers, and not just those engaged in cinemas, there was a further important aspect to their policy, well expressed by Roberts:

> If Sunday Opening is going to become an established fact, if it is claimed
> by the public of Great Britain, we ask that you should give a fair
> Sunday opening and let all places of entertainment enjoy the same
> facilities. But the tendency in the stampede . . . was to give a very clear
> advantage in the cinema section.
>
> The general public have only a certain amount of money to spend on
> entertainment, and if the bulk of it is spent on Sunday, or desired to be
> spent on Sunday, it is only fair that all the entertainment houses should
> have a fair crack of the whip and fair competition.[65]

In other words, though the Association was lukewarm about Sunday opening, in the end it went along with the more extreme position of George Isaacs, John Beckett and others: if cinemas should open, then so too should theatres, music halls, ice rinks and the rest. It is also fascinating to know that the great film comedian of the late 1930s, Will Hay, when King Rat of the Grand Order of Water Rats in the earlier part of the decade, wrote to Clynes to 'respectfully demand equality of treatment in the matter of Sunday opening of Entertainments'.[66] Needless to say, protests were also made that workers in all branches of the entertainment industry should work no more than six days each week.

To be sure, unions in the entertainment sector had mutual interests to protect. With this in mind, joint meetings were held between the various unions concerned to ensure that workers received fair and equal treatment, culminating in the formation of a Sunday Entertainments Equality League in 1931 and the petitioning of MPs.[67] In furtherance of their campaign they in fact enlisted the support of a group of Labour MPs and the TUC.

In the light of the 1932 TUC resolution calling for fair and equitable

Sunday opening, together with safeguards against a seven-day working week, the General Council convened a special conference of the main unions in the entertainment industry, held in May 1932. It was decided to seek a major amendment to the Sunday Entertainments Bill:

> The conditions of employment of any person employed in public entertainments on Sunday shall be such as are fixed by Trade Union agreements, but where no Trade Union agreements exists [sic] then such as may be fixed by conciliation boards consisting of an equal number of representatives of associations of employers and employees engaged in public entertainment on Sunday, together with an independent Chairman.[68]

However, though Arthur Greenwood of the Parliamentary Labour Party sympathized that the amendment should have official Labour support, this was not possible as a free vote in the Sunday entertainment debates had already been agreed. Yet this did not mean that the union's case was abandoned in Parliament.

Union interests were in fact stoutly defended by that most vocal of Parliamentary Labour spokesmen, Rhys Davies. As an active trade unionist he claimed that the Sunday Performances (Regulation) Bill was 'the first real challenge not only to the British Sunday, but to the institution of a general one day's rest in seven in this country'. He commented that at a time when Continental union leaders and social reformers wished to introduce a weekend on English lines, it was ironic that the British Parliament was trying to institute the Continental Sunday. Davies was not a Sabbatarian, but simply believed that the English Sunday was 'one of the best safeguards which the Labour movement in this country ever had against inroads into their hours of labour by unscrupulous employers'.[69] Apparently speaking in the name of 150,000 entertainment workers, it was clear to him that the unions opposed the measure, though they were compelled to moderate their opposition because of the force of public opinion: 'With regard to the trade union attitude I know of no trade union in this or any other country that would agree to its members working on Sundays if they could avoid it.'[70] Moreover, he was genuinely concerned about the spread of Sunday opening into other areas of employment, particularly retail distribution. This is hardly surprising as Davies had played a leading role in both the Amalgamated Union of Co-operative Employees and the National Union of Distributive and Allied Workers, writing in co-authorship with Joseph Hallsworth, *Working Life of Shop Assistants*.

More specifically, George Hicks, the Labour member for Woolwich East, proposed the TUC amendment already cited. Even so, it was defeated by 248 votes to 52, together with one intended to ensure that workers did not work more than 26 Sundays in a year and for more than two consecutive

Sundays. In the end, therefore, workers received little but elementary protection in the Sunday Entertainments Act. The TUC General Council were eager 'to register their very deep regret' at this failure. Hugh Roberts, in his last year as secretary of NATE, deplored the legislation and particularly the preferential treatment given to the cinema industry. His response showed a certain antipathy to the fact that the American product was usurping live theatre: 'Such preference gives an unfair advantage to the mechanical form of entertainment (which is mostly foreign), to the detriment of the human factor'.[71] From the Musicians' Union came a more muted response. Ratcliffe seems to have moderated his stance of the mid-1920s. He appreciated that as musicians 'their job was to entertain the public, and that the public required entertainment as much, if not more, on a Sunday night as on any other night'.[72]

In essential respects the union campaign had not been a total failure. After all, the legislation guaranteed a weekly day's rest for entertainment workers. Nevertheless, it is apparent that the Labour movement was split over this issue. Even within union ranks there was some disquiet about the activities of NATE and the musicians. Charles Milne of the National Union of Vehicle Builders shrewdly pointed out at the 1927 Scottish TUC that the cinema workers 'should perhaps be glad that their resolutions were left to the end, as in that way they slipped through without opposition'.[73] At local level, too, trades councils like the one at Birmingham backed a 'Brighter Sunday Movement' to open cinemas and other places of amusement. Anyway, the vast majority of political activists in the working-class movement were enthusiastic about Sunday leisure, excepting, that is, the Sabbatarians.

The Labour movement and Sabbatarianism

The final perspective on Sunday cinemas had much in common with the Sabbatarian cause. During the Victorian age a number of Socialists had been attracted to Sabbatarianism. Very simply and briefly, the Labour Socialist tradition had been as much influenced, if not more so, by the teachings of the Bible, as by the dialectical materialism of *Das Kapital*. Most of all, it was the ethical and spiritual wing of the Labour movement who were captured by Sabbatarian ideals. This was partly due to the fact that Sabbatarianism was linked to nonconformity and temperance, both of which had a base within the Labour movement. At any rate, for those Labour followers particularly close to the church, Sabbatarianism had an appeal.

By the inter-war years, it is evident that Sabbatarian influences in the Labour movement had been toned down, though they had not disappeared altogether. As noted in chapter two, the Bible continued to play a part in the lives of some Labour activists, and it was they who assumed a religious and moral opposition to Sunday entertainment. One trade unionist on the railways thus complained about the spread of Sunday games, suggesting that 'we might have one day set apart, which our Creator knew we should need for rest of body as well as soul'.[74] Likewise, Charles Ammon, the Labour County Councillor for North Camberwell and a Methodist lay preacher – he was the author of *Christ and Labour* – though denying he was a Sabbatarian, opposed Sunday games in public parks in order 'to retain the old British Sunday, which had done so much to build up the British Character'; he was totally against the Continental Sunday.[75] Gordon MacDonald, the Labour MP for Ince, made a similar point in his denunciation of Sunday films. Like Ammon he denied having Sabbatarian sympathies, yet his views were essentially Sabbatarians, fused with a concern for rational recreation:

> If ever there was a time for a stricter censorship of films it is when we are considering the question of allowing films to be shown on a Sunday. . . . If there is anything that is of vital importance to this and every other country, it is the use which the younger people make of their leisure. On that depends the future of this country. If this or any other country fails, it will fail because its young people have refused to make a right and proper use of their leisure. . . . We have to realise that a vital question is at stake, namely the continuance of the English Sunday. I do not mind people of materialistic and atheistic tendencies decrying a religious attitude, but I do feel that our standard in this country is the highest in the world, and that is largely due to the fact that no other country has the same regard for the Sabbath day as we have.[76]

It is not too surprising to find this source of opposition to Sunday entertainment, considering that there were numerous supporters of organized Labour who held official positions within the Church.

The most famous instance of all is that of Hewlett Johnson. Though never formally attached to the Labour movement, Johnson was a radical social reformer and became known as the 'Red Dean' of Canterbury. As the product of a Sabbatarian upbringing, he was very much against Sunday cinemas. Hence during his term of office as Dean of Manchester in the 1920s he played an important part in the agitation against the opening of Sunday cinemas. His views were revealingly stated in a letter to *The Times* in March 1927. In this he defends the interests of the working class, and especially that section of it who would be called upon to service Sunday amusement. Again the link between Sabbatarianism and trade union fears of Sunday working is apparent. In fact, Johnson also claims that he is 'by no means Sabbatarian in the old sense of the word and far from averse from healthy bodily activity on Sunday'. Yet this denial was to some degree contradicted by the caveat that such activity should 'not hinder worship nor disrupt the family and social circle for ourselves or others'. He continued:

> It misgives us to see the extension to the seventh day of the excitements and amusements of the other six, especially in the case of children. . . . But the nerve of the opposition [to Sunday entertainment] lies, I suspect, in a love for Sunday as Sunday. That is obviously so in the ranks of organised religion. I believe it is also a main impulse acting outside those ranks, and it is at bottom a religious impulse. To multitudes of men and women who cross no Church threshold Sunday itself is still a sacrament.[77]

For Johnson, the working man would indeed be hindered 'by crowding further excitement and noise into his one quiet sacramental day'. His views were clearly a diluted and less extreme form of Victorian Sabbatarianism.

The Labour MP for Oldham, the Reverend Gordon Lang, advanced a similar Sabbatarian line. Lang was a nonconformist minister, interestingly appointed honorary chaplain of the Showmen's Guild of Britain and Ireland in 1930. As with other Socialists who held holy orders, he was in a somewhat curious and contradictory position. On the one hand, he was critical of Communism, but on the other emphasized 'Labour's Challenge to the Churches'.[78] Indeed, gauging from the files of the *Oldham Chronicle*, he was a member of the ILP, though by 1931 increasingly estranged due to his lack of criticism of the Labour government. The ambiguity of his position comes out clearly during the debates on the Sunday Performances (Regulation) Bill. Whilst conscious of the fact that the Commons should have been spending more time 'upon matters of far greater importance to the general welfare of the community than the question of yea or nay with regard to Sunday entertainments', he was none the less, to use his own words, a 'rigid sabbatarian'. In a rather nostalgic way he discerned that there was still a need for a 'quiet' and 'peaceful Sunday', centred on home and chapel with 'simple hymns and songs'. In addition, he clearly feared that films on a Sunday would 'throw open this one precious retreat to the commercialisation and secularisation of the age'. In short, he opposed the Bill on the grounds that the Christian church had 'the duty of rendering back to its Creator certain specific acts of worship, of praise and of dedication'.[79]

To probe a little deeper, it is interesting to note that Lang appears to have had the wholehearted support of his constituents. Take the view expressed by a leader in the local paper:

> The Rev Gordon Lang spoke and voted against the Bill. . . . Mr Gordon Lang's speech against the Bill was clear and persuasive. We agree with him wholly. This is not a beginning and an end of a changing English

Sunday. If picture houses are open, why not every other facility, public and private, for Sunday travel, amusement, shopping, and refreshment, just as on a Saturday? The plea that part of the takings go to charitable purpose is mere camouflage. . . . Our guiding principle on this matter is that neither locally nor nationally should any official sanction be given to encroachments on Sunday as a day of rest and peace, one day in seven free as much as possible from the noise and the hurrying to and fro of restless beings who, the more they are incited to lose quiet, the more excitement they want.[80]

Furthermore, even though Lang was deposed at the 1931 General Election, the question of Sunday opening of cinemas was heavily defeated at the local poll: 3,227 people were in favour of Sunday films as compared with 12,092 against.[81] The popular will was perhaps the biggest tribute to Lang's integrity.

One last point, it does appear that some temperance advocates in Labour ranks were also advocates of the 'English Sunday'. Even by the 1930s the temperance and Sabbatarian lobbies still shared common members, ideas and tactics. Ben Turner, that great Yorkshire textile leader and Labour MP for Batley (most well known for lending his name to the 'Mond-Turner' talks of the late 1920s), is a case in point. During the period he spoke regularly on the platform of the National Temperance League and adhered to a fairly strict morality. Unsurprisingly therefore he rose from the Labour benches in 1931 to vote against Sunday entertainments. Squeezed between a critique of cinema proprietors who were apparently 'filling their own pockets' and the power of the 'almighty dollar from America' – 'I do not want Great Britain to be Americanised or commercialised' – was a strong attack on Sunday cinemas 'and all the other awful things like boxing matches'. As he concluded: 'We want a sweet Sunday, not one with boisterous film exhibitions or theatrical displays, or boxing tournaments.'[82]

By the same token, Ernest Winterton, the prohibitionist and Labour MP for Loughborough – who had once campaigned to secure the police one day's rest in seven – also made a tirade against the desecration of the Lord's Day:

In my judgment it is not the Puritans whom the working classes have to fear, but the profiteers, the people who want to commercialize Sunday . . . this House ought not to encourage the commercialisation of entertainment on Sundays . . . it marks a deterioration of our national spirit, and shows how feeble and weak we are, when we have to pay people to entertain us not only on six days of the week but on the seventh day also.[83]

Winterton made his first temperance speech at the age of sixteen and later served the Temperance Union in various capacities, helping to form the Temperance Committee of the Houses of Parliament in 1930. Given this experience of the temperance movement, his position on the Sunday question showed a lack of vision, extending into myopia. As a number of Labour supporters insisted, the spread of Sunday entertainment was an antidote to heavy drinking. Indeed, Winterton himself had once suggested that the reduction in drinking among the population had been due to the rise of the cinema and other leisure activities.[84] Like other Labour Socialists, Winterton's approach to Sunday films was full of ambiguities, bringing together religious and Socialist precepts in an uneasy alliance.

This chapter has rehearsed the competing claims of organized Labour on the Sunday films' question in some detail. Again, there has been a need to concentrate on the views of Labour leaders, and it is not certain whether they reflected fairly the views of the rank and file. Nevertheless, it is very apparent that there were differences of individual conscience in Socialist circles. The Parliamentary debates reveal that there was discord in the Socialist conception of Sunday and the uses of the cinema. Whereas Labour members such as George Isaacs and John Beckett did not think the Sunday Entertainment Bills progressive enough, others, like the Reverend Gordon Lang, Ben Turner and Ernest Winterton wanted the preservation of the traditional English Sunday. Indeed, colourful characters like the Reverend Wilcockson, the Labour leader of Farnworth, actually resigned from the party because of its reluctance to oppose Sunday cinemas.[85] The trade union position was different again, with its emphasis on the statutory protection of entertainment workers against Sunday exploitation. Admittedly, there was little consensus in other parties, and in the last resort Rhys Davies was probably quite right to point out that if the National government had not imposed the Whip in favour of the Sunday Entertainments Bill then there would have been further delays.

For many Socialists, the Sabbath was an anachronistic ritual, plainly against the interests of the working class. It was this approach, based on working-class experience, which received the support of the broad Labour movement. Sunday cinemas were considered in a favourable light because they offered workers rest and relaxation, a greater variety of life. For George Buchanan, of course, Sunday was an opportunity to escape from the problems of Capitalism, poor housing, poverty and a lack of domestic leisure facilities; this was the authentic voice of Socialism and not of morality.

It may be further suggested, however, that many of the claims made by Labour supporters, particularly those against further incursions into the English Sunday, were based on an unrealistic and, it must be added, atavistic reading of prevailing conditions. The truth of the matter was that no law was going to stop the gradual erosion of traditional religious practices. Organized religion was in decline, whilst organized recreation was mushrooming. The inter-war years were crucial in the development of modern leisure as commercial, voluntary and municipal forms all expanded. It was only to be a matter of time before they made an irreversible impact on the shape and character of the British Sunday. Many picture houses, for example, had already opened their doors to the Sunday public in the 1920s and before, despite the anachronisms of the 1780 Act. There were pockets of resistance to these trends both in a political and geographical sense. Organizations like the LDOS continued to defend the Sabbath, and some of the rural areas in Wales and Scotland were strongholds of Sabbatarian sentiment. There is also a need to acknowledge that vocal support for a quiet, church-based Sunday continued after 1945. As J.A.R. Pimlott has asserted, there was a failure to modernize the law because of the puritanical opposition to Sunday amusement.[86] Even so, by the 1980s most leisure activities are allowed on Sundays, and at the time of writing there is a strong movement for Sunday trading. Despite the defeat of the Conservative government's Sunday Trading Bill in April 1986, which was opposed by the Labour party on the grounds that shopworkers' conditions of employment would deteriorate, the question of Sunday deregulation has lost none of its ability to excite constituencies of public opinion.

The Labour Film Movement

In any investigation of the Labour movement's approach to film it is important to appreciate the ideological traditions informing that approach, the influences at the point of production and presentation, and the interventions of the State. Previous chapters have therefore focused on Labour's atttitudes to and perceptions of the cinema, the role of trade union representation in shaping the form of the final product, and lastly the interaction between Labour interests and the State on such issues as protection and Sunday entertainment. As yet, however, very little has been said about film provision within the structures of the Labour movement. In fact, Labour's interest in film manifested itself not only in the form of a distinctive policy approach, but also in the character and texture of the Labour Socialist and Marxist cultural formation. The British Labour movement, in brief, spawned a variety of organs in the inter-war years catering directly for film.

A number of historians have examined the workers' film groups of the 1930s. As previously mentioned, the work of Trevor Ryan and Bert Hogenkamp has revealed that British Labour gave rise to a rather small but none the less exciting and politically significant cinema movement.[1] Despite the detailed nature of this work, there is still a need to relate developments in the workers' film movement to the broader Labour history of the period, as well as the themes already raised in this study. The final two chapters of the study will therefore situate the workers' film movement in the wider social and political context, and provide a critical appraisal of the existing historiography.

Broadly speaking, the workers' film movement of the 1920s and 1930s was a form of oppositional culture, though divided according to the ideological perspectives and politics of Labour Socialism and Marxism. On the one hand, a number of film groups were formed and initiatives made under the auspices of the official Labour movement; that is, the Labour party, trade unions and co-operative societies. On the other hand, the Communist party and aligned organizations also supported, and some-times sponsored, Marxist activity on the film front. Needless to say, Labour Socialist and Marxist film groups often overlapped, and indeed those Labour activists interested in film often patronized the range of initiatives on offer. This chapter will concentrate on developments on the Labour party side, and the final chapter will turn to the Communist party.

The Labour party and film

The history of the inter-war Labour party has been relatively well researched. The party emerged from the First World War under its new constitution, complemented by the explicitly Socialist document, *Labour and the New Social Order* (1918), with its commitment to common ownership, economic planning, minimum wage legislation, and improvements in social welfare benefits financed out of progressive taxation. Stimulated by this new organizational and policy strength, Labour formed minority governments in 1924 and again in 1929–31, though on both occasions they were largely impotent faced by an insecure Parliamentary position and mounting economic dislocation. The fall of the second Labour administration in August 1931 signalled the start of a period of much political thought and policy discussion in Labour circles. The period after 1931 is particularly relevant to this study, as it coincided with the halcyon days of the workers' film movement.

It is true that the 1920s witnessed important landmarks in the evolution of Labour party thinking on economy and society; but it was in the following decade that policy formulation was to reach new heights of sophistication. One or two historians have been sceptical about the progress made in the Labour party's economic and social thought in the 1930s. Ben Pimlott, for example, in his work on the Labour left, writes that 'the published work of Left-wing leaders and thinkers contains remarkably little on policy that rises above the level of sophisticated propaganda'.[2] And elsewhere he has suggested that the left 'showed a disastrous insensitivity to the realities of political power and influence within the Labour Movement'.[3] Then again, Alan Booth has claimed that Labour failed even to understand Capitalism and come up with remedies for its defects.[4] Certainly there was discord in Labour's ranks – between the Socialist League and the party leadership, for example. However, to characterize party thinking as sterile is to miss some of the richness and diversity of policy debate. As long ago as 1948, G.D.H. Cole, that doyen of the left, remarked 'the Policy Reports which were put forward at every Conference from 1932 onwards did serve as the foundation of the Third Labour Government's legislative and administrative programme in 1945'.[5] More recent contributions have arrived at a similar conclusion. Take the view of David Howell, writing about the period after 1931: 'Labour began to develop a much clearer perception of the measures that it would introduce when next elected to office.'[6] The work of Elizabeth Durbin on the party and the economics of democratic Socialism points to the crucial importance of the 1930s in the development of a more rigorous and analytical approach to difficult economic, industrial and financial questions. As Durbin comments: 'By the outbreak of war the Labour party had travelled light-years in the depth and sophistication of its knowledge of British financial institutions and economic policy options since the dark days of 1931.'[7] A practical programme had certainly been outlined on unemployment, investment, finance, and nationalization within the inner sanctuaries of the party, as well as in unofficial bodies like the XYZ club – composed of those in the City sympathetic to the Labour cause – the National Fabian Research Bureau, and groups of young party intellectuals, most notably Hugh Gaitskell, Evan Durbin, Douglas Jay and James Meade. By the same token, Arthur Marwick has shown that party committees and closely aligned bodies such as the Socialist Medical Association, with its call for a State medical system 'free and open to all', contributed to a more mature welfare policy, a policy which anticipated the National Health Service.[8] Labour's approach to film in the 1930s must therefore be placed alongside other aspects of party thought as part of a highly original policy discourse. After all, the new medium of film had the potential to popularize Labour's new economic and social programme. Having outlined the salient aspects in the evolution of party policy, it is now possible to turn to film.

By the end of the Great War Labour was certainly interested in the question of culture and recreation. As was outlined in *Labour and the New Social Order*:

> The Labour Party holds, moreover, that the municipalities and county councils should not confine themselves to the necessarily costly services of education, sanitation, and police, nor yet rest content with acquiring control of the local water, gas, electricity, and tramways, but that they should greatly extend their enterprise in housing and town planning, parks, and public libraries, the provision of music and the organization of popular recreation.[9]

Presumably, film fitted into this scheme of things. Sir Leo Chiozza Money, a new convert to the Labour cause, in protesting that the 'great cinematographic industry has been unfortunately resigned to all sorts of capitalists', thus sought the public organization and provision of film.[10] However, party stalwarts regarded the film medium largely in terms of propaganda.

The Labour party first became involved in the film question as early as 1917. In April of that year the National Executive considered a letter from a supporter recommending 'the adoption of the cinema to Party propaganda', whilst three months later a call was made for 'the possibility of carrying on propaganda by means of a travelling daylight cinema'.[11] Despite the lack of evidence showing whether these suggestions were followed up or not, in November 1919 the party's Sub-Committee on Literature, Publicity and Research again considered suggestions for utilizing film as propaganda. At one level a proposal was made for the production of a film illustrating working conditions in the mining communities, no doubt to be used in conjunction with the campaign for the nationalization of the coal industry. And more generally, Charles Kendall – a barrister and later legal advisor to the Labour Committee on Ireland, as well as the party's first Parliamentary candidate for Stroud – submitted a scheme 'proposing the formation of a company to produce films which could be used by local organisations in local halls'. The Sub-Committee recommended that the party Executive approve Kendall's scheme.[12] Though the Executive referred the subject back for further consideration,[13] a Labour Committee on Film Propaganda was set up. Significantly, Committee members included such well known names as Sidney Webb (chairperson), Arthur Henderson, J.S. Middleton, Rebecca West and Bernard Shaw. The Committee also received letters of interest from Ramsay MacDonald, Arthur Greenwood, J.J. Mallon and others. According to the first set of minutes,

> Mr Webb explained that the purpose of the meeting was to discuss the formation of a syndicate with the double object of producing films that could be used by the ordinary trade, but which would be more or less of a propaganda character; and secondly, to produce other films for use in a portable projector which could be hired out or sold to local labour organisations for propaganda, especially in rural constituencies.[14]

Subsequently, reports were written on projectors, propaganda films and a proposed syndicate. These reports were rather short and on the whole unconvincing. It is interesting, however, that in providing details of the ways to raise capital for a film syndicate, the cinema experiments of the Bishops of Bath and Wells, and Bristol were cited as possible models; and indeed contacts were made with the Bishop of Bath 'in order to find out how the Church works in the matter'. The Church of England may have been the 'Tory Party at Prayer', but this did not seem to compromise Labour's regard for their efforts at film.

More seriously, problems were envisaged with the availability of films sympathetic to the Labour interest. Information was received from the principal film distributors which made it clear 'that the manufacturers of films have not made any films presenting directly or indirectly the Labour point of view'. Therefore, Labour was faced with financial and technical problems associated with the raising of capital and the purchase of suitable projectors, together with the need for original film scenarios with a Socialist content.[15] As a temporary measure, commercial films with some kind of moral such as *Jo, the Crossing Sweeper* (adapted from Dickens' *Bleak House*), and *Les Miserables* were to be adopted. In the long run, however, once Labour film distribution was established on a profitable basis, the party was to produce films of a fully propagandist nature itself.[16] At least in retrospect such a hope seems rather misplaced given the cost implications and the state of party finance.

In very general terms the party leadership seems to have accepted the proposals of the Committee on Film Propaganda. The Finance Sub-Committee in discussing the proposed syndicate thus resolved 'That a sum of £100 be granted from the Special Fund to assist in the preliminary work involved'.[17] Furthermore, a circular on cinema propaganda by means of portable projectors was sent to all local party branches.[18] Unsurprisingly, it was suggested that the cinema was a potent propaganda mechanism, and, since commercial films were said to be hostile to the Labour interest, the circular concluded that 'no time should be lost in utilising such a powerful weapon in the cause of labour'.[19] At least at local level in Yorkshire there is evidence of some interest. The Colne Valley Divisional Labour party made further inquiries, whilst a correspondent in the Yorkshire-based *Labour Pioneer* commended 'the proposition to the careful consideration of Parliamentary candidates and other officials'.[20] In reality, however, Labour film production was to prove too costly a proposition – £2,500 for a film of the agricultural workers' struggle, for example. After the summer of 1920, moreover, wider economic and political circumstances were not exactly propitious for radical experiments. In brief, the scheme went no further for want of funds and local interest.

It is of little more than academic interest that in March 1922 a Frank Coulthard urged the party Executive to make available a film about, of all people, Lord Kitchener.[21] Yet, apart from this and the inquiries of the party's national agent, Egerton Wake, on a phono-film device, the idea of film propaganda was shelved until towards the end of the decade. For the full significance of Labour's rather apathetic stance on film, it should be stressed that the party was far more enthusiastic about drama and music.

As a number of historians have discussed, there was a rich proletarian theatre in the inter-war years.[22] Moreover, in the 1920s music was perhaps the most important of the performing arts sponsored by Labour. Musical activity was a very popular working-class recreation, ranging from the Welsh male voice choirs, the Yorkshire and Lancashire brass bands and the workers' jazz bands of the North-East, to the new dance music and gramophone records of the Capitalist leisure industry. The popularity of music undoubtedly influenced the Labour movement, and music was a major Labour cultural activity in its own right. Indeed the success of a London Labour Choral Union created a demand for a national organization – Labour party head office constantly received inquiries regarding song books and song sheets – and in 1925 the party approved the constitution of the National Labour Choral Union. By 1926 there were about ninety four Labour choirs involved in all kinds of musical activity – co-op music days, annual festivals and competitions, community singing, and organ recitals.[23]

There were, of course, real financial difficulties in harnessing film to political propaganda, difficulties which were not so apparent for theatre and music. After all, dramatic and musical performances could be carried out without expensive and sophisticated stage lighting, props, musical instruments and the rest. In the case of film, relatively expensive technology was a prerequisite. Yet, it is also possible that drama and music were more easily assimilated within the Socialist sub-culture. As already noted, a number of activists regarded film as an inferior cultural product by comparison with theatre, music and other 'high arts'. None the less, aroused by the Conservative party's use of film, the coming of the talkies, and the realization that the cinema was a central cultural institution of the working class, the Labour movement returned to the films' question in 1928.

This time the party investigated the opportunities for film production and the possibility of using cinema vans to display films, though the high costs again proved prohibitive. It is true that at national level there were experiments with lantern slides, but this was only a passing infatuation. Moreover, there were few responses to a party circular on political films.[24] Interestingly, the Colne Valley branch made inquiries about exhibition facilities, but found that there were 'restrictions and difficulties in the way of film propaganda'.[25]

Even so, towards the end of 1928 the *Daily Herald* published a number of contributions on workers' film; Huntley Carter, a well known Socialist critic, advocated the establishment of a Labour Cinema Guild.[26] The article written by Ellen Wilkinson, who as we have already seen was very concerned about film, was the most interesting. Wilkinson described the cinema as the greatest social attraction for women because of its depiction of health and beauty, dress and house decoration, cookery, and royalty and society gossip. She thus concluded that, 'If these were the women's interests, then, somehow they must be linked with our labour propaganda'. Significantly, there was a hint of feminism in her analysis: films about women's problems should be shown to audiences composed exclusively of women. Yet the main message conveyed by Wilkinson and others was that films critical of Capitalism 'could be built up that would raise our masses to fury'.[27] In fact by the end of the 1920s a visible Labour cinema movement can be discerned.

In 1929 the ILP Arts Guild, which had been set up four years earlier with some sixty drama, music and art groups,[28] provided the launching pad for the rise of the Masses Stage and Film Guild (MSFG). The Guild had a number of prominent Labour and theatrical personalities on its advisory council, including J.R. Clynes (soon to be Labour Home Secretary, of course, with responsibilities for film censorship), J.F. Horrabin, George Lansbury, James Maxton, Charles Trevelyan, Miles Malleson, Henry Oscar and Sybil Thorndike. Its main aim was to bring plays and films of an international and democratic character to working-class audiences.[29] Certainly, judging from 'Benn's' contributions in the ILP weekly, the *New Leader*, the party was beginning to appreciate the cultural, recreational and political potential of film.[30] The MSFG hoped to present three Russian films in its first season, and to make arrangements for the exhibition of films in London and the provinces, though, as discussed in chapter four, the Guild ran into trouble with the Censors.[31] At the end of its first season the Guild had a recorded membership of 2,300 and there seemed every possibility of progress. There were also attempts to publicize and extend the Guild beyond London. The MSFG even organized a dance for Birmingham Labour followers who travelled to London to watch the 1931 FA Cup Final between West Bromwich Albion and Birmingham City.[32] However, not only did the MSFG fail to embark on any production initiatives of its own, but was also fairly inactive in film distribution. The ILP claimed that the film regulations of the London County Council had 'to some extent crippled the work of the Guild'.[33] But it is more likely that its early demise was intimately linked to the political difficulties faced by the ILP, which disaffiliated from the Labour party in 1932, together with a lack of resources and commitment. In 1932 the Arts Guild was wound up altogether.[34]

Fortunately for the Labour cinema movement the gap left by the downfall of the MSFG was soon filled, this time by the Socialist Film Council (SFC). The Council was formed in the summer of 1933 by a number of left-wing intellectuals in the Labour party. Indeed, the Council's first president was none other than the Labour leader, George Lansbury, who was joined by his son-in-law and Labour historian, Raymond Postgate, and the Socialist film critics, Rudolph Messel and Terence Greenidge. As an article by Postgate pronounced, the aim of the SFC was quite straightforward: 'Making Films to Make Socialists'.[35] The Council made three films, though one of these, the anti-war *Blow, Bugles, Blow!*, apparently produced in 1934 was actually released by the ILP in 1938.[36] The other two films, *The Road to Hell*, about the degradation of the means test, and *What the Newsreel Does Not Show*, were both available for distribution by August 1933. As far as the workers' newsreel is concerned, Terence Greenidge wrote an interesting review which is worth quoting at some length:

The Socialist Film Council presents 'What the Newreel Does Not Show', by Rudolph Messel and others. This film is good technically – I mean in camera angles and editing. But its strength lies in its propagandist effectiveness. One learns too much about Russia from dingy, unenlightened textbooks, and it is wonderful to see factories, railways, dams all erected so quickly not to mention masses of enthusiastic workers, in the first Socialist country. When the scene becomes England a close-up of Britannia above the legend 'No Foreign Apples' and some telling shots of London slums dispose of Tariff nonsense and discussions about housing, such as you get in the intelligent weeklies, absolutely and on the instant. And the May Day celebrations in various British towns made my blood tingle as it has not tingled since I first read William Morris's picturesque writings several years ago. A specially effective film in days when the commercial newsreels are so bad. Tattoos, Navy weeks and sports are about their level, and everlastingly they flee from reality. The truth of the Labour newsreel should ensure its popularity, and ultimately the others will have to conform to the standard set by it.[37]

The SFC also sought and received permission to organize a film display at the Labour party conference in Hastings in October 1933.[38] According to the *Daily Herald* the display was staged at the end of the proceedings in front of a large majority of delegates, and included a film of the conference itself, shot only forty eight hours before, together with *The Road To Hell* and *What the Newsreel Does Not Show* which 'was greeted with much cheering'.[39] From then on, however, the Council appears to have fallen into abeyance. It is probable that contact was made with other Socialist agencies like the Labour Fellowship in Stockport, and the Labour movement in Leeds where large audiences watched the Council's releases.[40] Also, *Blow, Bugles, Blow!* was still to be made, but it seems that the Council's main role was to stimulate further discussion of the film question. In December 1934, for example, 'It was reported that the officers of the Socialist Film Council desired a consultation with representatives of the Party to discuss the subject of film propaganda'. As a result discussions took place between representatives of the Council and the Labour party.[41] In the final analysis, as Bert Hogenkamp has commented, the SFC failed 'to create a broad movement among Labour organisations, that would use the film medium as a means of propaganda'.[42] Yet by using non-inflammable 16 mm film stock for production and distribution purposes it avoided the censorship problems which had plagued the MSFG.

At this point, we can return to the discussions about film within the Labour party. It certainly does appear that the SFC revived interest in film in the upper echelons of the party. In February 1935, William Henderson, who as secretary of the Press and Publicity Department took an active interest in film, 'reported on discussions that were taking place on the matter'.[43] Seemingly, by the following month definite commitments had been made about cinema propaganda: the National Executive, in conjunction with the TUC, was to guarantee the interest on a capital loan of £4,000 for a period of five years to enable the movement to embark on film work.[44] Despite a number of delays, a definite scheme emerged from the deliberations of a Joint Film Committee of Labour party and TUC representatives, who communicated their intentions in a circular to local

parties in April 1936.[45] The scheme, in short, envisaged the production
and exhibition of special documentary and Labour propaganda films, the
provision of suitable portable projectors, the organization of a centralized
film service and the establishment of film societies. Matters were further
consolidated with a special conference on film propaganda during the
Labour party meeting at Edinburgh in October 1936.[46] J.S. Middleton,
the party secretary, outlined the purpose of the conference:

> A principal feature of the Conference will be an Exhibition of a Special
> Programme of Films in which it is hoped to include a selection from the
> range of Films produced by Socialist Parties in Scandinavia and on the
> Continent. The Films will be projected by a British International Film
> 16-mm Sub-Standard Sound Film Reproducer which is the Portable
> Projector selected by the Committee and recommended as suitable for
> purchase by Film Societies and Local Labour or Trade Union
> organisations. . . . The Committee is confident that all Affiliated
> Organisations . . . will recognise the importance of the proposed
> Conference. Party propaganda services have to be kept efficient and up-
> to-date, and the Party must be ready to adopt modern instruments and
> to make use of new methods. An effective propaganda technique is being
> developed in association with Film production, and it is desirable that
> our Movement should be enabled to take advantage of it as soon and
> as fully as possible.[47]

At local level, too, Labour organizations at Cambridge, Sheffield and South
Shields, for example, began to consider the possibility of adopting the
cinema for political purposes.[48] The scene was therefore set for a more
enduring initiative, the Workers' Film Association – about which further
discussion later.

Underlying Labour's growing interest in film was an obvious appreciation of the effectiveness of the 'silver screen' as a means of communication,
particularly a means of communicating their new ideas and policies. But
perhaps more important was the influence of the documentary movement.
As noted in the opening chapter, under the sponsorship of first the Empire
Marketing Board and then the Post Office, the British non-fiction film
came of age in the 1930s. Interestingly, a number of documentary
producers had sympathy for and links with the Labour movement. John
Grierson, the king of them all, who had been 'alerted to the political
possibilities of the cinema . . . by his study of Lenin', thus emphasized the
importance of film in Labour politics.[49] Equally, Paul Rotha, the director
of such memorable films as *Shipyard* (1934) and *The Face of Britain*
(1935), was billed to present a short talk at the 1935 party conference 'on
the development and significance of the cinema as an educative and
cultural medium'.[50] And still at the 1937 conference, arrangements were
'made for the exhibition of a number of documentary films suitable for

propaganda and publicity purposes'.[51] There was certainly a great deal of enthusiasm evinced in Labour circles for non-fiction films like *Industrial Britain* (1931), *Housing Problems* (1935) and *Coal Face* (1935), as well as *The Peace Film* (1936) which had been specially produced for the party by film experts.[52] The problem remained, of course, of developing the documentary form so as to capture the Labour message.

The trade unions

The trade unions were also aware of the political and industrial advantages to be derived from film. As is well known, the unions emerged from the first world war having benefited from an upsurge in membership and an improved negotiating position. Unsurprisingly, they were therefore able to extract major concessions from the employers, most notably higher wages and reduced working time. Though the union movement was hampered by both rising unemployment and the set-backs connected with the General Strike of 1926, they were able to maintain their organizational base and essential strength, partly due to the amalgamation movement of the 1920s and the increased effectiveness of the TUC. Indeed, as a number of recent histories have confirmed, the TUC General Council acquired easy access to central government and became a 'governing institution' in the 1930s.[53] In each year between 1932 and 1937, government ministers received more deputations from the TUC on issues other than industrial disputes than their predecessors had done in any year since the First World War, excepting 1925.[54] Furthermore, according to Henry Pelling, the Labour party became more or less the TUC General Council's party during the 1930s, with Ernest Bevin and Walter Citrine in particular playing such important parts.[55] Clearly then, any study of Labour and film which ignores the influence of the trade unions is far from complete.

As the union movement matured and became more aware of its external responsibilities and image, it began to search for new ways of presenting itself. Here film was perceived as one means of publicizing the identity, aims and objectives of the unions. During the inter-war period, both individual unions and the TUC General Council were to take an interest in the film medium.

It seems that the first union to use film for propaganda purposes was the Union of Post Office Workers (UPW). Under the guidance of Horace Nobbs, the national organizing secretary of the union, a forty minute production simply called *The U.P.W. Film* was made in 1924. It received a first showing at the Kilburn Picture Palace, interestingly enough on a Sunday morning. The film has four important themes. Starting with a historical sketch of the attempts to organize postal workers in the latter half of the nineteenth century, it proceeds to show the contemporary experience of the post office employees at work. The third theme, and by all accounts the most interesting, depicts how the union catered for a membership 100,000 strong. The film closes with animated diagrams stressing the outstanding work and accomplishments of the union. The review which appeared in the union's journal, *The Post*, explained that the aim of the film was to acquaint the membership with the role played by the leadership and so widen the outlook and appeal of the union. Apparently the film was successful in this regard: 'The result so far as the UPW film is concerned is that many of the audience at the Kilburn Palace went away with a clearer idea as to what happened as a result of Union effort with regard to wages, and London and Provincial classification than they would have gained from any number of speeches or the reading of printed matter'. The review concluded by anticipating that 'The film will be shown in every part of the country as time goes on.'[56] Judging from a detailed examination of *The Post* in the years 1924–27 this is indeed what appears to have happened.[57]

Significantly, *The U.P.W. Film* was welcomed by other Labour and union organizations. The Constituency Labour party in Llanelly, for instance, praised the UPW on its 'forceful plea for industrial solidarity'.[58] Similarly, the National Amalgamated Union of Shop Assistants, Warehousemen and Clerks commented that the post office workers had succeeded in their objective of using the cinema for union propaganda:

> The lasting impression that one gained from the film, which was exhibited at the Kilburn Picture Palace, before an assembly of postal workers, was that it marks the birth, in industrial propaganda, of a new era which has remarkable potentialities, and there is no doubt that Mr Horace Nobbs . . . will be repaid for the efforts that he has expended on its preparation.[59]

A start had been made in presenting the face of trade unionism on the screen.

At a different level, the miners were also exhibiting films of one kind or another. In coal-mining communities, miners' institutes and halls were central cultural and recreational institutions providing an array of facilities for independent working-class education, sport, drinking, and the rest. Recently, Bert Hogenkamp has shown that a number of such institutes in the South Wales valleys also had cinemas. A Bioscope Committee was convened at the Ogmore Vale Workmen's Hall and Institute as early as 1912, and by 1919 miners' cinemas were found in Abercynon, Abergwynfi, Blaenavon, Llanbradach, Llanhilleth, Mardy, Mountain Ash, Nantymoel, Ton Pentre and Ynyshir. This was not the end of the story for there were further additions to the list in the 1920s.[60] Further north in the English county of Durham there were eight miners' cinemas by the late 1920s at Blaydon-on-Tyne, Burnhope, Easington, East Hetton, Esh Winning, Ferryhill, Sacriston, and Wheatley Hill.[61]

Many of the cinemas were financed by the Miners' Welfare Fund, created by the Mining Industry Act of 1920. This piece of legislation introduced a levy of one penny per ton of output which was to go to a welfare fund for the education, recreation, and general well-being of miners. Though the provision of cinemas was advocated by such influential figures as Viscount Chelmsford, there was a certain degree of ambiguity in the official approach to film. The departmental committee of inquiry into the welfare fund thus made the following observation:

> Some schemes have cinema installations operated by the miners themselves, while others let their hall to a commercial cinema undertaking. We see no objection to this in an isolated place where there is no ready access to any form of indoor entertainment, especially as the cinema has the advantage of providing amusement, if suitable films are shown, for children as well as adults, and we also think it can be justified where the receipts help to pay for the general upkeep of an institute which might otherwise have difficulty in maintaining itself, provided in both cases that it does not interfere with the provision for social gatherings. Where, however, there are already other cinemas in the vicinity and the receipts are not absolutely necessary for the upkeep of other activities or where a hall is intended for use as a cinema and nothing else, we do not think this is a suitable purpose for expenditure from the Fund, which was not intended to be used for what, in these cases, are simply commercial enterprises, which may justly be regarded by other cinema proprietors as in the nature of unfair competition.[62]

Yet, this did not appear to reduce the range of miners' cinemas in South Wales. Indeed, a Miners' Welfare and Workmen's Halls Cinema Association was eventually formed in March 1939 with 27 member organizations. But what kind of material was shown at these cinemas?

Hogenkamp has indicated that all manner of films were exhibited, from commercial successes like the imperialist epic, *The Lives of a Bengal Lancer* (Paramount, 1935), documentaries, and Labour films. Needless to say, the Soviet classics were also on offer. Though the Miners' Federation of Great Britain had no direct control over such cultural initiatives, it is apparent that they broadly supported miners' cinemas and the distribution of Russian films. This at least is the impression conveyed by the union's journal, *The Miner*. In December 1928 a report appeared under the headline, 'Soviet Russia on the Film', which stated that 'Workers who have not been to Russia, and have no chance of getting there, have at last a chance of seeing something of the Russian workers' life and condition for themselves'. Seemingly, the film, dealing with the tenth anniversary celebrations in Moscow, had been passed by the British Board of Film

Censors (BBFC) and could be booked by any working-class organization for £3: 'No projecting apparatus is available, and the film can only be shown in halls already fitted and licensed, such as Co-operative halls, Miners' cinemas, etc.'[63] During the period of the Spanish Civil War a number of films were also shown which were sympathetic to the Republican cause. It is important to stress, however, that the staple diet of miners' cinemas was probably the American film, for these were most accessible and more popular among working-class audiences.

The UPW and the miners were not the only Labour Socialist organizations interested in film. Herbert Tracey, for example, writing in the railwaymen's union journal, appreciated that the talking film was a new method of propaganda which could be used in trade union campaigns.[64] At a higher level, the International Federation of Trade Unions published a circular stressing the importance of cinema as a central working-class hobby; hence the talk about the use of film in independent working-class education.[65] Indeed, the National Council of Labour Colleges was well aware of such trends. Under the guidance of the general secretary, James Millar, lantern slides were applied to educational work.[66]

The TUC General Council was also appreciative of the political and educational possibilities offered by film. In 1924 a film was made of the TUC tour of the Soviet Union. This was eventually exhibited to the General Council in May 1925: 'The Council, having been present during the morning of the private exhibition of the Cinematograph Film of the Delegation's tour to Russia, gave consideration to the offer of the Censor to go carefully into the matter and make certain alteration [sic] which would make it possible for him to pass the film for exhibition purposes.'[67] Albert Purcell, of the National Amalgamated Furnishing Trades Association and a member of the Soviet delegation, was given the job of collaborating with the BBFC in editing sub-headings, though unfortunately it is not known what became of the film. Even so, the Council continued to keep abreast of developments. In 1929 the TUC acceded to a request from the Japanese trade union movement to make a film of the General Council.[68] And in the following year the General Council acquired a film record of the international Socialist youth demonstration in Vienna, which was available at a nominal rent to all Labour and Socialist organizations. Apparently the film had glimpses 'of the leading personalities of the international Socialist and Labour Movement', including Walter Citrine. It was first shown at a 'No More War' meeting in Glasgow and received publicity from unions like the Transport and General Workers' Union.[69]

Certainly then, by the early 1930s the TUC had been exposed to film. It is true that the General Council was reluctant to systematize its use of film and embark on a production plan on the grounds of cost and technical difficulties. Yet, the TUC's Organization Committee was empowered 'to bring the matter forward for further consideration when they feel such a course available'.[70] Unfortunately when Walter Citrine examined the question of 'Cinema Film in Trade Union Propaganda' in March 1935 financial factors were again cited as the major hurdle to overcome. Even so, pressure was being exerted from other quarters within the Labour party and the wider trade union movement which would have more positive results.

It is interesting that trade unionists, like J.W. Smith of the Amalgamated Engineering Union, were discussing the need for working-class film. As Smith expressed it: 'The cinema as a feature in the life of the worker cannot be ignored, and in the social side of our movement why should there not be a workers' cinema, just as there should be a workers' theatre or a workers' sports movement?'[71] In the same vein, Labour activists such as Ritchie Calder, writing in the TUC's official magazine, urged the working-class movement to adopt this most 'Powerful Propaganda Medium'.[72] Here, it is appropriate to recall that Labour's impression of film was shaped by a wide range of ideological influences from the elitist to the libertarian and the Marxist, which came together in a rather complex way in the making of a form of oppositional culture. Interestingly enough, some trade unionists exploring the nature and character of film were motivated by a curious mixture of views which, though responsive to working-class leisure preferences, synthesized rather elitist perceptions of the vulgarity of commercial films and quasi-Marxist notions of their wider cultural and political significance. This point is ably demonstrated by Edgar Harries, a trade unionist in the shipbuilding industry and secretary of the Organizing Department of the TUC. He aimed to widen union organization into the cultural field precisely because there was a 'necessity for counteracting some of the evils of mechanised entertainment':

> The position at the moment is that the cinema has rapidly attained the position of being the principal instrument of working-class amusement, and speaking generally the cinema is in the hands of people who are convinced that the only stories which have box office appeal are either those concerned with the eternal triangles or a mixture of sham romanticism and shoddy melodrama. . . . The result is that often . . . films which are an insult to average intelligence are produced in order to absorb working-class money.[73]

At the same time, it was appreciated that film could be useful in a recruitment drive. Take the view expressed by Miss F. Edwards of the National Union of Tailors and Garment Workers:

> This Conference [of women trade unionists] requests the General Council to explore the possibility of giving further additional assistance

in Trade Union propaganda by providing the Movement, particularly in recruitment campaigns, with film vans – loud speakers. The films used should be descriptive of the growth of the Trade Union Movement; the benefits secured for the workers; and the part played by Trade Unions in the social life of the workers.[74]

As is often the case, female trade unionists seemed to be more advanced in their arguments than their male colleagues. It was a leading male trade unionist, Andrew Naesmith, secretary of the Weavers' Amalgamation, who thus came out against film activity at the 1937 conference of unions catering for women workers.[75] But notwithstanding such antagonism, it was still the case that progress was being made.

There were one or two notable initiatives at local level. In 1935 a group of rank and file building workers produced a ten minute short film entitled *Construction*, about a nine-day strike and the type of work undertaken by builders. The film was released in early 1936 and exhibited successfully to various union branches in the London area.[76] Equally interesting was the decision of the South Shields Labour party to launch a 'talking Cinematograph Fund' which received donations from a number of local unions, including the electricians, miners, distributive workers, railwaymen, and general and municipal workers.[77] Returning to the national arena, the TUC was able to exhibit publicity material at about eighty cinemas in the spring of 1938. This provided the opportunity for trades councils to distribute union literature at the cinemas concerned.[78] But even before this publicity experiment, the TUC had committed itself to film, serving on the Joint Film Committee with the Labour party and eventually helping to form the Workers' Film Association.

The co-operative movement

The third wing of organized Labour was the co-operative movement. The co-operative ideal dates back to the nineteenth century, and was based upon working-class notions of collective strength, mutual assistance, equity and solidarity. By the 1920s the movement had clearly become more professionalized and bureaucratized, yet the older values of co-operation and fellowship survived, albeit in a somewhat diluted form. There were three main groupings in the movement – the Co-operative Wholesale Society (CWS), the Co-operative Union and the Co-operative party – all of whom had links with the Labour party and the trade unions. In addition, there was a thriving Women's Co-operative Guild, co-operative youth clubs and a widely circulated popular Sunday newspaper in *Reynolds' News*.[79]

By the 1930s the CWS was one of the largest concerns in the British food and consumer industry. In order to develop new market opportunities, as well as protect existing ones, the Society began to harness film to advertising. According to the historian of the CWS, Percy Redfern, films were first produced in 1904, though motion pictures were used at lectures as early as 1898. The first story film, *The Magic Basket*, was not made, however, until 1928.[80] It was to be shown in 1,000 public cinemas as a way of publicizing the trading and productive activities of the Society.[81] This was followed by a number of films produced by the CWS Publicity Film Unit, including *The King and the Cakes* about flour mills, *Bubbles* dealing with soap manufacture, *CWS Toffee, Round the Clock* about biscuit manufacture, and *A Matter of Form* about corsetry.[82] Furthermore, by the 1930s sound films were being produced. One of these, the *Milk 'Talkie' Film*, was made by the Midland Sectional Committee of the Co-operative Milk Trade Association, with the financial backing of the National Executive Committee.[83] In 1934 the film was exhibited in cinemas in various districts of the North-West, as well as in Bradford-on-Avon, Bridgewater, Exeter, Torquay and Trowbridge.[84] Significantly, by 1936 the publicity department of the CWS was using sound films only.[85] One final point here, it is apparent from the *Kinematograph Year Book* that a number of local co-operative societies had their own cinemas, though these tended to decline 'with the arrival of the "talkies", when heavy investment in new equipment was required'.[86] CWS sound films therefore had few 'natural' outlets of their own.

Aside from publicity, co-operative organizations began to use film for educational purposes. The Education Committee of the Royal Arsenal Co-operative Society (RACS), for example, purchased a portable projector in 1919 and film shows were a constant feature of educational work.[87] Moves in this direction were also taken at the national level. In 1921 the annual congress of the Co-operative Union reported that the Central Education Committee had 'given some consideration to the question of securing a film representation of the history of the Co-operative Movement'.[88] Unfortunately, the project had to be aborted due to 'the present financial position of the Union', though the broad principle was not rejected.[89] In fact, by the 1930s a number of societies were using film in educational work.[90]

Given these developments on the publicity and educational fronts, it is of little surprise that co-operators began to investigate the propaganda value of film. To a certain extent, the wish for a co-operative film society was inspired by the view that smaller cinemas should remain under British control and so be protected from the American monopolies, and more specifically the strong distribution companies.[91] By the mid-1930s, the movement was beginning to provide an articulate case for the adoption of film, based on an oppositional culture with its political and ideological motivations. A.S. Graham, in responding to the use of film by the

Conservative party, spoke for a number of co-operators: 'More and more it is being realised that films, hitting through the eyes and making people actually see for themselves, are the most forceful weapons in the hands of advertisers, educationalists, and propagandists alike.'[92] Moreover, in advocating a National Co-operative Film Society, Frank Cox of the London Society's Political Committee, claimed in 1936 that 'until we take advantage of radio, Press, and films to the fullest extent of which we are able we shall remain at the mercy of capitalism'. He was obviously influenced by certain quasi-Marxist notions that the cinema served the needs of the Capitalist State: 'It is a soporific and helps to keep the masses satisfied with their lot in life.'[93] Interestingly enough, a similar view that Capitalist institutions manipulated the screen in their own interests was advanced by S. Moir, the director of the London University Film Society and producer of four films for the unofficial Co-operative Film Council.[94] But the catalyst in the development of co-operative film was undoubtedly the work and effort of that great co-operator, Joseph Reeves.

Reeves was a Labour journalist who served as educational secretary of the RACS in the years 1918–38. It was in this capacity that he persuaded the Society to use film for educational, recreational and propaganda purposes. By 1937–8 over fifty film displays were held, including the exhibition of *Workers' Education* – a talking film depicting the educational work of the Society.[95] In 1936 he began to press for some kind of national initiative, and, as the principal organizer of an educational conference on the use of film, outlined a number of proposals for a National Co-operative Film Society. His paper presented to the conference, 'The Film and Education', is a useful synopsis of the co-operative approach to film, with sections on education, the advantages of the 16 mm projector, and the various film categories on offer.[96] The efforts of Reeves were not without their reward. He became secretary of the Co-operative Film Committee (which was to receive £1,000 a year for five years from the co-operative movement), and in this role was responsible for getting Ralph Bond's excellent picture, *Advance Democracy* (1938), off the ground.[97]

The first film circuit under the National Co-operative Film Society was launched in the summer of 1937 in Scunthorpe, and by the end of the year the Society had organized more than 400 shows throughout the country.[98] As one co-operator announced: 'The CWS and the Co-operative Union have now definitely decided to spend the money that is necessary to give the film services which will be worthy of the movement.'[99] In fact, by 1938 the CWS and Co-operative Union had introduced a National Film Service which in its first season was very popular, distributing 300 educational and entertainment films and 1,620 publicity films.[100] Elsewhere, the Co-operative party also resolved in favour of propaganda films.[101] And last but by no means least, the Co-operative Film Committee joined forces with the Labour party and the TUC, and was instrumental in the establishment of the Workers' Film Association, to which we turn next.

Workers' Film Association

The discussion up to now has shown that by the mid-1930s film was a salient issue in Labour party, trade union and co-operative circles. As the TUC and Labour party Joint Film Committee acknowledged in 1937, there was 'a general interest throughout the Movement in film propaganda'.[102] At this point a crucial decision was taken to rationalize the movement's investigation of film:

> To prevent overlapping and duplication and to get the fullest value out of existing programmes, there should be established forthwith a National Joint Film Committee, including the Labour Party, the Trades Union Congress and the Co-operative Film Committee, with power to invite the Workers' Travel Association and the Workers' Educational Association to take part.[103]

It appears that a Joint Film Committee of party members, trade unionists and co-operators first met in January 1938, with Herbert Elvin, the leader of the National Union of Clerks and TUC president, in the chair. A sub-committee was appointed to provide information on four main areas: a central office and film library; the supply of films; film production; and the possibility of establishing an organization for the production and circulation of films. The details cannot be entered into here, though it is important to note that the Committee finally decided to set up a joint film organization, to be known as the Workers' Film Association (WFA).[104] Joseph Reeves became first secretary-organizer of the WFA which seems to have started its operations in October 1938.[105]

The Workers' Film Association Limited was eventually registered in May 1941 under the Industrial and Provident Societies Act. The main aim of the WFA was 'to produce documentary and other cinematograph films of an educational character beneficial to the community and to undertake and arrange their supply and distribution for display through the Co-operative, Trade Union and Labour Movement and to undertake any business ancillary thereto'.[106] Before this, the WFA had already embarked on some important projects which progressed with a fair degree of success. At an early stage contacts were made with Labour organizations ranging from the Post Office Engineering Union and other unions, Labour women and local Labour parties at Leeds, Newcastle and elsewhere.[107] Also interesting is the fact that the WFA decided to assist the Labour party with general election propaganda. A free film service was to be provided at marginal constituencies, together with short films of party leaders – Attlee, Dalton, Morrison and the rest. The estimated total cost of £1,500 was to be a charge on the General Election Special Fund.[108] Though such propaganda was not required because the outbreak of war duly postponed the election, is it possible that these short films of leading Labour party personalities were the forerunners of the modern party political broadcasts on television? At least they were intended to popularize new aspects of party policy.

In overall terms, the results of the first year's activities were encouraging. Apart from the development of an extensive library and distribution service, films were produced, distributed and exhibited, and film equipment was sold.[109] Orders to the value of £5,462 came from such bodies as the RACS and the Joint Educational Committee of the London Co-operative Society; and the services of the Realist Film Unit were engaged to produce two co-operative films, *People with a Purpose* and *The Voice of the People*.[110] Further films were commissioned by the Camberwell Borough Council, British Workers' Sports Association, Woodcraft Folk and two unions, NATSOPA and the Amalgamated Union of Building Trade Workers. Most interesting of these was the film sponsored by the building workers, *The Builders*, which dealt with the life of bricklayers and masons, as well as the benefits of trade unionism. As the National Federation of Building Trade Operatives commented:

> Men are seen busy on the job, and arising from their working conditions there are numerous interesting glimpses of the Union's administrative machinery, seen through the branch meeting place, through the active life of a branch officer, and through the Head Office. . . . The member's life is touched at many points, his union keeping a benevolent eye on him from the first day of his joining it. In sickness, in accident and in unemployment, the members' interests are safeguarded: in matters of compensation nothing is neglected. In short, the Union is shown to be the workers *Alma Mater*.[111]

Having made the point that initial successes were recorded, it also has to be stressed, however, that the war adversely affected the work of the Association. Though films like *The Builders* and the *Jubilee of Natsopa* were distributed, activities were seriously curtailed.[112] Moreover, the WFA failed to build bridges and form a unified organization with the CWS which, as already noted, had its own National Film Service.[113] The fact that Joseph Reeves was transferred to the Ministry of Information for the duration of the war could only have aggravated the Association's difficulties.[114] Even so, in view of the pioneering work in the fields of production, distribution and presentation, it is little wonder that the Labour party National Executive was 'highly gratified by the progress the Association has Made'.[115]

Generally speaking, historians have been somewhat critical of the Labour cinema movement. Timothy Hollins in his excellent doctoral dissertation claims that the Labour party failed to develop film publicity to the high standards reached by the Conservative party.[116] Likewise, Bert Hogenkamp has written that 'the Labour leadership was foolish enough simply to leave the use of the medium to its opponents', whilst Ralph Bond has made the succinct point that the Labour party and TUC 'showed little awareness of the value of film'.[117]

There is a degree of validity in such claims. After all, the official Labour movement lacked the resources to establish a fully-fledged film service. This was the main reason for the breakdown of those schemes proposed by, for instance, the Labour party in 1919–20, the Co-operative Union in 1921–2, and the TUC in 1931 and 1935. Furthermore, Labour failed to fuse the schemes introduced by the Labour party and TUC on the one hand, and the co-operative movement on the other. Clearly this led to a certain duplication of effort and in turn a waste of scarce resources. But more than this, the Labour party leadership had an attitude of intransigence towards the cultural initiatives of the organized Communist movement. As early as February 1930, the Labour Executive was making enquiries as to whether the London Workers' Film Society was 'communistic in character'.[118] Similarly in 1935 and 1936 the party leadership refused to co-operate with the Communist-influenced Kino Films.[119] Even at local level, groupings like the Sheffield Trades and Labour Council were investigating the Communist nature of the district workers' film societies.[120] In fact, attitudes of this kind merely reflected the Labour leadership's opposition to the Popular Front movement against Fascism, which the Communist party, ILP and other left-wing bodies were deeply involved in. Julian Symons' point that the Labour party's attitude to the Left Book Club was one of 'stiff distrust' could equally be applied in the world of left-wing film.[121] To be fair, though, the anti-Communism of the Labour hierarchy found little support in many local parties, trade union branches and co-operative societies, where the work of Unity Theatre, the Left Book Club and Kino were welcomed with open arms. In particular, Labour Socialists and Marxists came together in raising funds for the Republican side in the Spanish Civil War. In March 1937 the Ashton and District Trades Council organized a picture show at the local Queens cinema in furtherance of the Spanish Relief Fund, whilst just about a year later the Gloucester Labour party supported the Spanish film show held at the local Hippodrome.[122] Moreover, the WFA even established links with the Progressive Film Institute, which produced the Communist party's only film of the period, *Peace and Plenty*.[123]

Accepting the problems of finance and disunity, in the last resort Labour's inter-war film activity was credible. Huntley Carter's quip in November 1930 'that the incipient Labour Cinema Movement is suffering from stagnation', certainly does not apply at the end of the decade.[124]

Between 1929 and 1939 there was a great deal of Labour production and distribution. The SFC produced three films, the London Co-operative Society nine, the RACS five, and the WFA also five. In addition, there is some evidence that local Labour parties, like the one at Nottingham, also experimented in the field of production, whilst some groups, most notably the CWS and the WFA, had thriving distribution networks. Then again, one must not forget co-operative publicity films or the cinemas directly controlled by the miners. This record was by no means a poor one. Given the industrial and political setbacks of the General Strike and the 1929–31 Labour government, together with the mounting problems posed by economic realignment, unemployment and varying degrees of class passivity, the Labour film movement is to be commended on its steady, if unsure, development. This point is even more pertinent when one considers that Labour had to compete against a commercial cinema product which was genuinely popular among workers, and an integral part of their collective culture.

In other respects, Labour's growing interest in film, particularly in the 1930s, fits in with the general re-evaluation of policy and strategy which was taking place at a variety of levels. If the movement was laying the foundations for electoral victory – eventually gained in 1945 – as well as industrial advance, film was perceived as one possible avenue of achieving this. It is indeed rather curious that historians should claim that Labour leaders were apathetic to the film question. The likes of Attlee, Bevin, Citrine, Lansbury, Morrison and Webb were interested in the newsreels, Socialist film production or the possibility of a Labour cinema service, precisely because they sought to publicize fresh Socialist ideas and policy.

Finally, for many Socialists, film was never solely a means of political propaganda, it was also there to entertain. Though Terence Greenidge urged the need for films produced by Socialists, he could still write about the damaging effects of overt propaganda:

> Socialistic films we do not want. Propaganda is always an unwelcome stranger in the home of entertainment, and anybody who talks about a production needing to have a special function ought to be burnt at the stake.[125]

By the same token, Joseph Reeves never perceived the film to be just a political medium. As Paul Swann has asserted:

> Reeves had been responsible for organising many non-theatrical displays for ordinary working people in the 1930s. He was certainly more in touch with audiences of this type than the middle class intellectuals who comprised the documentary movement. He had little doubts about the impact of non-theatrical displays which consisted entirely of documentary films unleavened with entertainment films. . . .

People generally, he thought, were unwilling to accept programmes which consisted completely of propaganda and documentary films.[126]

As Reeves said to the 1937 Co-operative Union Congress, 'we cannot expect the general public to visit cinema exhibitions when the programme consists exclusively of trade and propaganda films'.[127] Film, Socialism and propaganda were thus not necessarily complementary. There had to be a balance between politics, creativity and entertainment. Little wonder then that Reeves looked to films like *The Private Life of Henry VIII* (London Film Productions, 1933), *The Ghost Goes West* (London Film Productions, 1935) and *A Midsummer Night's Dream* (Warner Brothers, 1935) to provide entertainment and light relief.[128] Further, A.S. Graham noted the importance of films 'of the Mickey Mouse type to give the lighter side'.[129] Indeed, the 'go-ahead' Leicester Co-operative Society showed cartoons and even a 'technicolour picture taken at the arrival of Father Noah and Father Christmas to the society's Christmas bazaar'.[130] Despite the view that the Co-operative National Film Service was not an 'entertainment bureau', Mickey Mouse-like films were included in the Service's catalogue.[131] Elsewhere in the Labour movement, the Labour party and the trade unions were not closed to the entertainment value of film. Even during the General Strike, the TUC General Council noted the significance of 'Cinema Shows to Women and Children – say once a week'.[132] Film, therefore, also became an element in the Labour Socialist cultural formation which sought to link Socialism to recreation and to brighten up the social life of workers.

The Communist Movement and Film

The Communist Party of Great Britain (CP) was formally launched at the Unity Convention held in London on 31 July and 1 August 1920. The Convention brought together such diverse organizations as the British Socialist party, branches of the Socialist Labour party, the Socialist Prohibition Fellowship, branches of the Herald League, as well as a variety of local Socialist societies, Guild Communists and shop stewards. From then on the CP was to make a significant impact on inter-war politics and society. Though never a mass organization in terms of membership – 3,200 members in December 1929, rising to 7,700 in July 1935 and 17,756 by July 1939 – the party was able to exert an influence far greater than its formal support would suggest. The CP had a considerable degree of control over a wide range of quite important pressure groups such as the National Minority Movement (NMM) in trade union circles, National Unemployed Workers' Movement (NUWM) and a variety of politico-cultural organizations like the Workers' International Relief (WIR), Friends of the Soviet Union (FSU), League Against Imperialism (LAI), Workers' Theatre Movement (WTM), British Workers' Sports Federation (BWSF) and the rest. Consequently the party was able to intervene in a positive way in industrial relations through its influence in the trade unions and the militant shop stewards' movement, and make inputs into the formal political and economic policy-making process.

In very broad terms, the political perspective and strategical position of the CP underwent a number of changes in the inter-war years. It is possible to discern at least three crucial phases of development. In the first phase taking up most of the 1920s, the CP adhered to a united front line by which it sought to establish links with the leadership of the official Labour movement. Indeed, following the instructions of Lenin, the party attempted to affiliate to the Labour party, though without any success. The second phase, lasting roughly from 1929 to the mid-1930s, was linked to the world economic slump which Capitalism found itself in. The 'Class Against Class' approach of this phase aimed to show that the Labour party, the official trade union leadership and Labour Socialism in general helped to maintain Capitalist rule. Thus the party and its industrial, political and cultural satellites sought to expose and oppose the Labour party and other so-called 'Social Fascists' whenever the opportunity arose. The third phase began to take shape in 1933 and lasted until the end of the decade. These years were characterized by the movement for unity, firstly by the united front of Socialist forces and then the popular front of progressive forces against Fascism. Clearly it was the Nazi seizure of power in Germany in 1933 which was the crucial turning point in the policy transformation of the international Communist movement and in turn the British CP. Quite simply, the aim of the unity movement was to prevent the spread of Fascist ideology and reaction.[1] Most importantly here, these three specific phases in the CP's inter-war history imparted an influence on the Marxist film movement. Bearing this in mind, what can be said about Communism and workers' film?

Workers' film societies

As early as 1919 two leading Marxists, William Gallacher and J.R. Campbell, articulated the case for proletarian social organizations 'to supersede the existing social organisations of capitalism, and organise the social side of the workers' life'.[2] From then on until the end of the 1930s there were frequent calls for workers' cultural and recreational bodies which would act as alternatives to their bourgeois counterparts. Soon after the CP had been founded the influential organization commission comprising R. Palme Dutt, Harry Pollitt and Harry Inkpin, noted the political importance of entertainments as a means of recruitment and disseminating Marxist ideas.[3] The party was influenced by this recommendation and at least by the end of the 1920s attempts had been made to establish facilities for sport, drama and film. As already intimated, the Communist movement spawned a number of recreational and cultural agencies all similarly opposed to the Capitalist system. Insofar as this opposition went, these agencies wished to challenge the assumed cultural hegemony of the British ruling elite. Without knowing it, they were therefore following aspects of the social theory of the Italian Marxist, Antonio Gramsci.

The key Gramscian concept, as outlined in chapter one, is that of hegemony. To recap, Capitalist hegemony is apparently exercised when the working class consents to the norms and values of the ruling bourgeois order. Such consent is not guaranteed, however, for it has to be produced incessantly by ideological processes acting on the economic, political and cultural fronts. According to Gramsci, one of the ways in which Capitalist hegemony is tested is through the autonomous intervention of the proletariat at all levels of society, including the cultural level. In order for Marxists to oppose and counter Capitalist ideology, Gramsci suggested that the proletariat had to produce its own cultural institutions. It was the task of Communists – the so-called vanguard of the proletariat – to provide the leadership of these institutions so as to create an autonomous and hegemonic Socialist culture.[4]

In some respects the cultural satellites of the CP can be seen in this way: as Socialist counters to bourgeois values, ideology and culture; that is, a form of oppositional culture, also mentioned in the opening chapter. Alun Howkins has thus described the 'non-political' agencies of the CP during the 'Class Against Class' period in quite glowing terms as laying 'the foundations at least of a visible revolutionary and oppositional culture':

> the very sectarianism that divided the [working-class] movement produced, in Britain as well as on the Continent, a remarkable revolutionary culture. This culture was revolutionary because the politics of the Party, no matter how misguided, were also revolutionary. The political break with social democracy forced a cultural break – the party now had to differentiate itself artistically, intellectually and socially from its former allies. It also had to embrace its members into the differentiation. The organizational forms produced by this moment bear the stamp of the moment. They were sectarian and often puritanical. Yet they presented a challenge, formally and organization- ally at least both to social democracy and capitalism.[5]

The informal cultural world of the London CP revolved around the BWSF, WTM, Marx House, Shoreditch Town Hall, Nanking Chinese Restaurant and a 'honeycomb' of bookshops, cafes and clubs. And into this world fitted the Communist-inspired workers' film societies.

During the 1920s the Communist movement often exhibited Russian films, in their wish to challenge Capitalism and promote the ideals and achievements of Soviet Russia. This study has already alluded to Soviet films in the context of censorship, but it is important to know more about the conditions of exhibition. Such films were shown under the auspices of the WIR, FSU, LAI, and like-minded bodies. In 1924, for example, the WIR released two films depicting 'the revived activities of Moscow and Leningrad' and the days of serfdom. It was hoped that both of these would be presented at Labour organizations so as to aid Soviet relief work.[6] Judging from Communist papers like the *Sunday Worker, Workers' Life* and the *Worker*, Russian films gained a fairly wide distribution in Labour circles.[7] Indeed, according to a report which appeared in *The Times*, the distribution of Russian films was systematized by 1929. Seemingly, the Soviet government through its Trade Delegation in Berlin concluded an agreement with British Instructional Films Limited whose renting organization, Pro Patria Films Limited, would thereby distribute the work of Eisenstein, Pudovkin, Trauberg and other masters of the Soviet screen.[8] Though it is not known what came out of this initiative, Soviet films were certainly making some impact on Labour audiences – a point to some

VELL PARK, SEPT. 1932

23 Meeting of the British Federation of Film Societies in 1932, to which the
Manchester and Salford Workers' Film Society was affiliated

24/25 One of the most sought after Soviet films of the period was Eisenstein's masterpiece, *Battleship Potemkin*

26 Another Russian classic was Pudovkin's *Storm Over Asia*, which was banned by
the Salford Watch Committee in 1931

27 (left) Ivor Montagu, the Communist aristocrat, was one of the leading lights in the workers' film movement of the 1930s

28 (above) Ivor Montagu and company with the great Russian film maker, Sergei Eisenstein, in Hollywood

29 Kino Films (1935) Ltd was perhaps the most successful distributor of workers' films in the 1930s. Here we see their mobile van

30 One of the most dramatic worker films of the period was the Kino Production Group's *Bread*, produced by Sam Serta

31/32 The Workers' Film and Photo League, founded in 1934, was one of the most important working-class film organizations of the period

extent confirmed by the reactions of the censorship authorities. Further-more, by the end of the decade the Agit-prop department of the Red International of Labour Unions (RILU), which had some currency in the British Communist movement, was proclaiming the need for cultural work as one way of mobilizing the working class. At least by implication, film was to be an integral part of such cultural struggle.

Also important in the exhibition of the Soviet product was the London Film Society. The Society was formed in 1925 as a private cine-club, 'To afford people interested in the Cinema an opportunity of seeing films which were not otherwise available to them.[9] Huntley Carter was quite correct in describing the Society as bourgeois and to the right of the Labour film groups.[10] As Ralph Bond has remarked, 'the Society inevitably attracted to itself the type of audience that would probably never be seen dead in a local fleapit'.[11] Nevertheless, the Society did show such masterpieces as the *Battleship Potemkin* which had been censored for public but not private exhibition. The film was about a mutiny which took place on board the battleship *Potemkin* in the Black Sea at a time in 1905 when the Tsarist regime was experiencing social upheaval, including the destruction of the Imperial Fleet by the Japanese. Directed by Sergei Eisenstein, with a musical score from Nikolai Kryukov, the film was shot during the summer and autumn of 1925 at Leningrad, Odessa and on board the *Potemkin's* sister-ship, the *Twelve Apostles*. Interestingly, Eisenstein addressed the Society in 1929, having been booked into an expensive West End hotel by a member of the CP.[12] Together with *The End of St Petersburg, Mother* and *Bed and Sofa*, the exhibition of *Potemkin* suggests that there was a certain Communistic influence in the London Film Society. Indeed, as is well known, the leading Communist intellectual, Ivor Montagu, was an active member of the Society. Moreover, in the view of Erik Barnouw, 'The London Film Society already tending leftward in its membership, became more so during the depression years'.[13] It is therefore hardly surprising that the Federation of Workers' Film Societies (FWFS) should attract leading lights from the London Film Society.

Since the London Film Society was not catering for working-class audiences, towards the end of 1929 a group of trade unionists and activists committed to the realistic film launched the London Workers' Film Society (LWFS). The provisional council of the new body was dominated by CP members and sympathizers: Ralph Bond (secretary), Emile Burns, Ivor Montagu and Harry Pollitt. According to the *Sunday Worker* the objects of the Society were 'stated to be the presentation to its members of film productions of a definitely working-class character, together with films of outstanding educational, artistic, and technical merit'.[14] In addition, as the *Worker* made clear, while the main activities would be in the area of projection, the Society would also 'endeavour to co-operate with and assist any film producing group or company which has for its objective the production of films depicting the lives and struggles of the workers'.[15] The LWFS was established on a private membership basis to avoid censorship regulation, though the annual subscription of twelve shillings with an additional one shilling entrance fee was too high to encourage mass working-class affiliations. Even so, Ralph Bond in a retrospective account, has claimed that 'The immediate success of the Workers' Film Society was astonishing. Hundreds applied to join and soon the Scala Theatre was packed for the evening performances once a month.'[16] Gauging from the reports which appeared in the *Daily Worker*, admittedly not the most reliable of sources, the claim seems to be justified. At the Society's first general meeting it was recorded that membership was increasing and that there were possibilities of extending activities to attract factory workers.[17] By the end of the first season the Society had in fact increased its membership from 300 to 1,200.[18] During the same period, links had been forged with proletarian organizations like the Association of Women Clerks and Secretaries.[19] Furthermore, audiences were quite large – in February 1930 over 1,000 attended the Chinese film, *Shanghai Documents*, while in April of the same year 2,000 attended Pudovkin's famous production *The End of St Petersburg*.[20]

Certainly there was optimism about the possibility of harnessing film to the workers' movement, and, soon after the LWFS had started to operate, a FWFS was officially established, again with a Communist-inspired leadership which included Harry Pollitt and William Gallacher (possibly the two most influential working-class Marxists in Britain). The Federation had a number of aims, but perhaps the most pertinent were 'the formation of local workers' film societies' and 'the exhibition and production of films of value to the working class'.[21]

Following the London initiative, workers' film societies were established in ten or more British cities. For instance, in February 1930 the *Daily Worker* reported that a Merseyside Film Society had been formed to show Russian films and films about working-class life in Germany. At about the same time, the Edinburgh Workers' Film Society with its 'essentially working-class' membership, presented its first show consisting of the Soviet *Two Days* and the German *Shadow of the Machine*[22]. By the middle of 1931 there were six workers' film societies functioning in Edinburgh, Glasgow, Liverpool, London, Newcastle and Salford with a combined membership of 3,000, together with provisional committees in Derby, Middlesborough and Nottingham. Significantly, a number of these societies had established contacts in factories, engineering and print shops, and tram depots.[23]

Even more significant was the fact that the Federation set up its own distribution network through the Atlas Film Company Limited, formed in December 1929 with a nominal capital of £2,000. It is particularly interesting that the *Daily Telegraph* drew attention to this 'astounding story of Communist intrigue'. G.A. Atkinson, the paper's film critic, revealed that the main subscribers, shareholders and directors of the company were Communists: Emile Burns, a member of the CP, RILU, International Class War Prisoners' Aid Executive and the FOSU Executive; Ralph Bond, a member of the CP and RILU, chairman of the Communist First of May Committee and an advocate of 'the abolition of the British monarchy and of the British Empire'; Joan Beauchamp Thompson, the 'treasurer of the Meerut Prisoners' Defence Committee, a body actively engaged in fomenting sedition in India and England', and wife of a Communist lawyer; and Herbert Ward, a journalist connected with the Workers' Defence Corps and the NUWM.[24] Notwithstanding the fact that this was a rather crude form of 'red' baiting, it is again apparent that Atlas Films was to all intents and purposes a Communist body. In any case, the company's major objective was the importation and distribution of Soviet films, and the production of films depicting authentic British working-class life. The figures provided by Trevor Ryan show that Atlas distributed twenty four Russian films and produced six films in all.[25] What appears to have happened is that all the various workers' film societies rented Russian classics, like *The General Line, Mother, Turksib, Battleship Potemkin* and *New Babylon*, directly from Atlas. As far as production was concerned, Atlas was mainly responsible for a variety of working-class newsreels.

In 1929, 'Benn' (Gary Allighan), the Independent Labour Party (ILP) film critic, proposed that a Socialist newsreel was needed to combat the militarism, jingoism and sabre-rattling of the major commercial companies. Such a newsreel would show 'industrial and political demonstrations; the social causes leading up to strikes; co-operative activities; the effects of the miners' eight-hour day on the miners and their families; the contrast of nine-to-a-room in workers' homes with one-in-nine-rooms in the homes of the upper class, etc.'[26] In fact, Atlas Films produced a number of these newsreel-type actuality films, depicting various social and political problems. Film was again regarded as 'a valuable weapon in the class struggle'.[27] Atlas seems to have sponsored about four newsreels in all. These *Workers' Topical News*, as they were called, were mainly about unemployment, hunger marches and working-class demonstrations.[28] Not surprisingly, they were exhibited by workers' film societies, at London and Liverpool for example.[29] Atlas also made a compilation film about the economic and social life of the USSR, entitled *Glimpses of Modern Russia*, and a further production, *1931 – The Charter Film*, which was linked to the NMM's fight against rationalization, speed-up, lowered standards at the workplace, unemployment, poverty, poor housing and inadequate recreational facilities.[30] As such, Atlas production was obviously related to the wider campaigns of the British Communist movement.

Apart from the display and production of proletarian pictures, the Communist-inspired workers' film movement contributed to an emerging theoretical discourse. More specifically, conferences were held and literature distributed in an attempt to advance the aesthetic, technical and political aspects of the medium. In 1931, for instance, the LWFS held its first summer school at which papers were presented by John Grierson on the Soviet cinema, Ralph Bond on 'The Theory and Practice of Workers' Cinema', and by a number of other speakers. As the Marxist press put it: 'The school proved of great value in thrashing out the ideological as well as the practical basis for the Workers' Film Movement in Britain, and the fifty members and friends present favoured the holding of similar events in the future.'[31] Later in the year the FWFS even ventured into publishing with the one penny edition of *Workers' Cinema* (the only known copy of which is in the John Grierson archive, University of Stirling). Apparently the first number of the paper 'exclusively devoted to films from a working-class viewpoint' contained articles on Eisenstein in America, Soviet cinema under the Five Year Plan, reviews, international news and reports from local societies.[32] There appears to have been considerable interest generated in the first number which quickly sold out, leading to a second run. Little wonder then that one review felt that it was 'going to be a great little paper, and of great importance in the working-class struggle'.[33] However, though a second number appeared with material on working conditions in the British cinema industry, entertainments tax, and the Gaumont British Film Trust, this first experiment in workers' film publications soon came to an end.[34] Quite simply, the rather impetuous rise and fall of *Workers' Cinema* was related to a lack of worker correspondents and to the fortunes of the FWFS which fragmented in 1932. Nevertheless, the working-class movement was experimenting with all aspects of the film medium; not only production, distribution and exhibition, but also education and publication.

The FWFS and Atlas Films were undoubtedly cultural arms of the British Communist movement. The officials of the two organizations were by and large party functionaries, and the films distributed or produced aimed to disseminate the Soviet message and support the CP's political and industrial programme. Furthermore, as Trevor Ryan has cogently argued, 'The work of the FWFS was clearly of the cadre type, conforming to general Communist Party practice. . . . Audiences for the FWFS shows therefore consisted largely of members and sympathizers with the Communist Party and its auxiliary bodies.'[35] The Marxist personality of the workers' film movement at this time is also revealed by its ideological position and its connection with other Communist bodies.

Reading through some of the articles written by Ralph Bond, undoubtedly the leading personality in the workers' film movement, it is apparent that he was motivated by a Marxist view of society. Bond, like many other 'organic intellectuals', linked the dominant culture and ideology as apparently expressed in film to the Capitalist totality:

> The cinema today is a weapon of the class struggle. So far this weapon
> has been the exclusive property of the capitalists. We cannot hope to
> wrest it completely from their hands until relations in society have
> been changed, but we can and must fight capitalist influences in the
> Cinema by exposing, in a Marxist manner, how it is used as an
> ideological force to dope the workers. That can be done by exhibiting the
> films of the only country where the workers are the ruling class and by
> making our own films, not to initiate 'new spirits' and 'new religions',
> but to aid and encourage the workers in their fight against capitalism.[36]

This did not necessarily mean that Bond failed to appreciate the technical merits of the Capitalist film industry, but rather that he was highly critical of the ideological messages and signs conveyed by that industry. In reviewing Gainsborough's successful musical comedy, *Jack's the Boy* (1932), which starred Jack Hulbert as a policeman trying to sort out traffic jams, he made one or two favourable remarks: 'A technically excellent production, if a little on the long side, it provides plenty of good humour and laughter.' Even so, he went on to criticize the fact that 'the leading characters of the film all belong to that class of wealthy idlers who cheerfully cut unemployment benefit and wages to maintain their dividends', and further that 'the police are used by the ruling class to baton unemployed demonstrations'.[37]

At a time of rising unemployment, the notorious means test and hunger marches, it is quite understandable why Marxists took this line. Unsurprisingly, Bond therefore recommended the films of the Soviet Union, though he had to come to their defence against the opposition triumvirate of the ruling class, Censors and 'sleuths of the Tory Central Office'.[38] In brief, the films of Eisenstein, Pudovkin, Vertov and others were heralded as both an expression of Communist rule in the one country where Capitalism had been overthrown, where cinema was planned for service instead of profit, and a model for economic and social advance. Soviet films were thus deemed ideally suitable for projection by those bodies sympathetic to the Communist cause.

In a slightly different context, the workers' film societies were involved in joint activities with the political and industrial wings of the Communist movement, as well as the workers' sport and drama groups. Film exhibitions were an opportune time for making contacts, discussing political events and distributing party literature – at the first meeting of the Nottingham Society, for example, seventy one copies of the *Daily Worker* were sold.[39] Also, film groups co-operated in exhibiting *Spartakiade* – about the 1928 Moscow equivalent of the Olympic Games – to working-class audiences interested in sport.[40] Contacts also appear to have been made between the hierarchies of the BWSF and the LWFS, as was the case over Red Sports Day which took place in April 1930.[41] Likewise, proletarian drama was often supplemented by the exhibition of Soviet and other films. In May 1931, for instance, the NMM's charter campaign was supported by a presentation at Bethnal Green library of a WTM sketch on rationalization and *1931 – The Charter Film*.[42] All in all, the evidence is conclusive enough – the workers' film societies of the early 1930s were fairly effective auxiliaries of the CP.

In some respects the fact that the FWFS and Atlas Films were aligned to Communism was debilitating. It should be recalled that at this time the CP labelled Labour Socialism as 'Social Fascism', a fact hardly conducive in warming the hearts of the official Labour movement to workers' film. At its most extreme, Marxist analysis of the silver screen failed to acknowledge that there were elements in the commercial product which reflected and responded to working-class culture and tastes. This too could well have alienated an otherwise potentially quite sympathetic audience. The burden of this relationship with Communism is perhaps one reason why the FWFS and Atlas Films had disappeared by 1932, though by no means the only reason. After all, the workers' film movement had to face the negative intervention of the State through censorship and police regulation. In the last analysis, it was the lack of resources which hampered the movement most of all. By the end of 1931 Atlas Films faced serious financial problems, as did a number of film societies. Moreover, complaints were voiced that the pricing of workers' film was simply uncompetitive by the standards of the commercial cinema.[43] In a similar vein, delegates to a meeting of the Birmingham Society called for lower rates of subscription.[44] As many cultural agencies of the inter-war Socialist movement found, a lack of hard cash was often an insurmountable problem.

The Manchester and Salford Workers' Film Society

Though the FWFS had been disbanded by 1932 this does not mean that all individual societies experienced a similar fate; some lapsed, it is true, but others survived and new societies were formed. In 1934, for example, a workers' film society was started in the Medway towns of Kent 'with the object of showing educational and cultural and documentary films which do not appear in the commercial cinema', whilst in the following year workers' film groups in Hull and Doncaster were formed to produce and exhibit working-class film.[45] At the same time, the Manchester and Salford Workers' Film Society (originally the Salford Workers' Film Society) was still functioning. Indeed, the Society founded during the 'Class Against Class' period went on to survive Popular Frontism. Here, it is appropriate to use the Society as a case study.

The need for workers' film in Salford was first articulated by a group of trade unionists and cinema enthusiasts following a trades council meeting in February 1930, at which the documentary film *The Vienna Congress of International Youth* (already discussed in the previous chapter) was shown. A provisional committee was formed, which in turn launched the Salford Workers' Film Society to encourage 'the most progressive elements in the cinema by exhibiting artistic, cultural and scientific films, particularly those dealing with economic and social questions'.[46] The leading figures were all working-class activists; Tom Cavanagh as secretary, Tom Savage as chairperson, and Alfred Williams as treasurer. The Society was in fact formally established under the auspices of the Salford Social Democratic Land and Builders' Society Limited (1903) which had been re-constituted in 1930 among other things to 'erect, purchase or hire any buildings for the exhibition of Cinematograph Film'.[47] As such the Film Society fitted into a rich Marxist cultural formation centred on Hyndman Hall and the Workers' Art Club with its range of sporting and cultural activities. Interestingly, one member of the Club was Ewan MacColl who has since given a life's work to Communism and workers' culture – with Joan Littlewood, his first wife, he was responsible for the Manchester Theatre of Action, he inspired the post-war folk revival, and more recently was awarded the coveted miners' lamp by Arthur Scargill and the National Union of Mineworkers.

Returning to the Salford Workers' Film Society, from all accounts it appears that the first season was a success. The inaugural performance in November 1930 featured *Two Days, The First Time in History* and *Glimpses of Modern Russia*, which were viewed by an enthusiastic audience of several hundred.[48] From then on until the end of the season in May 1931 all manner of films from Soviet classics to workers' newsreels and a Disney cartoon were shown at the Prince's cinema, described by Alf Williams as a 'bughut . . . terrible that was'.[49] In all, the eight performances in the first season attracted average attendances of 450. There was also an interchange of delegates with the Arts Club, the South East Labour College and the Lancashire and Cheshire Federation of Trades Councils. Councillor Jack Brewin, a leading Society member, was also a Labour College lecturer in psychology, chairperson of the Manchester Plebs League, and vice-chairperson of the Federation of Trades Councils. Furthermore, the Society affiliated to the FWFS and as such played an important part in the Federation's work, attending the London council meeting in May 1931. Alfred Williams has recalled that there was much correspondence with Ralph Bond over the Russian classics, and in fact in the initial stages the Society was dependent upon the central organization for its supply of films: a member collected the films from Salford station and immediately the display had finished they were dispatched back to

London by rail. Yet the most important and interesting link with the FWFS was in the field of production. With the support of the Federation, the Society made a film, no longer extant, of the textile dispute in the Burnley area in 1931. Apparently two members with borrowed equipment and technical advice shot a film of demonstrations, protest marches and soup kitchens, lasting approximately twenty minutes. Though the film was shown at Hyndman Hall, it was very primitive due to a lack of resources and the terrible weather conditions the production team faced – it was snowing in the Rossendale Valley when the picture was made. Moreover, when exhibited the film actually caught fire, and though not totally destroyed, this incident does illustrate the lack of technical expertise of the Society.[50]

In the first stages the Society had meagre resources, notwithstanding the subscription of eight shillings per season and an entrance fee of 6d, and thus relied on the Salford Social Democratic Land and Builders' Society to cover its expenses. As already noted in chapter four, the Society was hampered by the censorship decrees of the Salford Watch Committee, hence the presentation of films outside the Salford city boundaries and the change of name to the Manchester and Salford Workers' Film Society. Even so, given these financial and political constraints the historian has to admire the Society's enthusiasm and perseverence. At least this is the verdict arrived at by the Society itself:

> To summarise, we have no hesitation in stating the first season has been most successful. To have carried through eight performances without hitch, to bring to the Manchester district films that otherwise would never have been seen here, despite lack of funds, experience and facilities, and to have built up a substantial membership in addition, is an achievement of which we are proud, though it has not been accomplished without hard work.[51]

More independent sources also acclaimed the achievements of the Society. On more than one occasion the liberal *Manchester Guardian* was full of praise. In January 1931 under the headline 'Intelligent Films' the paper reported that

> The Salford Workers' Film Society is making good progress in the screening of unusual films which rarely come to ordinary kinemas.[52]

And three months later there was support for the exhibition of Soviet films:

> The belief that the intelligent film will one day prosper grows with each visit to the kinema shows organised by the Salford Workers' Film Society. This society packed the Princes Kinema, Liverpool Street, on Saturday afternoon, when Eisenstein's magnificent film *The General*

Line was screened for the first time out of London.[53]

From then on the paper was to provide a great deal of favourable media coverage which possibly helped to stimulate or, at least, sustain the Society.

Going into the second season in the summer of 1931, it is apparent that the Society was by then firmly established. Membership had increased to 350 and valuable financial and technical experience had been gained. It is not the place here to examine the subsequent history of the Society in any detail, though one or two salient developments are worthy of note. The work of the Society clearly extended into the educational and theoretical side of film. In the second and third seasons, for instance, lectures were given by leading experts on amateur film, the study of cinema, and production problems.[54] Members also gave talks to working-class organizations like the Hyde Socialist Church.[55] On the exhibition side, progress continued to be made, based not only on the Soviet classics, but also on cartoons and increasingly documentaries such as *Industrial Britain, Men and Jobs* and *Today We Live*. Significantly, though, the Society was compelled to use up to eight widely-separated picture houses for viewing purposes due to the conservatism of cinema proprietors – as already noted, at one point the Society was blacklisted by the Cinematograph Exhibitors' Association. Fortunately by 1933 a more permanent home was found in the Rivoli Cinema, Rusholme, with its 1,250 seats, latest Western Electric sound apparatus, and a stage 18 feet deep.[56] Efforts were also made to raise funds to purchase production equipment, and there were even suggestions to build a workers' cinema, though in the last resort money worries continually plagued the affairs of the Society.[57] Despite an increase in annual membership fees to ten shillings in 1933, at the end of the following year the Society was making an annual loss of £18 6s. 11d. Although the figure was not particularly burdensome, it almost crippled the movement for workers' film in the Manchester area, as there was also a hefty tax liability of some £50.[58] Faced with the possibility of extinction, the programme secretary, Reg Cordwell, and others were able to raise the necessary funds and also gain exemption from payment of entertainment tax.[59] Thus the Society weathered the storm, increasing its membership to 1,400 by the end of the decade.[60]

In the first half of the 1930s, like the various other workers' film societies, the one in Manchester and Salford conformed to wider Communist practice. It is apparent from Ruth and Edmund Frow's excellent short study of the Manchester CP that functionaries of the Society were embroiled in Communist politics.[61] Jack Brewin was treasurer of the Salford branch of the National Unemployed Workers' Committee Movement and, though secretary of the Crescent Ward Labour party between 1927 and 1932, remained sympathetic to the Marxist cause.

Tom Cavanagh was a founding member of the CP and secretary of the Salford branch in the 1920s, whilst Tom Savage was a party member. Likewise, Mick Jenkins, whose home was used initially by the Society to recruit members, and Larry Finley both gave a lifetime's service to the Communist and Labour movement. Furthermore, some of the members were influenced by the political events of the period, and the Marxist analysis of those events: the Russian revolution, General Strike and the Capitalist economic crisis. Alf Williams has thus referred to the feeling of imminent change in the late 1920s and early 1930s, and the ways in which Soviet films like *Earth* – 'I have never seen anything more beautiful in my life' – would be a means of political education and change.[62] In essence, the Society was an integral part of the Communist political culture which surfaced in the Manchester district of the early 1930s. Communist activists would often view the films of the Society, perform in the agit-prop sketches of the Salford Red Megaphones, ramble and camp with the Manchester BWSF, and of course demonstrate against unemployment, wage cuts and the rest. At a time when the commercial cinema was so ubiquitous – there was one for every 6,139 persons in Manchester in 1930 – the workers' film society offered a rich and vibrant alternative, providing a different view of the world. Between the winter of 1930 and the summer of 1937 the Society's forty five exhibitions included over 100 films drawn from 13 countries.[63] True, the vast majority of the working class were not attracted to the 'red' screen, but at least an alternative to Hollywood and London had been created.

Having said all this, the Society was never a formal Communist organization. Mick Jenkins has recalled to the author that the left cultural groups in Manchester, though Communist-dominated, never excluded non-Communists from participation.[64] Similarly, the *Manchester Guardian*, in an editorial entitled 'The Film as Propaganda', suggested that the Society would find little difficulty in drawing support from 'dispassionate lovers of kinema' outside the membership of the Third International.[65] In some respects this imitated the 'Class Against Class' line of the 'united front from below', which took the form of joint agitation between Communists and Labour supporters at local level. Moreover, by the mid-1930s it was acknowledged that future development lay in gaining the support of all progressive elements in and outside the ranks of organized Labour. In fact, as the supply of Russian films dried up, often replaced by avant garde movies and in turn petty-bourgeois ideas, Alfred Williams resigned from the Society to direct his energies to more pressing political matters. By 1937 the Society dropped the prefix 'Worker' from its name, and the new Manchester and Salford Film Society stressed that its aim was 'to present artistic, scientific and cultural films of a progressive character'.[66] This change in direction reflected wider changes in the economic and political situation and a general shift in political priorities. Whereas the earlier workers' society had to develop against a background of political division, the new 'progressive' society was to some extent a logical outcome of political unity. It is to film and the unity movement which we turn next.

Films and the unity movement

In March 1933 the Comintern took up the slogan of the 'United Front Against Fascism' as a direct response to the rise of National Socialism in Germany. Put simply, the international Communist movement sought to unite, or at least collaborate with, Socialist organizations of all descriptions. If 'Class Against Class' can in some ways be portrayed as the 'united front from below' and a rejection of organizational co-operation at the national level, in contrast the new line led to attempts to establish formal links with the national leadership of rival social democratic and left-wing organizations. This obviously had implications for the political strategy of the British CP and in turn the workers' culture movement, which ceased to attack the Labour party and TUC leadership. At first the 'united front' established links between the CP, ILP and the left-wing of the Labour party – the Socialist League – but towards the end of the decade this had given way to the 'popular front'; that is, a non-party alliance of all progressive forces opposed to Fascism from dissident Tories on the right to Marxists on the left. How did the workers' film movement fit into this political transformation?

In May 1933 the WTM sent a delegation to the Moscow Olympiad. It was here that the cultural side of the British Communist movement was persuaded to broaden its methods and co-operate with other Labour organizations. At the same time, the delegation was also encouraged to develop workers' film. Soon afterwards, Charles Mann, a leading figure in the WTM, reported that a new film section had made a street presentation of *Soviet Russia, Past and Present*: 'Here is a new medium which will add yet another weapon of intense cultural and propaganda value.'[67] Towards the end of 1933, as Paul Marris has contended, it was CP members who again played the leading role in the founding of the 16 mm production and distribution group, Kino.[68] Ostensibly, Kino was formed to distribute Soviet films and to produce films of workers' life. As early as the summer of 1934 the group had made two one-reel films, *Hunger March* and *Bread*, and the first of its *Workers' Newsreels*. In November of that year, the Kino group and the Workers' Camera Club – formed in 1932 to 'Help the Movement by providing photographs for the Press and propaganda lantern slides'[69] – combined to create the Workers' Film and Photo League (WFPL). Those members who remained in Kino constituted themselves into a new distribution network, Kino Films (1935) Limited, which later also developed its own production group, the British Film Unit.

Terry Dennett has shown that in its early stages the League sought to oppose and contest Capitalism by promoting proletarian films. As the League's manifesto of 1935 stated:

The League will produce its own films giving a true picture of life today, recording the industrial and living conditions of the British workers and the struggle of the employed and unemployed to improve their conditions.

It will popularize the great Russian films and endeavour to exhibit them to the widest possible audiences.

It will carry out criticism of current commercial films in the press and its own literature and expose films of a militarist, fascist or anti working class nature.[70]

Given such political and ideological aims it comes as little surprise to find that the League had links with the Communist movement, though members were drawn from all strata of political society, the clergy as well as the CP. In essence the WFPL was a creature of the popular front. Its activities extended from production, distribution and exhibition – around twenty to thirty films were produced and distributed by the League – into film education. In addition, the League had quite a thriving photographic section. In sum, before its demise in 1939, the League attempted with some success to oppose the dominant culture by exposing through film and photographs the ills of Capitalist society.

Kino Films (1935) Limited, after a few teething problems, advanced to become the largest distributor of working-class films in the inter-war years. According to the figures collected by Trevor Ryan, it distributed some 158 Labour films in the 1930s. Ryan has claimed that by 1937 the company had 'an extensive distribution/exhibition service based on a web of regional agents and a large number of local contacts in branches of the Labour Party, the Communist Party, trade unions and Left Book Club groups'.[71] Indeed, as early as the spring of 1936 Kino had already given shows to over 250,000 people in the previous twelve months, turnover thus increasing threefold and provincial groups being formed in Birmingham, Doncaster, Glasgow and Manchester.[72] The scale of operations broadened in the first half of 1937: 1,023 film shows were organized, an increase of 200 per cent over 1936, and the company's twenty silent projectors were scrapped in favour of six new sound units at £150 each. Certainly, judging from one of Kino's catalogues there was a range of silent and sound films on offer – films on peace, films of China, Russia and Spain, and films on trade union problems.[73] Most fascinating of all is the fact that a move to Wardour Street, the heart of the Capitalist film industry, was even mooted.[74] After all, Kino was a profit-making concern and activities were burgeoning.

Together with the Communist-influenced Progressive Film Institute

(PFI), which had been registered as a company in March 1935, Kino was the major Labour film organization by the end of the decade. Though both Kino and the PFI produced their own films – most important of these were the PFI's *Spanish ABC, Behind the Spanish Line* and *Peace and Plenty* – their major role was in the field of distribution and exhibition; the former to distribute and exhibit 16 mm films and the latter 35 mm films to Labour organizations and where possible to independent cinema owners. To be sure, they both provided an important service to the Labour movement in supporting political campaigns and offering opportunities to extend Labour's cultural and social milieu.

These various initiatives on the film front were assimilated within the united front strategy and links were forged with the broad Labour movement. The films actually produced by the League, Kino and the PFI exuded unity. *Bread* stressed that the way out of poverty was to 'build the united front of employed and unemployed', while *Workers' Newsreel* number two showed that the united front 'is the only possibility to act against Mosley and his Blackshirts'.[75] By the same token, *Peace and Plenty*, the PFI film commissioned by the CP, with its scenes of poor housing, ill-health, under-nourishment and unemployment, ended 'with an appeal for a united front against Fascism and against the present [National] Government'.[76] Also, the Sussex district organizer of the CP, Ernie Trory, was the leading figure behind People's Newsreels which interestingly made a number of films which had shots of Labour officials in joint activities with Communists.[77] As Victoria Wegg-Prosser has commented, the message of these and other films was that 'Unity Wins'.[78]

As previously noted, the Labour party was reluctant to promote Kino Films (1935) Limited and was still suspicious about the Communist origins of workers' film, yet there were attempts to build unity. Thus at the first general meeting of Kino, there were delegates from the Labour party, trade unions, co-operative societies, film societies and other bodies, as well as Communists. As one of the delegates expressed it: 'The move towards unity by all working-class organizations has led to an increasing use of films as a powerful weapon of propaganda'.[79] There were also some local attempts at unity. In 1934, the Kino group acquired its first print of Eisenstein's *The General Line*, and the Royal Arsenal Co-operative Society gave 100 performances of this film to 40,000 co-operators, while in the following year the Colne Valley Labour party purchased fifty copies of *Kino News* for local distribution.[80] The CP member and film activist, Frank Jackson, could therefore write about a 'People's Cinema':

Gone are the days when small crowds huddled fearfully in halls in back streets to see forbidden films.

Today Kino is part of the entire progressive movement. It gives shows to all political parties, to unions, to peace organisations, to religious and missionary bodies, to Left Book Clubs, to professional organisations, to the Co-ops, to Spain organisations, to China organisations, to Nationalist organisations (our operators several times, in fear of their lives, give [sic] shows to fierce crowds of Irish Nationalists).[81]

Similarly, the Hull Workers' Film Society, which exhibited Russian films and also had a photographic sub-section associated with the Film and Photo League, was characterized as free from 'inter-party friction'.[82] Indeed, a further sign of the times was that the WFPL dropped the word 'Workers' from its name in order to fit in with the multi-class concepts of the united and popular front – it wished to work 'in conjunction with Left books, artists and all United and People's Front Organisations'.[83] By the second half of the 1930s Kino, the PFI, the Film and Photo League and other bodies were providing an avenue for cultural co-operation between the various wings of the Socialist movement. Communist-sponsored populist movements, ranging from Kino to the Artists' International, Writers' International, Workers' Music Association, Young Workers' Ballet, London Workers' Choir and the Architects' and Technicians' Organization, promoted the prevailing orthodoxy of unity, which was to reach its zenith with the creation of Unity Theatre.[84]

The fact that from the mid-1930s workers' film was coupled to the progressive movement is shown by its willingness to learn from and accept the help of the non-Socialist, yet progressive documentary movement. The *Left Review*, the journal of the Marxist-dominated Writers' International, published a number of favourable reviews of non-fiction film. Edgar Anstey's production, *Enough to Eat?* (1936), was said to convey 'a piece of socialist propaganda' with its depiction of inequality, poverty, malnutrition, while Paul Rotha's *To-day We Live* (1937), was reviewed as showing 'those ultimate realities of our social system'.[85] Interestingly enough, some commercial films were acclaimed. Take, for example, Metro-Goldwyn-Mayer's first quota film of 1938:

'*A Yank at Oxford* is a British film, but practically everything that is good in it came out of Hollywood. It has all the efficiency, speed and dramatic tension of an M-G-M. product. England has provided only a background, a very excellent though involuntary caricature of the amazing uselessness of university life.'[86]

It is doubtful whether left film critics would have written such favourable reviews of the commercialized product at the height of 'Class Against Class'. Fundamentally, left-wing film was clearly influenced by the documentary movement in their construction of social facts, the reality of everyday life struggles against Capitalism and the concomitant problems of unemployment, low wages, poverty, Fascism and so on. After all, Labour film-makers often mixed in the same circles as the Griersonians.

The workers' film movement best reflected the prevailing mood of unity in its support of the Republican side in the Spanish Civil War. At one level, several members of the Electrical Trades Union and the Association of Cine-Technicians filmed the return of the International Brigade from Spain in order to drum up support for the Brigade and the Wounded Aid Committee.[87] But more significantly, all Labour film groups were involved in raising funds for the Republicans and presenting a Socialist interpretation of the Spanish situation. In this they gained adherents from all progressive elements in and around the Labour movement. As noted in the previous chapter, notwithstanding the fact that the Labour party Executive was concerned about the Communist influence in such broadly-based organizations as the Left Book Club, Marxists and Labour Socialists often came together to view films about Spain and bolster the anti-Fascist campaign. John Lewis, the historian of the Club, has shown that joint initiatives were made with both Kino and the Film and Photo League.[88] Evidently a number of films dealing with Spanish events were shown to Club members drawn from all shades of Labour opinion. In May 1938, for instance, the film *News from Spain* was shown at Woking to a mixed audience of blue-coated and white-collar workers at which the local Labour party was well-represented and money raised for the National Joint Committee for Spanish Relief.[89] Kino and the Film and Photo League were certainly involved in the Spanish campaign. Kino presented *Defence of Madrid* all over the British Isles, raising some £3,000 for relief funds.[90] At local level, the film was shown by the Manchester Film and Photo League and the Manchester and Salford Film Society with much success, having raised cash for the Medical Fund and the International Brigade.[91] In fact, during the three seasons 1936–9 the Manchester Society made numerous collections for Spanish Medical Aid and Basque Children. Finally here, it is interesting that the Central Committee of the CP made the following claim in 1937: '"The Defence of Madrid" film has been shown in over 400 centres, in most cases by our Party organisations or through their initiative.'[92] If the use of film in support of the Spanish campaign was essentially an out-growth of unity, then seemingly the CP was taking the credit for it.

The position of the Communist Party: some conclusions

It is apparent that the British Communist movement generated a number of film groups in the 1920s and 1930s. However, the party never had a formal production, distribution or exhibition unit of its own. Indeed, the party only commissioned one film, *Peace and Plenty*, in all the years in question; though it must be added that at least in the early 1930s the party paper, the *Daily Worker*, had fairly regular columns on 'Films Which

The Workers May Not See' covering Russian pictures, and 'Films They Show You' dealing with the commercial cinema. Like the official Labour movement, this inability to harness film possibly reflected a lack of resources and greater interest in pressing political matters. Kazimierz Zygulski, in his study of popular culture and Socialism has indeed suggested that for Marxist parties, cultural questions play a subordinate role to political and socio-economic questions in the years immediately preceding the revolution.[93] Yet it is also arguable that the party leadership remained apathetic and ignorant of the political possibilities of the new medium.

Certainly party workers were not insulated from those ascetic and puritanical values which characterized certain aspects of Fabian Socialism. For them, time spent in cultural work was wasted time – all efforts had to be chanelled into achieving revolutionary economic and social change. Such political commitment has been vividly described by John McArthur in his recollections of the Scottish Marxist, David Proudfoot:

> I remember when we had our first meeting of recruits. We had to take the biggest hall in Methil. It was bigger than a normal mass meeting. My old friend David Proudfoot opened the meeting. He had the most awkward way of attracting people to the Party. He told them that this was a Party of a new kind that they were joining. It was not a Party that was interested in having socials and dances and tea parties. It was a Party in which everybody had to do work and devote themselves entirely to the work of the Party. They had got to participate in strike activity, go on picket work if it was needed, participate in the communal feeding activity, sell the Party organ, and attend regular classes. Unless they were prepared to do all these things the door was open and they would be better to go away. Proudfoot laid down all the rigid rules that were to be carried through until we had even the old Party members wondering where they were. . . . It was no surprise that many of the recruits vanished like thieves in the night.[94]

Indeed, on one occasion Proudfoot wrote laconically to the Communist author, George Allen Hutt, that during the New Year celebrations 'it is next to impossible to get anyone to take an interest in anything other than pantos, football matches and shortbread guzzling'.[95] This revolutionary puritanism, more likely than not influenced by a Calvinistic upbringing, was perhaps evinced only by a minority of Communist activists, yet it did strike a chord throughout the party ranks.

With this in mind, the kind of spare-time interests which Marxists consistently espoused as strategically correct were those with political benefits, particularly independent working-class education. In the 1920s and 1930s self-taught worker intellectuals were given the opportunity to study Marxism at classes arranged by the CP, National Council of Labour Colleges, the Plebs League and the like.[96] For them, a meagre leisure had to be spent profitably on political education; workers would be advised to spend their leisure absorbing revolutionary education, learning the tactics of the class struggle and trying to subvert the bourgeois order. There was thus little enough time for assimilating the principles of Marxist science, let alone time for watching a Hollywood film. The autodidactic nature of Communist life gives a clue to why some of the party faithful resented leisure activities like cinema-going. What was the use of intensive study if the working class paid no attention to revolutionary propaganda? Moreover, a stock excuse for the failure of propaganda was that workers were diverted, in the pub or the cinema, from the harsh realities of political truth. These types of recreations were not viewed as intrinsically immoral, but as irrational because they were the antithesis of a revolutionary strategy.

It should not be forgotten, however, that the CP was a predominantly working-class organization. The rhetoric of the party might have been one of Marxist purity, but this did not mean that party members were isolated from the pleasures of the people. Communists worked and lived in proletarian communities, so they were hardly immune from the day-to-day interests of work-mates and neighbours. It is not surprising that in trying to build up a 'mass' party, the demand for entertainment was acknowledged. It has already been revealed that the CP planned to organize social activities, though there was little in the way of an integrated entertainment policy. Social activity was neglected by many branches, or, if practised, opposed by political stalwarts. As a number of first-hand accounts have recently shown, Proudfoot was not alone in considering social events to be a way of avoiding political work, such as selling the *Daily Worker*, participating in industrial action and organizing meetings.[97] Even where social facilities were provided they invariably played second fiddle to politics. Education and those spare-time interests which furthered Marxist understanding and contributed to the class struggle were regarded as legitimate; popular entertainment was illegitimate, though often tolerated, because it was thought to be ideologically and politically unproductive. It is in this respect that Proudfoot could enthuse about 'a lantern lecture on Co-operative Russia'.[98] Likewise, film which could serve as a form of Marxist education was looked upon as politically desirable. Alfred Williams has thus explained: 'if we could get these Russian films . . . in to trade union branches, and get trade union members talking about them, it would be a means of political education. Now that was my prime and only concern – using films as a means of political education'.[99]

In any case, party functionaries did play a role in the workers' film movement, and at least during the period of the popular front there was a recreational side to their activity. Unfortunately, internal party records have not survived so it is difficult to tell whether any formal support was forthcoming, though it is very unlikely that finance was provided. Yet, party members formed the backbone of the various workers' film groups in the inter-war years. In the 1920s they played a part in the distribution of proletarian films through the WIR, FSU and the London Film Society; and in the following decade, were deeply embroiled in the work of the FWFS, Atlas, WFPL, Kino and the PFI. Communists like Ralph Bond, Ivor Montagu, Henry Dobb (the film critic of the *Sunday Worker*), Eva Reckitt, Charles Mann, Frank Jackson, Jean Ross, Sime Seruya, Ernie Trory and others, though by no means the only leading personalities, formed the nucleus of the inter-war workers' film movement.

The development of the movement also has to be placed in its proper political and economic context. Obviously, workers' film in the early 1930s, a time of 'Class Against Class' and the assumed imminent collapse of Capitalism, was very different than in the later part of the decade, a time of Capitalist recovery and unity against Fascist aggression. Accepting this, the FWFS and to a lesser extent Atlas Films were building blocks in a Marxist cultural formation which had something in common with Gramsci's notion of a proletarian counter-hegemony whereby working-class intellectuals showed a commitment to cultural and ideological struggle, as well as the seizure of the organs of the Capitalist State. In other words, Communist-inspired film was a form of oppositional culture, as already noted. On occasions, film was being offered as a form of both political education and entertainment, perhaps providing some kind of counter to the ideological messages of the silver screen. In fact many of the workers' film societies presented comedies, as well as the more serious film: humorous items in Bradford; *Cut It Out*, an English comedy in Nottingham; a Disney cartoon in Salford 'which caused much amusement'; and a revival of Chaplin's *A Dog's Life* in London.[100] The LWFS began to appreciate the importance of showmanship 'and realised that our programmes needed to be leavened with variety and humour. Some of the best of the early Chaplin, Charlie Chase, and Laurel and Hardy comedies were regularly included'.[101] Yet, it was in the exhibition of Socialist films that the workers' film movement made its mark. By using these films, the workers' cinema societies, like the WTM and the BWSF, were able to assist the CP in its struggle against the injustices of the dominant social order. Notwithstanding the numerous problems encountered, this initial experiment had not been a waste of time: Marxists had gained access to the screen and working-class audiences were given the opportunity to view films that were not shown at the commercial cinema.

Having reached such a favourable conclusion however, there is a need for at least two caveats. In the first place, the CP was only a small organization with meagre resources and so was not in a position to offer unconditional help. And even if it was, a number of activists were against cultural work, as just discussed. Sections of organized Communism in Britain were economistic in emphasis, no doubt influenced by the Leninist proposition that cultural and ideological work should play a secondary role to economic and political struggle. In the second place, the workers' film movement had a tendency to dogmatism in argument and sectarianism in position. It is true that some of the films exhibited were rather crude, lacking in political subtlety; as Huntley Carter said of the Soviet film, 'The worst are rotten'.[102] It is also true that those Marxists interested in the cinema often failed to make allowances for the tastes of working-class audiences. Arguably, the workers' film groups were wrong when they rejected the best in bourgeois and commercial culture, and in subordinating entertainment to politics.

This rather dogmatic approach and sectarian position was diluted by the mid-1930s. The popular struggle against Fascism had given rise to a more balanced perspective and a willingness to heed 'the norms of bourgeois cultural liberalism'. As John Coombes has asserted: 'in general, the dominant trend in Communist cultural politics was directed ... towards the enthusiastic concessions to liberal cultural practice'.[103] Be this as it may, there were some real benefits to be gained from the change in line. Not only were those Marxists in the workers' film movement more prepared to accept some of the richness of bourgeois practice, but also to learn from the documentary and commercial cinema. Comedies and cartoons may have been shown during the 'Class Against Class' period, but it was only during the 'United Front' era that they began to command interest. As Kino stated: 'we can obtain for you a number of first-rate general interest films from other purely commercial libraries, including well-known successes in the world of Comedy, Romance, Musicals, Wild West and Detective Thrillers, etc'.[104] There is little doubt that this offer was taken up by Labour organizations.

Cultural links were established between the Communist and Labour Socialist traditions. Notwithstanding the antipathy of the official Labour leadership, Communists and social democrats united in the search for a viable Socialist creativity, mainly working through informal channels like Kino, Unity Theatre and the Left Book Club. By moderating class-struggle film – though never rejecting it altogether – stressing unity and promoting the technical and recreational side of the medium, much was accomplished; learning and instruction was combined with entertainment and fun. As the interesting work of Douglas Allen on Scotland has shown, in the popular front atmosphere of the late 1930s leftist cultural activity, such as Glasgow Kino's production of *Hell Unlimited* (1936) and *May Day 1938: Challenge to Fascism* (1938), achieved its finest hour: 'The popular front era was to provide the opportunity for their talents to flourish, in the Glasgow left's most creative period – a result of the merging of the most radical elements and traditions of the reformist counter-culture with the by now diffused revolutionary ethos of the Communist tradition.'[105] Indeed, in the summer of 1939 the Glasgow Labour party took over the Kino group, though any hope of producing their own films was cut short by the outbreak of the Second World War.

Conclusion

This study has shown that the British Labour movement's approach to film in the inter-war years was wide-ranging. Labour's approach involved a consideration of the ideological and cultural role of film in Capitalist society, trade union organization at the point of production and presentation, the questions of State regulation and Sunday entertainment, and perhaps most important of all the need for film organizations directly accountable to the working-class movement. All along, however, we have seen that differences in political traditions and perspectives gave rise to tensions within the Labour approach. To take but one example. Sabbatarian Socialists viewed the opening of cinemas on Sundays with some distress, whilst those Socialists in a more secular position were very much in favour of Sunday amusement. Broadly speaking, of course, the main distinction was between the Labour Socialist and Marxist traditions which manifested themselves in fairly distinctive Labour and Marxist film movements. Bearing in mind the danger of caricature and over-simplification, Labour Socialism and Marxism were the ideological parameters, as worked out during the changing economic and political environment of the period, which determined the nature of the Labour movement's approach. Having said this, there has been a need to acknowledge that neither Labourist nor Marxist ideas were captured by or the preserve of one particular party or sect. Indeed, different political forms clearly took root in similar cultural contexts.

More fundamentally there is a need to relate Labour's approach to film to broader changes in the inter-war political economy – the transformation of trade and industry, the growth of the State and in turn the character of working-class culture. At the outset it was suggested that tensions existed between working-class and Socialist culture. Again it must be stressed that it is difficult to differentiate the culture of the working class from that of the Labour movement. To an extent, this dilemma can be faced by assigning working-class culture as alternative to the dominant society, Socialist culture as oppositional. However, such a demarcation is not always very fruitful. To be sure, there have been times in twentieth-century Britain when a fairly diverse and wide-ranging working-class culture has been oppositional, particularly in a local context (1919 and 1926 spring to mind), and when Socialist culture has been little more than an alternative to bourgeois society. Indeed, the sub-culture of the Labour party and the trade unions has perhaps got more in common with working-class culture than it has with the construction of ideological opposition or forms of counter-hegemony. Thus Labour Socialists often accepted and worked within the dominant institutions and conventions of Capitalist society. On the whole the Labour cinema movement did not seek to disseminate oppositional values, simply to use the new medium as a form of political propaganda. That is to say, the Labour party, TUC and co-operative societies sought to use film as a means of ideological defence rather than attack. Additionally, film was to be an electioneering device, a way of gaining support and publicizing new economic and social policies. Moreover, the mainstream of Labour thought accepted that the working class had the right to watch commercial (or Capitalist) films of their own choice. Hence the Labour party's opposition to the 1927 Cinematograph Films Bill and their advocacy of Sunday cinemas. Certainly the Libertarian Socialist tradition, outlined in chapter two, was sympathetic to the aspirations of ordinary people and the organic character of working-class culture. Labour cinema groups, most notably miners' institutes and co-operative societies, thus exhibited commercial successes. This was evidence of a link between working-class culture and the sub-culture of the Labour movement. The fact that the cinema was a central leisure institution attracting some 1,000 million viewers each year by the end of the 1930s was understood by many Labour activists, and as far as possible accommodated within Labour policy and institutions. It is indeed axiomatic that the Labour cinema may have been as much a reflection of the recreational impulse within the Labour movement and the need to respond to working-class tastes, as it was a form of political propaganda.

On the other hand, there was much about the Marxist approach to film and the cultural forms of Capitalist society which was oppositional. At one level, of course, Marxists – often but not always in the CP – were critical of film in Capitalist society. It was somewhat crudely believed that commercial films were a means of ideological indoctrination by which working-class discontent was marginalized. Though such a view failed to take on board the alternative nature of working-class culture, and the fact that ideological construction and reproduction was an extremely complex process, those Marxists interested in film saw the need to expose and oppose the Capitalist product. This was attempted in an ideological way through the writings and film productions of Socialist intellectuals, and through the organizational forms of the workers' film movement. The Communist-inspired film movement of the 1930s was oppositional insomuch as it sought to help create a new kind of society. To this end Soviet and indigenous proletarian films were presented as a cultural critique of Capitalist society and the status quo. Once again, however, Marxism was neither a closed tradition nor impervious to broader cultural influences from the mass of the working class. After all, the CP and its related organizations aimed to defend and promote the interests of workers.

All of this helps to shed light on the ideological influence of film in Capitalist society. First of all, though, a note of caution. As Jeffrey Richards has intimated, the cinema's influence in society was somewhat exaggerated.[1] In terms of the maintenance of the Capitalist way of life, it was the wage form, capital accumulation, private ownership and the closely linked aspects of political society which were by far the most important influences. That taken, by focusing on the Labour movement's approach to film it can be shown that the dominant class could not simply impose ideology on the subordinate class without opposition. Palpably, imposed forms had some influence, but not without ideological struggle having taken place between, and even within, opposing classes. Thus film was not controlled by capital as a whole, but rather by fractions of capital. Divisions between individual film capitals or between production, distribution and exhibition meant that there was conflict over the purpose, content and form of film. Moreover, the search for profit concerned film capital most and not ideology. At another level, the cinema trade unions were able to have some bearing on production and presentation; not forgetting the undoubted economic power of film capital over film labour. Production in particular is well suited to aesthetic labour, in which film workers, be they directors, cameramen or make-up girls have some influence on the outcome of the final commodity. Even if film organization became more akin to factory organization with a highly disciplined division of labour it is still likely that workers were not stripped completely of control. In studios, and to a lesser extent cinemas, trade union formation was a way of defending independence and autonomy and, moreover, of improving wages and other conditions of employment. Unions such as NATKE, the ACT and ETU made sure that the film product was not a simple reproduction of the interests of capital. By the same token, since the film industry operated in an economic and political context shaped by the State, it is important to stress that working-class interests were being defended. At the national level, the Labour party, TUC and other representative organs of the working class contributed to the formulation and implementation of film policy – entertainments tax, censorship, protection, Sunday opening – as mediated by the State.

Once films had been produced and distributed the struggle over their meaning did not end there. It has been claimed that working-class audiences were far from passive recipients of ideological messages, and indeed were able to reshape such messages through an essentially communal cinema-going experience to accord with their own needs and culture. Furthermore, arguably the views expressed by Labour Socialists and, perhaps to a lesser extent, Marxists must have filtered through to working-class constituents providing alternatives, if not opposition, to the ideological position of film capital and its political advocacy. The workers' film movement was critical of the commercial cinema, and so provided oppositional modes of production, distribution and exhibition. As Ralph Bond has rightly concluded, 'It was in the thirties that films were used for the first time as a weapon in the class struggle in Britain, and their impact and importance should not be underestimated.'[2] Through its collective culture, and especially its Labour and trade union organizations, the working class was able to contest the ideological intentions that fractions of film capital may have had. To be sure, any considered study of the development of the British cinema industry and its economic, political and ideological importance can gain much by investigating the approach of the Labour movement.

Notes

1 Introduction

1 See E. Yeo, 'Culture and Constraint in Working-Class Movements, 1830–1850', in E. and S. Yeo (eds), *Popular Culture and Class Conflict 1590–1914: Explorations in the History of Labour and Leisure*, Brighton, Harvester, 1981, pp. 155–86. R. Samuel, E. MacColl and S. Cosgrove, *Theatres of the Left: Workers' Theatre Movements in Britain and America 1880–1935*, London, Routledge & Kegan Paul, 1985. S.G. Jones, 'Sport, Politics and the Labour Movement: The British Workers' Sports Federation, 1923–1935', *British Journal of Sports History*, vol 2, no. 2, 1985, pp. 154–78.

2 See B. Hogenkamp, *Deadly Parallels: Film and the Left in Britain 1929–1939*, London, Lawrence & Wishart, 1986. T. Ryan, 'Film and Political Organisations in Britain 1929–39', in D. Macpherson (ed.), *Traditions of Independence: British Cinema in the Thirties*, London, BFI, 1980, pp. 51–69; T. Ryan, '"The New Road To Progress": the Use and Production of Films by the Labour Movement, 1929–39', in J. Curran and V. Porter (eds), *British Cinema History*, London, Weidenfeld & Nicolson, 1983, pp. 113–28.

3 R. Williams, 'Base and Superstructure in Marxist Cultural Theory', *New Left Review*, no. 82, 1973, pp. 3–16. This section on Socialist and working-class culture has also been informed by E.P. Thompson's essay, 'The Peculiarities of the English', in *The Poverty of Theory*, London, Merlin Press, 1978, pp. 35–91; R. Hoggart, *The Uses of Literacy*, Harmondsworth, Penguin Books, 1977; G. Stedman Jones, 'Working-Class Culture and Working-Class Politics in London, 1870–1900: Notes on the Remaking of a Working Class', *Journal of Social History*, vol. 7, no. 4, 1974, pp. 460–508.

4 R. Williams, 'Ideas and the labour movement', *New Socialist*, no. 2, 1981, pp. 30–1.

5 A. Gramsci, 'Socialism and Culture', in Q. Hoare (ed.), *Antonio Gramsci, Selections from Political Writings (1910–1920)*, London, Lawrence & Wishart, 1977, p. 13.

6 R. Burns and W. van der Will, 'Working-Class Organisation and the Importance of Cultural Struggle: A critique of James Wickham', *Capital and Class*, vol. 10, 1980, p. 170.

7 R. Williams, 'Minority and popular culture', in M.A. Smith, S. Parker

and C.S. Smith (eds), *Leisure and Society in Britain*, London, Allen Lane, 1973. For a critique of concepts of 'alternative' culture, see S. Hall, 'Notes on Deconstructing the Popular', in R. Samuel (ed.), *People's History and Socialist Theory*, London, Routledge & Kegan Paul, 1981, pp. 232–3.

8 E. Hobsbawm, 'The Formation of British Working-Class Culture', in *Worlds of Labour: Further Studies in the History of Labour*, London, Weidenfeld & Nicolson, 1984, p. 178.

9 R.J. Evans, 'Introduction: The Sociological Interpretation of German Labour History', in R.J. Evans (ed.), *The German Working Class 1888–1933*, London, Croom Helm, 1982, p. 32. As far as Britain is concerned, the article by Stedman Jones, op. cit., 'attempted to establish a systematic linkage between culture and politics'. See G. Stedman Jones, *Languages of Class: Studies in English Working Class History 1832–1982*, Cambridge, Cambridge University Press, 1983.

10 D.H. Aldcroft, *The Inter-War Economy: Britain, 1919–1939*, London, Batsford, 1970. See also Professor Aldcroft's latest offering, *The British Economy. volume 1 The Years of Turmoil 1920–1951*, Brighton, Wheatsheaf Books, 1986.

11 For further discussion, see R. Middleton, *Towards the Managed Economy: Keynes, the Treasury and the fiscal policy debate of the 1930s*, London, Methuen, 1985, pp. 7–9.

12 J. Stevenson and C. Cook, *The Slump: Society and Politics During the Depression*, London, Quartet, 1979, p. 30.

13 See A. Howkins and J. Saville, 'The 1930s: A revisionist history', *Socialist Register* 1979, pp. 274–84.

14 See the interesting chapter in J.E. Cronin, *Labour and Society in Britain 1918–1979*, London, Batsford, 1984, pp. 51–69.

15 J. Richards, *The Age of the Dream Palace: Cinema and Society in Britain 1930–1939*, London, Routledge & Kegan Paul, 1984, pp. 12–15.

16 P. Corrigan, 'Film Entertainment as Ideology and Pleasure: A Preliminary Approach to a History of Audiences', in Curran and Porter, op. cit., p. 30.

17 C.L. Mowat, *Britain Between the Wars 1918–1940*, London, Methuen, 1955, p. 250.

18 E.H. Haywood, 'Where Films are Distributed in the United Kingdom', *The Kinematograph Year Book*, 1924, pp. 331–3. S. Rowson, 'A Statistical Survey of the Cinema Industry in Great Britain in 1934', *Journal of the Royal Statistical Society*, no. 99, 1936, pp. 67–129.

19 R. Low, *The History of the British Film 1918–1929*, London, Allen & Unwin, 1971, p. 51.

20 See S.G. Jones, *Workers at Play: A Social and Economic History of Leisure 1918–1939*, London, Routledge & Kegan Paul, 1986, ch. 1.

21 D. Caradog Jones (ed.), *The Social Survey of Merseyside,* vol. 3, Liverpool, Liverpool University Press, 1934, p. 279.

22 J. Stevenson, *Social Conditions in Britain Between the Wars*, Harmondsworth, Penguin Books, 1977, p. 44.

23 J. Power, 'Aspects of Working Class Leisure During the Depression Years: Bolton in the 1930s', unpublished MA thesis, University of Warwick, 1980, pp. 22–30.

24 L. Halliwell, *Seats in all Parts: Half a Lifetime at the Movies*, London, Granada, 1985, p. 45.

25 Calculated from *Kinematograph Year Books*.

26 F. Brockway, *Hungry England*, London, Gollancz, 1932, p. 39.

27 Cited in M. Chanan, 'The Emergence of an Industry', in Curran and Porter, op. cit., p. 40.

28 W.G. Jackson, 'An Historical Study of the Provision of Facilities for Play and Recreation in Manchester', unpublished MEd thesis, University of Manchester, 1940, p. 148.

29 Rowson, op. cit.

30 J.B. Priestley, *English Journey*, Harmondsworth, Penguin Books, 1979, first published 1934, p. 247.

31 W. Vamplew, *The Turf: A Social and Economic History of Horse Racing*, London, Allen Lane, 1976, pp. 68–9. G. Williams, 'From Grand Slam to Great Slump: Economy, Society and Rugby Football in Wales During the Depression', *Welsh History Review*, vol. 11, no. 3, 1983, pp. 338–57.

32 Cited in V. Porter, *On Cinema*, London, Pluto, 1985, p. 29.

33 Richards, op. cit., p. 14.

34 J. Walvin, *Leisure and Society 1830–1950*, London, Longman, 1978, pp. 134–5.

35 K. Burgess, *The Challenge of Labour*, London, Croom Helm, 1980, p. 205.

36 Quoted in Richards, op. cit., p. 23.

37 A. Barratt Brown, *The Machine and the Worker*, London, Nicolson & Watson, 1934, pp. 182–5.

38 B. Seebohm Rowntree, *Poverty and Progress: A Second Social Survey of York*, London, Longman, 1942, p. 413.

39 Caradog Jones, op. cit., p. 281.

40 H. Llewellyn Smith (ed.), *The New Survey of London Life and Labour*, vol. 9, *Life and Leisure*, London, P.S. King, 1935, p. 47.

41 E. Hobsbawm, *Industry and Empire*, London, Pelican, 1972, p. 221.

42 Caradog Jones, op. cit., pp. 282–3.

43 Hobsbawm, 'The Formation of British Working-Class Culture', op. cit., p. 188.

44 N. Pronay, 'British Newsreels in the 1930s 1. Audience and Producers', *History* vol. 56, 1971, pp. 414–5.

45 See the various working-class autobiographies which have appeared in recent years. More often than not these contain descriptions and recollections of inter-war cinema. J.P. Mayer in his book *British Cinemas and their Audiences*, London, Dobson, 1948, printed reports of the views of film-goers. There are also 500 handwritten questionnaire answers from Bolton cinema-goers dating from 1938, held at the Mass Observation archive, University of Sussex.

46 TUC, *Annual Report*, 1930, p. 330.

47 S. Shafer, '"Enter the Dream House": The British Film Industry and the Working Classes in Depression England, 1929–1939', unpublished PhD thesis, University of Illinois at Urbana-Champaign, 1982, p. 23.

48 *Ashton-Under-Lyne Reporter*, 19 June 1926.

49 Indeed, it has been stated that the 'regulars' of the Paramount of the 1930s were middle class. A. Donbavand interviewed by S. Robertson, North West Film Archive, Manchester Polytechnic.

50 C. Delisle Burns, *Leisure in the Modern World*, London, Allen & Unwin, 1932, p. 63.

51 R. Rosenzweig, *Eight hours for what we will: Workers and leisure in an industrial city, 1870–1920*, Cambridge, Cambridge University Press, 1983, pp. 191–221.

52 F.D. Klingender and S. Legg, *Money Behind the Screen*, London, Lawrence & Wishart, 1937.

53 Political and Economic Planning, *The British Film Industry*, London, PEP, 1952. Low, op. cit. R. Low, *Film Making in 1930s Britain*, London, Allen & Unwin, 1985. See also R. Murphy, 'Fantasy Worlds: British Cinemas Between the Wars', *Screen*, vol. 26, no. 1, 1985, pp. 10–20. Idem, 'Coming of Sound to the Cinema in Britain', *Historical Journal of Film, Radio and Television*, vol. 4, no. 2, 1984, pp. 143–60.

54 *The Economist*, 5 October 1935.

55 *The Economist*, 21 September 1935.

56 *The Economist*, 24 August 1935.

57 *The Economist*, 5 February 1938.

58 *The Economist*, 23 November 1935.

59 *Report of a Committee appointed by the Board of Trade to consider the Position of British Films*, cmd. 5320, London, HMSO, 1936, p. 12.

60 *Ibid.*, p. 5.

61 T. Aldgate, 'Comedy, Class and Containment: The British Domestic Cinema of the 1930s', in Curran and Porter, op. cit., pp. 259–64.

62 G. Perry, *The Great British Picture Show*, London, Pavilion, 1985, p. 53.

63 *Hansard* (Commons) 5th ser. vol. 238, col. 1952, 14 May 1930.

64 *Ibid.*, vol. 260, col. 536, 26 November 1931.

65 See P.M. Taylor, 'Propaganda in International Politics, 1919–1938', in

K.R.M. Short (ed.), *Film and Radio Propaganda in World War II*, London, Croom Helm, 1983, pp. 17–47.

66 P. Swann, 'The British Documentary Film Movement, 1926–1946', unpublished PhD thesis, University of Leeds, 1979, p. 147.

67 R.M. Barsam, *Nonfiction Film*, London, Allen & Unwin, 1974, p. 79.

68 *Ibid.*, p. 37.

69 T.J. Hollins, 'The Conservative Party and Film Propaganda between the Wars', *English Historical Review*, vol. 96, no. 379, 1981, pp. 359–69.

70 *The Times*, 1 September 1924, 8 April 1926.

71 *The Times*, 13 April 1926.

72 T.J. Hollins, 'The Presentation of Politics: The Place of Party Publicity, Broadcasting and Film in British Politics, 1918–1939', unpublished PhD thesis, University of Leeds, 1981, pp. 56–7.

73 *The Times*, 26 February 1931.

74 *Ashton-Under-Lyne Reporter*, 7 July 1934.

75 *Blackshirt*, 11–17 May 1934.

76 R. Benewick, *The Fascist Movement in Britain*, London, Allen Lane, 1972, p. 140.

77 K. Marx and F. Engels, *Manifesto of the Communist Party*, Moscow, Progress Publishers, 1977, first published 1848, p. 72.

78 L. Althusser, 'Ideology and Ideological State Apparatuses (Notes towards an Investigation)', in *Lenin and Philosophy and other Essays*, London, New Left Books, 1971, p. 146.

79 See Q. Hoare and G. Nowell Smith (eds), *Selections from the Prison Notebooks of Antonio Gramsci*, London, Lawrence & Wishart, 1971.

80 J. Joll, *Gramsci*, London, Pluto, 1977, p. 112.

81 Richards, op. cit., p. 323.

82 Aldgate, op. cit., pp. 270–1.

83 N. Pronay, 'The First Reality: Film Censorship in Liberal England', in K.R.M. Short (ed.), *Feature Films as History*, London, Croom Helm, 1981, p. 125. Shafer, op. cit., p. 249.

84 See the useful discussion in E. Buscombe, 'Bread and Circuses: Economics and the Cinema', in P. Mellencamp and P. Rosen (eds.), *Cinema Histories Cinema Practices*, Los Angeles, University Publications of America, 1984, pp. 3–16.

85 J. Richards and A. Aldgate, *Best of British: Cinema and Society 1930–1970*, Oxford, Basil Blackwell, 1984, pp. 1, 8.

86 P. Stead, 'Essays in Bibliography: British Society and British Films', *Bulletin of the Society for the Study of Labour History*, no. 48, 1984, p. 72.

87 Shafer, op. cit., pp. 84, 88.

88 *Ibid.*, p. 101.

89 E. Coxhead, 'Films Bear Left', *Left Review*, March 1938. The joint

secretary of the Prudential Assurance Company (which financed Korda's ideas), E.H. Lever, thus thought that in the last analysis the 'only real proof' of a film's quality was whether it made a 'reasonable profit'. Cited in S. Street's pioneering study of film finance 'Alexander Korda, Prudential Assurance and British Film Finance in the 1930s', *Historical Journal of Film, Radio and Television*, vol. 6, no. 2, 1986, p. 176.

90 Quoted in Shafer, op. cit., pp. 99–100.

91 J. Robertson, *The British Board of Film Censors: Film Censorship in Britain, 1896–1950*, London, Croom Helm, 1985, p. 86.

92 *Ibid.*, p. 90. But see also the mature analysis of Jeffrey Richards, 'Boy's Own Empire: Feature Films and Imperialism in the 1930s', in J.M. MacKenzie (ed.), *Imperialism and Popular Culture*, Manchester, Manchester University Press, 1986, pp. 140–64. Here it is argued that, while 'the audience is not a helpless and inert mass, bound hand and foot and forced to digest unpalatable messages', the working class accepted cinematic views of the Empire as authentic.

93 G. Orwell, *The Road to Wigan Pier*, Harmondsworth, Penguin Books, 1979, first published 1937, pp. 80–1.

94 Porter, op. cit., p. 20. This is not to say, of course, that Chandler or Hammett were themselves anti-Capitalist.

95 A. Howkins, 'Leisure in the Inter-War Years: an auto-critique', in A. Tomlinson (ed.), *Leisure and Social Control*, Brighton, Brighton Polytechnic, 1981, pp. 79–81.

96 T. Aldgate, 'The British cinema in the 1930s', in *The Historical Development of Popular Culture in Britain 2*, Milton Keynes, Open University, 1981, p. 27. See also Richards and Aldgate, op. cit., pp. 2–3.

97 T. Willis, *Whatever Happened to Tom Mix? The Story of One of My Lives*, London, Cassell, 1970, pp. 47–8. Cf. Richards, 'Boy's Own Empire', op.cit., pp. 157–8.

98 K. McDonnell and K. Robins, 'Marxist Cultural Theory: the Althusserian Smokescreen', in S. Clarke et al., *One Dimensional Marxism: Althusser and the Politics of Culture*, London, Allison & Busby, 1980, p. 168.

2 The Labour Movement, Ideology and Film

1 See chapter six.

2 T. Ryan, 'Film and Political Organisations in Britain 1929–39', in D. Macpherson (ed.), *British Cinema: Traditions of Independence*, London, BFI, 1980, p. 52.

3 The phrases have been taken from J.E. Cronin, 'Coping with Labour, 1918–1926', in J.E. Cronin and J. Schneer (eds), *Social Conflict and*

the Political Order in Modern Britain, London, Croom Helm, 1982, p. 113. M. Jacques, 'The Emergence of "Responsible" Trade Unionism, A Study of the "New Direction" in T.U.C. Policy 1926–1935', unpublished PhD thesis, University of Cambridge, 1976. See also K. Burgess, The Challenge of Labour, London, Croom Helm, 1980, pp. 195–251.

4 See K.D. Brown, The English Labour Movement 1700–1951, Dublin, Gill & Macmillan, 1982, pp. 252–3. H.A. Clegg, 'Some Consequences of the General Strike', Transactions of the Manchester Statistical Society, 1953–4. G.A. Phillips, The General Strike: The Politics of Industrial Conflict, London, Weidenfeld & Nicolson, 1976, pp. 280–95.

5 R.M. Martin, TUC: The Growth of a Pressure Group 1868–1976, Oxford, Oxford University Press, 1980, pp. 205–43.

6 S. Pollard, 'Trade Union reactions to the economic crisis', Journal of Contemporary History, vol. 4, no. 4, 1969, pp. 113–4. H.A. Clegg, 'Employers', in A. Flanders and H.A. Clegg (eds), The System of Industrial Relations in Great Britain: Its History, Law and Institutions, Oxford, Basil Blackwell, 1954, p. 214.

7 S. Macintyre, A Proletarian Science: Marxism in Britain 1917–1933, Cambridge, Cambridge University Press, 1980, p. 54.

8 C. Waters, 'Social Reformers, socialists, and the opposition to the commercialisation of leisure in late Victorian England', in W. Vamplew (ed.), The Economic History of Leisure, papers presented at the Eighth International Economic History Congress, Budapest, 1982, p. 117.

9 S. Pierson, British Socialists: The Journey from Fantasy to Politics, Cambridge, Massachusetts, Harvard University Press, 1979.

10 See, for example, S. Mayor, The Churches and the Labour Movement, London, Independent Press, 1967.

11 J.A. Lovat-Fraser, 'Leisure and its use', Forward, 26 July 1919.

12 Quoted in J. Richards, The Age of the Dream Palace: Cinema and Society in Britain 1930–1939, London, Routledge & Kegan Paul, 1984, p. 73.

13 Hansard (Commons) 5th ser. vol. 266, col. 775, 27 May 1932.

14 Ibid., vol. 291, col. 1181, 27 June 1934.

15 Ibid., vol. 267, col. 1838, 29 June 1932.

16 J.R.E., 'The Uses of Leisure', New Leader, 13 January 1933.

17 The Post, 2 June 1934, 1 June and 24 August 1935.

18 F.G.H., 'The Problem of Leisure', The Post, 17 October 1936.

19 Hansard (Commons) 5th ser. vol. 204, col. 246, 22 March 1927.

20 Cited in Daily Herald, 27 December 1928.

21 Cotton Factory Times, 1 November 1929.

22 C. Massie, 'The Colour of Life: Why the Workers are Restless', Daily Herald, 4 April 1919.

23 C.W.E. Bigsby, 'The Politics of Popular Culture', *Cultures*, vol. 1,
no. 2, 1973, pp. 21–2. For Britain's general response to Hollywood, see
P. Stead, 'Hollywood's Message for the World: the British response in
the nineteen thirties', *Historical Journal of Film, Radio and
Television*, vol. 1, no. 1, 1981, pp. 19–32.

24 *Hansard* (Commons) 5th ser. vol. 328, cols 1233–5, 4 November 1937.

25 A. Bourchier, *Art and Culture in Relation to Socialism*, London, ILP
Publications, 1926, p. 10.

26 *Ibid.*, p. 16.

27 A. Williams-Ellis, 'Why Not Jazz? The Socialists and the Highbrows',
Socialist Review, n.d. (October 1926?).

28 *Red Stage*, January 1932. Other Communists disagreed: 'We are not
out to raise the aesthetic standards of the workers nor to develop
artistic theories of working class art; our job is to spread the
revolution; our place is with the masses in their class struggle against
capitalism.' J. Morris, 'Do We Agree?', *Red Stage*, February 1932.
Also, S.R. Gough, 'One Up For Jazz', *Red Stage*, March 1932.

29 Quoted in J. Tilbury, 'The Significance of Hanns Eisler', *Red Letters*,
no. 13, 1982, p. 32.

30 I. Britain, *Fabianism and Culture: A study in British socialism and
the arts c.1884–1918*, Cambridge, Cambridge University Press, 1982,
p. 161.

31 London School of Economics Library, Beatrice Webb Diaries, 24 April
1921, vol. 36, pp. 3836–7.

32 Cited in Britain, op. cit., p. 242.

33 *Manchester Guardian*, 19 August 1930.

34 I. Wright, 'F.R. Leavis and the Scrutiny Movement and the Crisis', in
J. Clark *et al.* (eds), *Culture and Crisis in Britain in the Thirties*,
London, Lawrence & Wishart, 1979, p. 55.

35 F.R. Leavis, 'Mass Civilisation and Minority Culture', in *For Continuity*, Cambridge, Minority Press, 1933, pp. 13–46.

36 J.L. Hammond, 'The Background of the Problem of Leisure',
Industrial Welfare, September 1939. See also J.L. Hammond, 'The
Problem of Leisure', *The New Statesman and Nation*, 19 November
1932; Idem., *The Growth of Common Enjoyment*, London, Oxford
University Press, 1933.

37 A. Ponsonby, 'Socialism and the Arts', *Socialist Review*, September
1922. C.E.M. Joad, *Diogenes or The Future of Leisure*, London,
Kegan Paul, Trench, Trubner, n.d. (1928?), p. 56. As David
Neville pointed out in his review: 'Mr Joad leaps very far forward
indeed when he envisages a civilisation in which the enjoyment of
purely spiritual delights, the contemplation of beauty or truth, will be
the chosen recreation of mankind'. *Daily Herald*, 26 September 1928.

38 T. Greenidge, 'The Talkies and the Socialists', *Socialist Review*, June 1930.

39 *Cotton Factory Times*, 1 November 1929.

40 *Daily Herald*, 21 November 1935.

41 *Manchester Evening News*, 18 November 1919. *The Times*, 19 November 1919.

42 *Daily Herald*, 12 March 1920.

43 W. Citrine, 'The National Theatre: How It Interests the Trade Union Movement', *The Journal* (Post Office Engineering Union), 7 October 1938.

44 Quoted in M. Dickinson and S. Street, *Cinema and State: The Film Industry and the British Government 1927–84*, London, BFI, 1985, p. 156. (The relevant sections of this book are based on Sarah Street's excellent 1985 Oxford University thesis.)

45 *Reynolds' News*, 24 May 1931. *Hansard* (Commons) 5th ser. vol. 314, col. 2237, 16 July 1936.

46 Manchester and Salford Film Society, *Twenty One Years: 1930–1951*, Manchester, The Society, n.d., p. 2. *Manchester Guardian*, 17 November 1930.

47 R.B. Suthers, *Let the People Decide – What?: The Labour Programme and the Liquor Problem*, London, reprinted from the *Railway Review*, n.d. (1928?), p. 9.

48 *Hansard* (Commons) 5th ser. vol. 214, cols. 589–93, 14 March 1928.

49 *Labour Year Book*, London, Labour Publications, 1925, p. 418.

50 R.H. Tawney, 'Introduction', in W. Boyd and V. Ogilvie (eds), *The Challenge of Leisure*, London, New Education Fellowship, 1936, p. xiii.

51 J.J. Findlay, 'Spare Time', *Labour Magazine*, August 1922.

52 TUC, *Annual Report*, 1934, p. 209.

53 S. Hartog, 'State Protection of a Beleaguered Industry', in J. Curran and V. Porter (eds), *British Cinema History*, London, Weidenfeld & Nicolson, 1983, pp. 63–6.

54 V. Porter, *On Cinema*, London, Pluto, 1985, p. 77.

55 *Hansard* (Commons) 5th ser. vol. 204, col. 262, 22 March 1927.

56 *Ibid.*, col. 271.

57 *Ibid.*, cols. 271–6.

58 B. Pimlott, *Labour and the Left in the 1930s*, Cambridge, Cambridge University Press, 1977, p. 26.

59 *Hansard* (Commons) 5th ser. vol. 204, col. 295, 22 March 1927.

60 *Ibid.*, vol. 210, cols 906–7, 15 November 1927.

61 *Cotton Factory Times*, 21 September 1934.

62 Quoted in Macintyre, op. cit., p. 199.

63 H. Marcuse, *One-Dimensional Man*, London, Routledge & Kegan Paul, 1964, p. 5.

64 J.W. Smith, 'Why Not a Workers' Cinema?', AEU, *Monthly Journal*, June 1934.

65 'Benn', 'Imperialism on the Screen', *New Leader*, 17 January 1930.

66 E. and C. Paul, *Proletcult (Proletarian Culture)*, London, Leonard Parsons, 1921, p. 26. F.R. Cowell wrote in the 1950s that *Proletcult* was 'One example of the Marxian doctrine in its cruder form'. F.R. Cowell, *Culture: In Private and Public Life*, London, Thames & Hudson, 1959, p. 282.

67 E. Upward, 'The Island', *Left Review*, January 1935. More generally, the cinema and movie stars, particularly Greta Garbo, were a persistent theme of 1930s literature, in C. Day Lewis' 'Newsreel', Dylan Thomas' 'Our Eunuch Dreams', George Orwell's *Keep the Aspidistra Flying*, Graham Greene's *England Made Me*, and the rest. See B. Bergonzi, *Reading the Thirties: Texts and Contexts*, London, Macmillan, 1978, pp. 124–33.

68 A. Hutt, *The Condition of the Working Class in Britain*, London, Martin Lawrence, 1933, p. 177.

69 D. Bennett, 'News-Reel Poison', *Red Stage*, April-May 1932.

70 S. Macintyre, 'British Labour, Marxism and Working Class Apathy in the Nineteen Twenties', *Historical Journal*, vol. 20, no. 2, 1977, p. 489.

71 *Cotton Factory Times*, 1 November 1929.

72 E. Rickwood, *War and Culture: The Decline of Culture Under Capitalism*, London, CP, n.d. (1936?).

73 H. Carter, *The New Spirit in the Cinema*, New York, Arno Press, 1970, first published in 1930.

74 *Daily Worker*, 3 December 1937.

75 R. Bond, 'A Bit of Gristle for the Starving Dog: The British Film Industry between life and death', *Left Review*, March 1938.

76 'The Finance of the Film World', *The Monthly Circular of the Labour Research Department*, February, March and April 1929.

77 Public Record Office, London (hereafter PRO) LAB 2/2079/5, H. Roberts to J. Ramsay MacDonald, 30 May 1932.

78 PRO LAB 2/2079/5, H.H. Seller to Sir Basil Peto, 28 June 1932.

79 TUC, *Annual Report*, 1937, p. 367.

80 I. Montagu, 'The Film Achievements of the U.S.S.R.', *New Red Stage*, June–July 1932.

81 See *Russia To-day*, November 1935, September and December 1937.

82 G. Hicks, *Give New Life and Purpose to the Labour Clubs!*, London, Federation of Trade Union, Labour, Socialist, and Co-operative Clubs, 1928, p. 7.

83 *Labour News* (Llanelly), 29 August 1925. Cited in P. Stead, 'The people and the pictures. The British working class and film in the

1930s', in N. Pronay and D.W. Spring (eds), *Propaganda, Politics and Film, 1918–45*, London, Macmillan, 1982, p. 91.

84 Bourchier, op. cit., pp. 4, 6, 8, 16.

85 Richards, op. cit., p. 90.

86 *Daily Herald*, 23 July and 30 October 1931.

3 Trade Unionism in the Cinema Industry

1 *Reynolds' News*, 2 August 1931.

2 Quoted in A. Kohler, 'Some Aspects of Conditions in the Film Industry', *International Labour Review*, June 1931.

3 A.L. Chapman and R. Knight, *Wages and Salaries in the United Kingdom 1920–1938*, Cambridge, Cambridge University Press, 1953, p. 207.

4 Figures have been calculated from the *Census of England and Wales 1931*, London, HMSO, 1934.

5 *The Plebs*, March 1932. Interestingly, Simon Rowson had put the labour force at some 50,000 in 1925 – 43,000 in exhibition, 6,000 in distribution and 1,000 in production and printing. *Kinematograph Weekly*, 2 July 1925.

6 R. Low, *Film Making in 1930s Britain*, London, Allen & Unwin, 1985, p. 122.

7 M. Balcon, 'The Film Industry', in H. Schofield (ed.), *The Book of British Industries*, London, Denis Archer, 1933, p. 155–6.

8 Low, op. cit., p. 135.

9 *Morning Post*, 30 July 1931.

10 M. Chanan, *Labour Power in the British Film Industry*, London, BFI, 1976, p. 26.

11 *Minutes of Evidence Taken Before the Committee on Holidays with Pay*, 1937–8, London, HMSO, pp. 111, 115.

12 *Daily Herald*, 22 July 1936. For union organization in the acting profession, and the rise of Equity, see M. Sanderson, *From Irving to Olivier: A social history of the acting profession 1880–1983*, London, Athlone Press, 1984, pp. 229–54.

13 *News Chronicle*, 21 April 1936.

14 *Daily Express*, 9 November 1936. *Daily Herald*, 30 January 1937.

15 *Reynolds' News*, 8 August 1937.

16 TUC, *Annual Report*, 1933, p. 394.

17 See H. Braverman, *Labor and Monopoly Capital*, New York, Monthly Review Press, 1974.

18 C.R. Littler, *The Development of the Labour Process in Capitalist Societies*, London, Heinemann, 1982, pp. 99–145.

19 M. Chanan, *The Dream That Kicks: The Prehistory and Early Years*

of Cinema in Britain, London, Routledge & Kegan Paul, 1980, p. 23.

20 Chanan, *Labour Power in the British Film Industry*, op. cit., p. 7.

21 V. Porter, *On Cinema*, London, Pluto, 1985, pp. 66, 68.

22 Low, op. cit., p. 78.

23 *Minutes of Evidence Taken Before the Committee on Holidays with Pay*, op. cit., p. 149. As Ernest Betts has written: 'The director must gear his subject to the dimensions of a large factory turning out goods for the world. Those who built the studios were not usually film producers but entrepreneurs who thought in terms of manufactured goods to be sold at a profit.' E. Betts, *The Film Business: A History of British Cinema 1896–1972*, London, Allen & Unwin, 1973, pp. 108–9.

24 Low, op. cit., pp. 174, 175, 190. G. Perry, *The Great British Picture Show*, London, Pavilion, 1985, pp. 84–5. See also G. Perry, *Forever Ealing: A Celebration of the Great British Film Studio*, London, Pavilion, 1981. According to Charles Barr, production at Ealing was based on 'teamwork'. C. Barr, *Ealing Studios*, London, Cameron & Tayleur, 1977, p. 43.

25 Porter, op. cit., p. 69. Cf R. Murphy, 'A Brief Studio History', in S. Aspinall and R. Murphy (eds), *Gainsborough Melodrama*, London, BFI, 1983, p. 4.

26 J. Clarke and C. Critcher, *The Devil Makes Work: Leisure in Capitalist Britain*, London, Macmillan, 1985, p. 77.

27 *Hansard* (Commons) 5th ser. vol. 315, col. 1798, 30 July 1936. Interviews conducted with ex-cinema workers also point to the arduous character of work. See, for example, North West Film Archive, Manchester Polytechnic, tapes 727, 852, 1001. G.H. Carder, *The Man in the Box: Memoirs of a Cinema Projectionist*, Cornwall, United Artists, 1984, pp. 16–17, 20–7, 41–2, 63–70.

28 For details, see Low, op.cit., pp. 199–208.

29 *Amusement Workers' News*, August 1925.

30 Mrs Syd Field, *The First Thirty Years – a record of the first thirty years of the NATKE*, Glasgow, Civic Press, 1973.

31 See A. Marsh and V. Ryan, *Historical Directory of Trade Unions*, vol. 1, *Non-manual unions*, Farnborough, Gower, 1980.

32 *Amusement Workers' News*, June 1928. NATKE, *Annual Report*, 1937–8, pp. 13, 18.

33 Figures are from TUC, *Annual Reports*.

34 *Amusement Workers' News*, January 1928.

35 Figures from TUC, *Annual Report*, 1937; *Daily Worker*, 6 December 1937.

36 Broadcasting and Entertainment Trades Alliance Archives, London (hereafter cited as BETA), NATE, Finance Committee Minutes, 28 June 1921.

37 Quoted in Low, op. cit., p. 18. Alfred Donbavand, who worked at the Paramount cinema, Manchester, in the 1930s, has recalled that 'You

talk about unions and you'd be out of the door'; interviewed by
S. Robertson, North West Film Archive, Manchester Polytechnic.

38 BETA, NATE Management Committee Minutes, 14 February 1935.

39 PRO LAB 2/2079/5, Establishment of Joint Conciliation Board, 9
June 1932.

40 PRO LAB 2/2079/5, London and Home Counties Conciliation Board
Minutes, 1 and 4 April 1935. (This file holds the minutes of the
Board). For details of the disagreements between the ETU and
NATKE on this issue, see NATKE, *Annual Report*, 1936–7, pp. 7–9.

41 Cited in *Financial News*, 29 November 1937. BETA, NATKE
Management Committee Minutes, 16 and 22 December 1937.

42 *Daily Herald*, 29 November 1937. *Daily Worker*, 6 December 1937.

43 S.G. Rayment, 'A Year for the Statesman', *Kinematograph Year Book*,
1938, p. 10.

44 *Daily Herald*, 22 June 1935.

45 *Daily Herald*, 22 October 1935.

46 *Daily Herald*, 16 September 1935. BETA, NATE Management
Committee Minutes, 19 September 1935.

47 Low, op. cit., p. 22.

48 Quoted in *ibid.*, p. 20.

49 F.A. Tilley, 'The Story of the Year', *Kinematograph Year Book*, 1921,
p. 16.

50 *Daily Herald*, 21 October 1935.

51 *Daily Herald*, 3 July 1934.

52 *Daily Herald*, 10 January 1938.

53 See PRO LAB 2/2079/5, Ministry of Labour Conciliation Department
Weekly Report, 18 July, 8 August and 26 September 1936. *Electrical
Trades Journal*, July 1936.

54 Quoted in ACTT, *Action: Fifty Years in the Life of a Union*, London,
Pear Publications, 1983, p. 170. See also the interesting article by
J. Neill-Brown, 'Pioneers', *Cine-Technician*, July–August 1938.

55 R.J. Minney, *Puffin Asquith: The Biography of the Honourable
Anthony Asquith. Aristocrat, Aesthete, Prime Minister's Son and
Brilliant Film Maker,* London, Leslie Frewin, 1973, p. 88.

56 Quoted in *ibid.*, pp. 198–9.

57 *Daily Herald*, 22 December 1936.

58 Porter, op. cit., pp. 47–9.

59 *Daily Herald*, 21 May 1937.

60 *Cine-Technician*, May 1936.

61 S. and B. Webb, *The History of Trade Unionism*, London, Longmans,
1920, p. 1.

62 *Daily Herald*, 11 May 1936.

63 *Daily Herald*, 23 November 1936.

64 ACT, *Annual Report*, 1937.

65 *Daily Telegraph*, 23 November 1936.

66 *Daily Herald*, 2 July 1934.

67 *Daily Herald*, 27 October 1937.

68 See S.G. Jones, 'Trade-Union Policy Between the Wars: The Case of Holidays with Pay in Britain', *International Review of Social History*, vol. 31, part 1, 1986, pp. 40–67.

69 *Ministry of Labour Gazette*, March 1925. It should be appreciated, however, that many cinemas, like the Paramount in Manchester, discontinued holiday pay when trade was not so good. See *Daily Worker*, 7 June 1932.

70 See *Minutes of Evidence Taken Before the Committee on Holidays with Pay*, op. cit., pp. 110–15, 148–51.

71 BETA, Joint Committee Minutes, 23 March 1923; Report of the Joint Committee's deputation to the Ministry of Labour, 12 April 1923.

72 BETA, Report of the Conference in reference to the Restriction on Alien Artists, 26 November 1931.

73 *Daily Herald*, 15 November 1935.

74 *Daily Herald*, 4 November 1937. PRO LAB 8/75/9820, Note of a deputation from the ACT and British Association of Film Directors, 2 November 1937.

75 *Daily Express*, 26 February 1938.

76 R. Bond, 'The British Film Industry between life and death', *Left Review*, March 1938.

77 TUC, *Annual Report*, 1937, pp. 366–71. As a further twist to the tale, the Aberdeen branch of NATE had demanded disaffiliation from the IFTU as early as 1921. *Amusement Workers' News*, March 1922.

78 Scottish TUC, *Annual Report*, 1930, pp. 144, 147–8. See also C. Ehrlich, *The Music Profession in Britain Since the Eighteenth Century. A Social History*, Oxford, Clarendon Press, 1985, pp. 210–7.

79 *Daily Herald*, 10 September 1930.

80 PRO LAB 2/1367/ET 2035, A.V. Drewe to M. Bondfield, 27 January 1930.

81 PRO LAB 2/1367/ET 2035, A.V. Drewe to H.H. Seller, 17 February 1930.

82 PRO LAB 2/1367/ET 2035, Report of a deputation received by Margaret Bondfield from the Entertainments' Composite Committee, 20 February 1930.

83 PRO LAB 2/1367/ET 2035, Memorandum from the Board of Trade, 19 February 1930.

84 Scottish TUC, *Annual Report*, 1930, p. 147.

85 E.D. Mackerness, *A Social History of English Music*, London, Routledge & Kegan Paul, 1964, pp. 253–4.

86 For this, see chapter one.

87 Chanan, *Labour Power in the British Film Industry*, op. cit., pp.45–52.

88 *Ministry of Labour Gazette*, May 1939.

89 ETU, *The Story of the ETU: The official history of the Electrical Trades Union*, Bromley, ETU, 1952, p. 154.

90 TUC, *Annual Report*, 1936, p. 454. Interestingly enough, at a time when relations between the two unions were particularly bad in 1928, there is evidence to suggest that the Communist-inspired Minority Movement was beginning to take an interest in cinema workers. BETA, NATE Sub-Executive Committee Minutes, 17 October 1928.

91 BETA, NATE, Report of National Delegate Meeting, 1920, p. 12; NATE, Executive Committee Minutes, 6 and 11 June, 13 August, 5 November and 3 December 1920, 7 January, 5 March, 20 May and 3 August 1921.

92 *Musicians Journal*, July 1922. *Amusement Workers' News*, July 1922.

93 *Electrical Trades Journal*, June 1932.

94 PRO LAB 2/2079/5, London and Home Counties Conciliation Board Minutes, 24 October 1932.

95 PRO LAB 2/2079/5, Memorandum on Cinema organization in the Bristol area, 20 December 1935.

96 Conversation with J.L. Wilson, 28 January 1986.

97 *Daily News*, 8 October 1923. See also BETA, NATE Sub-Executive Committee Minutes, 9 August 1923.

98 BETA, NATE Management Committee Minutes, 5 July 1934.

99 NATE, *Annual Report*, 1934–5, p. 11.

100 BETA, NATE Management Committee Minutes, 16 July, 5 November and 22 and 31 December 1936.

101 BETA, NATE Sub-Executive Committee Minutes, 1921, *passim*.

102 TUC, *Annual Report*, 1928, pp. 512–3.

103 BETA, NATE Sub-Executive Committee Minutes, 12 September 1928.

104 BETA, Report of General Secretary's visit to Sheffield, 6 to 10 July 1928; H. Roberts to Secretaries of Sheffield trade union branches and Labour organizations, 8 October 1928.

105 BETA, NATE Sub-Executive Committee Minutes, 10, 17, 24 and 31 October 1928.

106 TUC, *Annual Report*, 1937, p. 401.

107 NATKE, *Annual Report*, 1936–7, p. 4. Trades councils also supported other entertainment workers – MU, VAF, Actors' Association and Equity. A. Clinton, *The Trade Union Rank and File: Trades Councils in Britain 1900–40*, Manchester, Manchester University Press, 1977, pp. 23–4, 173.

108 G.A. Atkinson, 'The Story of the Year', *Kinematograph Year Book*, 1920, p. 15.

109 *The Times*, 20 June 1929.

110 *Daily Express*, 18 December 1936, 4 August 1939.

111 BETA, NATE London Report for 1928. Bernstein controlled the Granada chain of cinemas in the 1930s, and contrary to the evidence here has been described as 'a left-winger in the centre of a predominantly right-wing Wardour Street and his interest in politics, in the arts, and in the film as a public service did not endear him to his Conservative opposite numbers'. Betts, op. cit., p. 90. See also, C. Moorehead, *Sidney Bernstein: A Biography*, London, Cape, 1983, especially pp. 84–5.

112 B. Hogenkamp, 'Miners' Cinemas in South Wales in the 1920's and 1930's', *Llafur*, vol. 4, no. 2, 1985, p. 69.

113 S.G. Rayment, 'Disillusion', *Kinematograph Year Book*, 1939, p. 14.

4 Labour, Film and the State

1 See A. Booth and M. Pack, *Employment, Capital and Economic Policy: Great Britain 1918–1939*, Oxford, Basil Blackwell, 1985.
R. Middleton, *Towards the Managed Economy: Keynes, the Treasury and the fiscal policy debate of the 1930s*, London, Methuen, 1985.
G.C. Peden, *British Economic and Social Policy: Lloyd George to Margaret Thatcher*, Oxford, Philip Allan, 1985, pp. 47–123.

2 S.G. Jones, *Workers at Play: A Social and Economic History of Leisure 1918–1939*, London, Routledge & Kegan Paul, 1986, ch. 4.

3 PRO BT 64/86/8227/32, Industries and Manufacturers Department Minute, 13 June 1932. Having said this, the Board of Trade's interest in the cinema was primarily commercial and even then it was reluctant to become involved in film finance.

4 See PRO BT 64/86/6267/31. Michael Chanan suspects that 'the government turned the offer down, unprepared to step on the toes of the film industry and of the powerful interests which ultimately lay behind it'. M. Chanan, 'The Emergence of an Industry', in J. Curran and V. Porter (eds), *British Cinema History*, London, Weidenfeld & Nicolson, 1983, p. 58.

5 Details from PEP, *The British Film Industry*, London, PEP, 1952, pp. 124–5. R. Stone and D.A. Rowe, *The Measurement of Consumers' Expenditure and Behaviour in the United Kingdom 1920–1938*, vol. II, Cambridge, Cambridge University Press, 1966, pp. 80–1.

6 PEP, op. cit., p. 125.

7 Scottish TUC, *Annual Report*, 1921, p. 75. TUC, *Annual Report*, 1921, pp. 341–2.

8 TUC, *Annual Report*, 1921, p. 341. See also J.B. Williams, 'Amusements and Taxes', *Daily Herald*, 17 February 1922.

9 Scottish TUC, *Annual Report*, 1922, pp. 98–9; 1923, p. 136; 1924, p. 146.

10 EP Microform Collection, South Shields Labour party and Trades Council Minutes, 21 February 1922.

11 Labour party Archives, Labour party Executive Committee Minutes, 24 June 1922.

12 Scottish TUC, *Annual Report*, 1929, p. 170. TUC, *Annual Report*, 1929, pp. 454–5.

13 Jones, op. cit., pp. 99–100.

14 For detailed discussion of the State, protection and the film industry, see M. Dickinson and S. Street, *Cinema and State: The Film Industry and the British Government 1927–84*, London, BFI, 1985.

15 The *Era*, 11 January 1928. There are references to Hugh Roberts' appointment to the sub-committee of the Theatre and Music Halls Committee in the LCC printed minutes 1925–27, though no mention of his recommendation of film protection. I am indebted to R.B. Heath for this information.

16 See University of Warwick Modern Records Centre, Mss 200/F/1/1/159; 200/F/1/2/25, Memorandum to H.M. Government from the FBI, 17 July 1925. Dickinson and Street, op. cit., ch. 1.

17 PRO CAB 24/178 (CP 69), The British Film Industry, Memorandum by the President of the Board of Trade, 16 February 1926.

18 PRO CAB 24/184 (CP 29), Memorandum by the President of the Board of Trade, 28 January 1927.

19 *Hansard* (Commons) 5th ser. vol. 204, cols 237–46, 22 March 1927.

20 *Ibid.*, col. 275.

21 *Ibid.*, vol. 210, col. 692, 14 November 1927.

22 *Ibid.*, vol. 204, col. 297, 22 March 1927.

23 *Ibid.*, vol. 210, col. 691, 14 November 1927.

24 *Ibid.*, vol. 204, col. 238, 22 March 1927.

25 S. Hartog, 'State Protection of a Beleaguered Industry', in Curran and Porter, op. cit., p. 64.

26 TUC, *Annual Report*, 1928, p. 509.

27 Dickinson and Street, op. cit., p. 46. G. Perry, *The Great British Picture Show*, London, Pavilion, 1985, p. 54. J. Richards, *The Age of the Dream Palace: Cinema and Society in Britain 1930–1939*, London, Routledge & Kegan Paul, 1984, p. 35. However, compare with the comments of Rachael Low: 'The 1927 quota legislation had a profound and damaging effect on the structure of the British film industry.' R. Low, *Film Making in 1930s Britain*, London, Allen & Unwin, 1985, p. 33.

28 TUC, *Annual Report*, 1930, pp. 416–7.

29 BETA, NATE Management Committee Minutes, 9 December 1931.

30 BETA, NATE to P. Ashley, n.d.

31 BETA, NATE, Annual Report, 1931.

32 TUC, *Annual Report*, 1931, pp. 300–1. See also University of

Warwick Modern Records Centre, Mss 200/F/1/2/40, FBI/TUC Film Industry Recommendations.

33 TUC, *Annual Report*, 1932, p. 194; 1933, p. 202. PRO BT 64/97/7749/33.

34 See, for example, PRO BT 64/99/7915/ 34, Memorandum on the present position of the Film Industry, and the difficulties which may be expected to arise under the Act in the near future, November 1934.

35 Hartog, op. cit., p. 69.

36 BETA, NATKE National Delegate Minutes, 19 July 1935.

37 PRO LAB 8/75/9820, Notes of a deputation from the ACT, 13 July 1937. It was at this deputation that George Elvin criticized the policy of Alexander Korda, who 'by virtue of his foreign experience and associations, had a decided preference for foreign technicians and held the view that the really expert British technician did not exist. As a result, a very large number of foreigners found employment at Denham Studios.' See also PRO BT 64/88/7411/35. Board of Trade, *Minutes of Evidence Taken Before the Departmental Committee on Cinematograph Films*, London, HMSO, 1936, pp. 71–8. *Cine-Technician*, February-March 1937; April-May, 1937.

38 TUC, *Annual Report*, 1936, pp. 221–3.

39 PRO BT 64/92/6757/38, Moyne Committee on Cinematograph Films [Private] Minutes, 19 May 1936.

40 See *Report of a Committee appointed by the Board of Trade to consider the Position of British Films*, cmd. 5320, London, HMSO, 1936.

41 *Hansard* (Commons) 5th ser. vol. 328, col. 1174, 4 November 1937.

42 Low, op. cit., pp. 47–50. See also PRO BT 64/89/6551/37.

43 BETA, NATKE Management Committee Minutes, 11, 18 and 25 November 1937. See also TUC, *Annual Report*, 1937, pp. 366–71. PRO BT 64/90/7880/37, TUC deputation received by the President of the Board of Trade, 24 November 1937.

44 PRO BT 64/90/7880/37, G.H. Elvin to O. Stanley, 3 February 1938.

45 PRO BT 64/94/6540/39, A.M. Crickett to O. Stanley, 12 May 1939. TUC, *Annual Report*, 1938, p. 431. *The Times*, 12 January 1939. Dickinson and Street, op. cit., pp. 99–100, 110–11.

46 R. Bond, 'The British Film Industry between life and death', *Left Review*, March 1938. In the government's defence, however, the demands of Hollywood and the Hays Office had been largely resisted. See S. Street, 'The Hays Office and the Defence of the British Market in the 1930s', *Historical Journal of Film, Radio and Television*, vol. 5, no. 1, 1985, pp. 37–55.

47 D. Macpherson (ed.), *Traditions of Independence: British Cinema in the Thirties*, London, BFI, 1980, p. 101.

48 J. Richards, 'The Secret Diaries of the Film Censors', Channel 4 television, 31 March 1986.

49   *Hansard* (Commons) 5th ser. vol. 204, cols 2240–1, 7 April 1927.

50   A.W. McIntosh, 'Russia Finds a New Art Form: Pudovkin Versus Hollywood', *Socialist Review*, March 1929.

51   *The Times*, 16 June 1930. Cf *Daily Worker*, 20 June 1930.

52   See *Hansard* (Commons) 5th ser. vol. 240, col. 972, 24 June 1930; cols 1587–8, 30 June 1930; col. 1934, 2 July 1930.

53   J.C. Robertson, *The British Board of Film Censors: Film Censorship in Britain 1896–1950*, London, Croom Helm, 1985, pp. 34, 37, 43–4.

54   *Sunday Worker*, 10 November 1929.

55   *Daily Herald*, 22 February 1930.

56   ILP, *Annual Conference Report*, 1930, p. 47. *New Leader*, 28 February 1930.

57   Greater London Record Office (GLRO), LCC Minutes of Proceedings, 11 March 1930. See also Richards, *The Age of the Dream Palace*, op. cit., pp. 96–7.

58   *The Times*, 10 and 12 March 1930.

59   GLRO, LCC Minutes of Proceedings, 27 May 1930.

60   GLRO, LCC Minutes of Proceedings, 17 October and 4 November 1930.

61   *Manchester Guardian*, 5 May 1931.

62   *Manchester Guardian*, 29 June 1931. *Daily Worker*, 4 July 1931.

63   H. Marshall, 'Eisenstein and others', *The Listener*, 22 March 1973.

64   For a general discussion of the political implications of filming working-class demonstrations, see T.J. Hollins, 'The Presentation of Politics: The Place of Party Publicity, Broadcasting and Film in British Politics, 1918–1939', unpublished PhD thesis, University of Leeds, 1981, pp. 647ff.

65   *Daily Worker*, 30 November 1931.

66   PRO HO 45/15208, Film Censorship Consultative Committee Minutes, 10 October 1932.

67   R. Cordwell interviewed by Seona Robertson, 21 July 1977; A. Williams interviewed by S. Robertson, 19 January 1978, North West Film Archive, Manchester Polytechnic.

68   PRO HO 45/15206, Deputation from the Parliamentary Film Committee, 17 March 1932.

69   D. Allen, '"Culture" and the Scottish Labour Movement', *Scottish Labour History Society Journal*, no. 14, May 1980, p. 34.

70   PRO HO 45/17067–8.

71   See *Daily Worker*, 20 February 1934. J.P.M., 'The Cinema Trades Blow at Workers' Education', *The Plebs*, November 1934.

72   See B. Hogenkamp, *Film and the Labour Movement in the North East – exhibition purposes*, Trade Films/Northern Film and Television Archive, August 1985, pp. 8–10.

73   PRO HO 45/14275, Notes of a deputation received by the Home

Secretary from the Parliamentary Film Committee and other Film Societies, 15 July 1930.

74 PRO HO 45/15206, Deputation from the Parliamentary Film Committee, 17 March 1932.

75 *New Leader*, 12 December 1930.

76 PRO HO 45/15208, Film Censorship Consultative Committee Minutes, 26 November 1931.

77 PRO HO 45/15208, Film Censorship Consultative Committee Minutes, 10 October 1932.

78 PRO HO 45/17955, Film Censorship Consultative Committee Minutes, 15 June 1934.

79 A. Aldgate, *Cinema and History: British Newsreels and the Spanish Civil War*, London, Scolar Press, 1979.

80 PRO HO 45/15206, Memorandum on Film Censorship, n.d.

81 PRO HO 45/15206, C. Wigram to F.A. Newton, 30 April 1932. Clive Wigram was the King's private secretary.

82 PRO HO 45/17072, Annexe to letter from National Cinema Inquiry Committee to Ramsay MacDonald, 30 November 1934.

83 PRO HO 45/15207, Circular letter from J. Brooke Wilkinson to British Producers, 18 October 1932.

84 PRO HO 45/14276, C.A. Loveless to J.R. Clynes, 11 April 1931.

85 PRO HO 45/14275.

86 PRO HO 45/17955, File on political censorship by BBFC on question asked by G. Mander in the House of Commons, 7 December 1938. Cf. Richards, *The Age of the Dream Palace*, op. cit., pp. 99, 104.

5 Labour and the Sunday Films' Question

1 J. Wigley, *The Rise and Fall of the Victorian Sunday*, Manchester, Manchester University Press, 1980, p. 205.

2 J. Lowerson, 'Sport and the Victorian Sunday: The Beginnings of Middle-Class Apostasy', *British Journal of Sports History*, vol. 1, no. 2, 1984, p. 204.

3 B. Harrison, 'Remembering the Sabbath Day', *Times Literary Supplement*, 26 December 1980. I am indebted to Mr Terry Wyke for this reference.

4 H. Llewellyn Smith (ed.), *The New Survey of London Life and Labour*, vol. 9, *Life and Leisure*, London, P.S. King, 1935.

5 C. Harris, *The Use of Leisure in Bethnal Green: A Survey of Social Conditions in the Borough 1925 to 1926*, London, Lindsey Press, 1927, pp. 70–1.

6 S. Rowntree, *Poverty and Progress: A Second Social Survey of York*, London, Longmans, 1942.

7 *Ibid.*, pp. 429–45.

8 *The Times*, 10 July 1922; 11 July 1923.

9 PRO HO 45/14102.

10 *Ibid.*, newspaper cutting from *The Times*, 20 January 1931. Cf E. Betts, *The Film Business: A History of British Cinema 1896–1972*, London, Allen & Unwin, 1973, p. 51.

11 *The Bioscope*, 12 February 1930.

12 Cited in *The Times*, 31 March 1927.

13 *Daily Telegraph*, 12 October 1928.

14 *Hansard* (Commons) 5th ser. vol. 251, col. 645, 20 April 1931.

15 PRO HO 45/14102, newspaper cutting from *The Times*, 26 January 1931.

16 See PRO HO 45/14102 for further details.

17 Labour party, *Annual Conference Report*, 1932, p. 98. The Board of Trade, in stressing that they were 'not concerned with the moral aspects of the question', drew attention to the 'wrecking amendments' which spelled doom for the future of the Bill. See PRO BT 64/86/8134/32.

18 *Hansard* (Commons) 5th ser. vol. 266, col. 715, 27 May 1932.

19 J. Richards, 'The cinema and cinema-going in Birmingham in the 1930s', in J.K. Walton and J. Walvin (eds), *Leisure in Britain 1780–1939*, Manchester, Manchester University Press, 1983, p. 43.

20 *Hansard* (Commons) 5th ser. vol. 275, col. 188, 28 February 1933.

21 S. Rowson, 'A Statistical Survey of the Cinema Industry in GB in 1934', *Journal of the Royal Statistical Society*, vol. 99, 1936.

22 G. Perry, *The Great British Picture Show*, London, Pavilion, 1985, p. 67. For details of the various local polls undertaken, see the following files in the PRO HO 45/14857–8, 15247–9, 15817–29, 18059–63.

23 A.J.P. Taylor, *English History 1914–1945*, London, Book Club Associates, 1977, p. 316.

24 R. Low, *Film Making in 1930s Britain*, London, Allen & Unwin, 1985, p. 60.

25 *Hyde Reporter*, 27 March 1920.

26 EP Microform Collection, Sheffield Federated Trades and Labour Council Executive Committee Minutes, 14 and 21 December 1920. Over a decade later the Sheffield Watch Committee was to ban the Sunday performances of the local workers' film society. *Daily Worker*, 5 October 1931.

27 *Labour's Northern Voice*, 14 February 1930.

28 Manchester and Salford Film Society, *Twenty One Years: 1930–51*, Manchester, The Society, n.d., p.1.

29 *The Worker*, 1 November 1929.

30 *The Times*, 29 February 1930.

31 GLRO, LCC Minutes of Proceedings, 27 October 1925, 2 November 1926, 19 July 1927, 10 July 1928, 29 October 1929.

32 *Daily Worker*, 12 December 1933. *New Leader*, 22 December 1933.

33 For details of the Association, see the files of the *Scottish Co-operator* for 1938.

34 Manchester and Salford Workers' Film Society, *Prospectus*, 1936–7.

35 J. Jones, *My Lively Life*, London, John Long, 1929, pp. 149, 152. Mowat described Jones as 'A wit and genial obstructionist in parliament for many years.' C.L. Mowat, *Britain Between the Wars 1918–1940*, London, Methuen, 1955, p. 184.

36 *The Times*, 7 July 1923.

37 *Hansard* (Commons) 5th ser. vol. 251, col. 677, 20 April 1931.

38 *Ibid.*, vol. 264, cols 940–4, 13 April 1932; vol. 266, cols 775–80, 27 May 1932.

39 *Ibid.*, vol. 251, col. 678, 20 April 1931.

40 See Lowerson, op. cit.; idem, 'Joint stock companies, capital formation and suburban leisure in England, 1880–1914', in W. Vamplew (ed.), *The Economic History of Leisure*, papers presented at the Eighth International Economic History Congress, Budapest, 1982, pp. 61–71; idem, 'Scottish Croquet: The English Golf Boom, 1880–1914', *History Today*, no. 33, May 1983.

41 H. Gosling, *Up and Down Stream*, London, Methuen, 1927, p. 102.

42 *Hansard* (Commons) 5th ser. vol. 251, cols 686–7, 20 April 1931.

43 *Daily Worker*, 16 December 1930.

44 *Hansard* (Commons) 5th ser. vol. 251, col. 755, 20 April 1931; vol. 264, col. 916, 13 April 1932.

45 *Ibid.*, vol. 251, col. 641, 20 April 1931.

46 *Ibid.*, cols 705–10.

47 *Ibid.*, col. 739.

48 *Ibid.*, vol. 264, cols 905–7, 13 April 1932.

49 *Ibid.*, vol. 267, col. 1853, 29 June 1932.

50 M. Pallister, 'Sunday Cinemas', *New Leader*, 19 December 1930.

51 Labour party, *Annual Conference Report*, 1931, p. 87.

52 *Daily Herald*, 4 April 1932.

53 E. Hughes, 'The Agitation about Sunday Sin', *Forward*, 30 April 1932. H. Tracey, 'The Sinful Cinema, the Censor, and the Sabbatarian', *Labour Magazine*, May 1932. H. Griffith, 'Open the Cinemas on Sunday', *New Leader*, 23 December 1932.

54 H.R., 'Open Cinemas on Sundays With Shorter Hours for Workers', *Daily Worker*, 27 December 1932.

55 S.G. Jones, 'Sport, Politics and the Labour Movement: The British Workers' Sports Federation, 1923–1935', *British Journal of Sports History*, vol. 2, no. 2, 1985, pp. 154–78.

56 For further details, see Wigley, op. cit., ch. 11.

57 TUC, *Annual Report*, 1925, p. 529.

58 Scottish TUC, *Annual Report*, 1925, p. 207.

59 TUC, *Annual Report*, 1927, pp. 445–6. Scottish TUC, *Annual Report*, 1927, pp. 200–2.

60 TUC, *Annual Report*, 1927, p. 446.

61 PRO HO 45/14102, Deputation from CEA to Home Secretary, 9 February 1931.

62 PRO HO 45/14102, H.H. Martin to J.R. Clynes, 29 January 1931; Council of Christian Ministers on Social Questions deputation to Home Office, 2 February 1931.

63 TUC, *Annual Report*, 1931, p. 470.

64 BETA, NATE Management Committee Minutes, 8 April 1931.

65 TUC, *Annual Report*, 1931, pp. 470–1.

66 PRO HO 45/14102, W. Hay to J.R. Clynes, 3 March 1931. However, Clynes declined to receive a deputation from the Water Rats 'in view of the exceptionally heavy demands which are at present being made on his time'. Home Office to W. Hay, 13 March 1931.

67 BETA, NATE Management Committee Minutes, 15 and 22 April 1931.

68 TUC, *Annual Report*, 1932, p. 116.

69 *Hansard* (Commons) 5th ser. vol. 264, cols 929–34, 13 April 1932.

70 *Ibid.*, vol. 266, col. 735, 27 May 1932.

71 TUC, *Annual Report*, 1932, p. 141.

72 *Ibid.*, p. 142.

73 Scottish TUC, *Annual Report*, 1927, p. 202.

74 R. Haslett, 'N.U.R. and Sunday Football', *Railway Review*, 13 August 1920.

75 *The Times*, 18 February 1920; 12 July 1923.

76 *Hansard* (Commons) 5th ser. vol. 264, cols 857–61, 13 April 1932.

77 *The Times*, 31 March 1927.

78 See *Labour Pioneer*, 30 June 1921. *Oldham Labour Gazette*, April 1923.

79 *Hansard* (Commons) 5th ser. vol. 251, cols 655–62, 20 April 1931.

80 *Oldham Chronicle*, 25 April 1931. See also *Oldham Evening Chronicle*, 21 April 1931.

81 *The Times*, 22 December 1932. Interestingly, the Oldham Town Council was of the 'opinion that the Sunday Licensing of Cinemas should be dealt with by the Government alone and not left to the option of Local Authorities'. PRO HO 45/14102, J.J. Williams [Oldham Town Clerk] to J.R. Clynes, 29 July 1931.

82 *Hansard* (Commons) 5th ser. vol. 251, cols 718–20, 20 April 1931.

83 *Ibid.*, col. 700.

84 *Minutes of Evidence Taken Before the Royal Commission on Licensing (England and Wales)*, 29 July 1930, q.33948 at p. 1929.

85 C. Ford, '"One Man's Town?" – the life and struggles of Wilcockson of Farnworth, a remarkable figure in the labour movement who dominated a town', paper presented to the Spring Conference of the North West Labour History Group, 1983.

86 J.A.R. Pimlott, *Recreations*, Studio Vista, 1968, pp. 54–5.

6 The Labour Film Movement

1 See B. Hogenkamp, *Deadly Parallels: Film and the Left in Britain, 1929–1939*, London, Lawrence & Wishart, 1986.

2 B. Pimlott, 'The Labour Left', in C. Cook and I. Taylor (eds), *The Labour Party: An Introduction to its History, Structure and Politics*, London, Longman, 1980, p. 185.

3 B. Pimlott, *Labour and the Left in the 1930s*, Cambridge, Cambridge University Press, 1977, p. 6.

4 A. Booth, 'Essays in Bibliography: The Labour Party and Economics Between the Wars', *Bulletin of the Society for the Study of Labour History*, no. 47, Autumn 1983, p. 39.

5 G.D.H. Cole, *History of the Labour Party from 1914*, London, Routledge & Kegan Paul, 1948, p. 279.

6 D. Howell, *British Social Democracy: A Study in Development and Decay*, London, Croom Helm, 1980, p. 10.

7 E. Durbin, *New Jerusalems: The Labour Party and the Economics of Democratic Socialism*, London, Routledge & Kegan Paul, 1985, p. 261.

8 A. Marwick, 'The Labour Party and the Welfare State in Britain 1900–48', *American Historical Review*, vol. 73, no. 2, 1967–68, pp. 380–403. See also the interesting comments of Richard Lyman, 'The British Labour Party: The Conflict between Socialist Ideals and Practical Politics between the Wars', *Journal of British Studies*, vol. 5, no. 2, 1965, pp. 140–52.

9 Quoted in J.S. Harris, *Government Patronage of the Arts in Great Britain*, Chicago, University of Chicago Press, 1970, p. 150.

10 *Daily Herald*, 7 and 8 May 1919.

11 Quoted in T.J. Hollins, 'The Presentation of Politics: The Place of Party Publicity, Broadcasting and Film in British Politics, 1918–1939', unpublished PhD thesis, University of Leeds, 1981, p. 184.

12 Labour party Archives (LPA), Labour party Sub-Committee on Literature, Publicity and Research, 11 November 1919.

13 LPA, Labour party Executive Committee Minutes, 12 November 1919.

14 LPA, Labour party Press Department, Film Propaganda Committee Minutes, 18 December 1919.

15 LPA, Reports filed under Film Propaganda Minutes, 18 December 1919.

16 Hollins, op. cit., p. 186.

17 LPA, Labour party Finance Sub-Committee Minutes, 18 March 1920.

18 LPA, Labour party Executive Committee Minutes, 9 March 1920.

19 Circular on Labour Cinema Propaganda, March 1920, cited in Hollins, op. cit., pp. 186–7.

20 EP Microform Collection, Colne Valley Divisional Labour party Executive Minutes, 8 May 1920. *Labour Pioneer*, 9 September 1920.

21 LPA, Labour party Executive Committee Minutes, 1 March 1922.

22 See, for example, R. Samuel, E. MacColl and S. Cosgrove, *Theatres of the Left: Workers' Theatre Movements in Britain and America 1880–1935*, London, Routledge & Kegan Paul, 1985.

23 See S.G. Jones, 'The British Labour Movement and Working Class Leisure 1918–1939', unpublished PhD thesis, University of Manchester, 1983, pp. 277–9.

24 Hollins, op. cit., pp. 188–9.

25 EP Microform Collection, Colne Valley Divisional Labour party Executive Minutes, 6 January and 3 February 1929.

26 *Daily Herald*, 10 September and 3 October 1928.

27 E. Wilkinson, 'Say it with Pictures', *Daily Herald*, 22 September 1928.

28 Jones, op. cit., pp. 273–6.

29 See H. Carter, *The New Spirit in the Cinema*, New York, Arno Press, 1970, first published 1930, p. 285.

30 'Benn' appears to have been the left-wing intellectual, Gary Allighan.

31 ILP, *Annual Conference Report*, 1930, pp. 33–4.

32 [Birmingham] *Town Crier*, 17 April 1931.

33 ILP, *Annual Conference Report*, 1931, p. 23.

34 ILP, *Annual Conference Report*, 1932, p. 24.

35 R. Postgate, 'Making Films to Make Socialists', *Labour*, September 1933.

36 According to a number of sources, *Blow, Bugles, Blow!*, written by Postgate, directed by Messel and starring George Hicks MP, was first shown at the Southport Conference of 1934.

37 T. Greenidge, 'Films of the Month', *Socialist Review*, September 1933.

38 LPA, Hastings Conference Arrangements Committee Minutes, 10 August 1933.

39 *Daily Herald*, 5 October 1933.

40 Stockport Public Library Archives Department, B/MM/3/23, Stockport Labour Fellowship Executive Committee Minutes, 5 December 1933. 'Socialist Films at Last', *Leeds Weekly Citizen*, 16 March 1934.

41 LPA, Labour party Finance and General Purposes Committee Minutes, 7 December 1934.

42 B. Hogenkamp, 'Workers' Newsreels of the 1920's and 1930's', *Our History*, no. 68, n.d., p. 17. Hogenkamp, *Deadly Parallels*, op. cit., ch. 4.

43 LPA, Labour party Research and Publicity Committee Minutes, 21 February 1935.

44 LPA, Labour party Research and Publicity Committee Minutes, 21 March 1935; National Executive Committee Minutes, 27 March and 22 May 1935; Finance and General Purposes Sub-Committee Minutes, 20 May 1935.

45 The circular is reprinted in D. Macpherson (ed.), *Traditions of Independence: British Cinema in the Thirties*, London, BFI, 1980, p. 153. See also Labour party, *Annual Conference Report*, 1936, p. 82.

46 LPA, Labour party National Executive Committee Minutes, 5 September 1936.

47 LPA, Special Conference on Film Propaganda, Letter signed by J.S. Middleton, September 1936, filed in Labour party Minutes.

48 EP Microform Collection, Sheffield Trades and Labour Council Delegate Minutes, 26 May 1936; Cambridge Trades Council and Labour party Executive Minutes, 19 April 1937; South Shields Labour party Minutes, 7 June 1938.

49 P. Swann, 'The British Documentary Movement, 1926–1946', unpublished PhD thesis, University of Leeds, 1979, p. 7. *Labour*, February 1936.

50 LPA, Labour party Finance and General Purposes Sub-Committee Minutes, 2 October 1935. Rotha's speech was published as a pamphlet, *Films and the Labour Party*.

51 LPA, Labour party National Executive Committee Minutes, 1 October 1937.

52 LPA, Labour party Research and Publicity Committee Minutes, 16 April 1936; Finance and General Purposes Committee Minutes, 17 December 1936.

53 See, for example, K. Middlemas, *Politics in Industrial Society: The British Experience of the System Since 1911*, London, Andre Deutsch, 1979. H.A. Clegg, *A History of British Trade Unions since 1889. vol. II: 1911–1933*, Oxford, Clarendon Press, 1985.

54 R.M. Martin, *TUC: The Growth of a Pressure Group 1868–1976*, Oxford, Oxford University Press, 1980, p. 207.

55 H. Pelling, *A Short History of the Labour Party*, London, Macmillan, 1978, pp. 71–88.

56 *The Post*, 4 October 1924. The London and Provincial Classification related to efforts to standardize wage differentials. See A. Clinton, *Post Office Workers: A Trade Union and Social History*, London, Allen & Unwin, 1984.

57 See University of Warwick Modern Records Centre, Records of the Union of Post Office Workers Mss 148.

58 *Labour News* (Llanelly), 14 October 1924, cited in P. Stead, 'The people and the pictures. The British working class and film in the 1930s', in N. Pronay and D.W. Spring (eds), *Propaganda, Politics and Film, 1918–45*, London, Macmillan, 1982, p. 90.

59 *Shop Assistant*, 25 October 1924. It must be added, however, that this comment may have been directly attributable to publicity notices circulated by the UPW itself.

60 B. Hogenkamp, 'Miners' Cinemas in South Wales in the 1920's', *Llafur*, vol. 4, no. 2, 1985, pp. 64–76.

61 B. Hogenkamp, *Film and the Labour Movement in the North East – exhibition purposes*, Trade Films/Northern Film and Television Archive, 1985, pp. 17–27.

62 *Report of the Departmental Committee of Inquiry into the Miners' Welfare Fund*, cmd 4236, London, HMSO, 1932, p. 27.

63 *The Miner*, 1 December 1928.

64 H. Tracey, 'Pictures that Tell a Story: The Talking Film as a New Method of Propaganda', *Railway Review*, 5 October 1928.

65 *The Post*, 8 January 1927.

66 *Daily Herald*, 26 September 1928.

67 TUC Archives, TUC General Council Minutes, 14 May 1925.

68 TUC Archives, TUC General Council Minutes, 24 July 1929.

69 *Daily Herald*, 14 January 1930. *The Record*, January 1930.

70 TUC, *Annual Report*, 1931, p. 123.

71 J.W. Smith, 'Why Not a Workers' Cinema?', AEU, *Monthly Journal*, June 1934.

72 R. Calder, 'We Must Learn to Shoot. . . . The Film as a Powerful Propaganda Medium', *Labour*, October 1936.

73 E.P. Harries, 'The Play's The Thing: A New Departure in T.U.C. Propaganda', *The Journal* (POEU), 18 December 1936.

74 *Summarised Report of the 5th Annual Conference (1934–5) of Representatives of Unions Catering for Women Workers*, 26 January 1935, pp. 19–20.

75 *Report of the 7th Annual Conference of Unions Catering for Women Workers*, 8 May 1937, p. 20.

76 See B. Hogenkamp, 'Making Films with a Purpose: Film-making and the Working Class', in J. Clark et al. (eds), *Culture and Crisis in Britain in the Thirties*, London, Lawrence & Wishart, 1979, pp. 262–5.

77 EP Microform Collection, South Shields Labour party Minutes, 7 and 21 June 1938, 1 and 15 July 1938, 13 January 1939.

78 TUC, *Annual Report*, 1938, p. 100.

79 For further details, see G.D.H. Cole, *A Century of Co-operation*,

London, Allen & Unwin, 1944.

80 P. Redfern, *The New History of the CWS*, London, Dent & CES, 1938, p. 430.

81 *Labour Magazine*, January 1928. *Labour's Northern Voice*, 3 February 1928.

82 Details from the North West Film Archive, Manchester Polytechnic.

83 *Co-operative News*, 20 August 1932.

84 Co-operative Union, *Annual Congress Report*, 1934, pp. 206, 227, 270.

85 Co-operative Union, *Annual Congress Report*, 1936, p. 332.

86 Hogenkamp, *Film and the Labour Movement*, op. cit., p. 15.

87 J. Attfield, *With Light of Knowledge: A Hundred Years of Education in the Royal Arsenal Co-operative Society, 1877–1977*, London, RACS and Journeymen Press, 1981, pp. 49–50, 105.

88 Co-operative Union, *Annual Congress Report*, 1921, p. 49.

89 Co-operative Union, *Annual Congress Report*, 1922, p. 41.

90 Co-operative Union, *Annual Congress Report*, 1932, p. 44; 1933, p. 75.

91 With this in mind even the independent commercial cinemas launched a Film Industries Co-operative Society in December 1931, though it failed largely due to the opposition of the powerful Kinematograph Renters' Society. See *Labour Magazine*, December 1931. R. Low, *Film Making in 1930s Britain*, London, Allen & Unwin, 1985, pp. 5–6.

92 A.S. Graham, 'A Film Plan: Why Not News Reels of Co-operative Events', *The Millgate*, September 1934.

93 F.H.W. Cox, 'A National Co-operative Film Society', *The Millgate*, October 1936.

94 S.E.L. Moir, 'Co-operative Films – When?', *The Millgate*, January 1937.

95 Attfield, op. cit., p. 55.

96 J. Reeves, *The Film and Education*, National Association of Co-operative Education Committees, 1936.

97 For a discussion of the film, see B. Hogenkamp, 'Film and the Workers' Movement in Great Britain, 1929–1939', *Sight and Sound*, vol. 45, no. 2, Spring 1976, p. 75.

98 *Co-operative News*, 3 July 1937. *Daily Worker*, 3 November 1937. Co-operative Union, *Annual Congress Report*, 1937, pp. 460–1.

99 *Co-operative News*, 30 October 1937.

100 Co-operative Union, *Annual Congress Report*, 1939, p. 80.

101 Co-operative party, *Annual Conference Report*, 1937, pp. 85–6.

102 LPA, National Joint Film Committee Report, filed under Labour party Publicity, Research and Local Government Minutes, 22 July 1937.

103 *Ibid.*

104 LPA, National Joint Film Committee Report on a National Film

Service, 24 March 1938, filed under Labour party National Executive Committee Minutes. TUC, *Annual Report*, 1938, pp. 238–9.

105 LPA, National Joint Film Committee Minutes, 4 August 1938; National Joint Film Sub-Committee Minutes, 7 October 1938. See also *Daily Worker*, 1 December 1938. *Reynolds' News*, 11 December 1938.

106 *Rules of the Workers' Film Association Limited*, 1941, p. 1.

107 WFA, *Annual Report*, 1939, p. 3. *The Journal* (POEU), 24 February 1939. *Labour Woman*, June 1939. Labour party, *Annual Conference Report*, 1939, p. 102. EP Microform Collection, South Shields Trades Council Executive Committee Minutes, 24 March 1939.

108 LPA, Labour party National Joint Film Committee Minutes, 21 March 1939; Finance and General Purposes Sub-Committee Minutes, 20 April 1939; National Executive Committee Minutes, 26 April 1939.

109 See WFA, *Annual Report*, 1939. TUC, *Annual Report*, 1940, p. 214.

110 For details of these two films, see *The Times*, 26 September 1939.

111 National Federation of Building Trade Operatives, *Annual Conference Report*, 1940, pp. 105–6.

112 WFA, *Annual Report*, 1940.

113 LPA, CWS to W.W. Henderson, 7 March 1939, filed in Labour party Minutes; National Joint Film Committee Minutes, 16 November 1939. TUC Archives, TUC General Council Minutes, 22 March 1939. Co-operative Union, *Annual Congress Report*, 1940, p. 76.

114 TUC, *Annual Report*, 1940, p. 214.

115 Labour party, *Annual Conference Report*, 1940, p. 49.

116 Hollins, op. cit., *passim*.

117 Hogenkamp, 'Film and the Workers' Movement', op. cit., p. 75. R. Bond, 'Cinema in the Thirties: Documentary Film and the Labour Movement', in Clark, op. cit., p. 254.

118 LPA, Labour party National Executive Committee Minutes, 26 February 1930.

119 LPA, Labour party Finance and General Purposes Sub-Committee Minutes, 21 June 1935; National Executive Committee Minutes, 22 January 1936.

120 EP Microform Collection, Sheffield Trades and Labour Council Executive Committee Minutes, 4 February 1936.

121 J. Symons, *The Thirties: A Dream Revolved*, London, Faber & Faber, 1975. The Labour Executive compiled a lengthy tirade against the 'Communist' Left Book Club, and sponsored a Labour Book Service as a kind of ideological counter. See LPA, Memorandum Concerning the Activities of the Left Book Club, 23 November 1938, filed in Labour party Minutes.

122 Tameside Local History Library, Ashton and District Trades Council Monthly Meeting of Delegates Minutes, 2 March 1937. *Gloucester*

Labour News, April 1938. See also Hogenkamp, 'Miners' Cinemas', op. cit., pp. 71–2.

123 WFA, *Annual Report*, 1939, p. 3. Even during the period of 'Class Against Class' in April 1931, the ex-Labour Cabinet Minister, Sir Charles Trevelyan, opened the first performance of the Communist-inspired Newcastle Workers' Film Society.

124 H. Carter, 'Labour and the Cinema', *The Plebs*, November 1930.

125 T. Greenidge, 'Present-Day Tendencies in the Cinema', *Socialist Review*, March 1930.

126 Swann, op. cit., p. 278.

127 Co-operative Union, *Annual Congress Report*, 1937, p. 461.

128 *News Chronicle*, 24 December 1936.

129 Graham, op. cit., p. 693.

130 *Co-operative News*, 4 December 1937.

131 Co-operative Union, *Annual Congress Report*, 1938, p. 538.

132 *General Council Bulletin*, no. 3, n.d. *The British Worker*, 6 May 1926.

7 The Communist Movement and Film

1 For the inter-war CP, see J. Klugmann, *History of the Communist Party of Great Britain*, 2 vols, London, Lawrence & Wishart, 1969. L.J. Macfarlane, *The British Communist Party. Its Origins and Development until 1929*, London, Macgibbon & Kee, 1966. N. Branson, *History of the Communist Party of Great Britain 1927–1941*, London, Lawrence & Wishart, 1985.

2 W. Gallacher and J.R. Campbell, *Direct Action: An Outline of workshop and social organisation*, London, Pluto, 1972, first published 1919, p. 27.

3 *Report on Organisation presented by the Party Commission to the Annual Conference of the CPGB*, 7 October 1922, p. 61.

4 For further discussion, see A. Showstack Sassoon, *Gramsci's Politics*, London, Croom Helm, 1980.

5 A. Howkins, 'Class Against Class: The Political Culture of the Communist Party of Great Britain, 1930–35', in F. Gloversmith (ed.), *Class, Culture and Social Change: A New View of the 1930s*, Brighton, Harvester, 1980, pp. 245, 254.

6 *Daily Herald*, 16 April 1924.

7 See *Sunday Worker*, 23 September and 14 October 1928. *Workers' Life*, 9 and 16 November 1928; 15 February 1929. *The Worker*, 7 December 1928.

8 *The Times*, 5 April 1929.

9 For the Society's first show, see *Sunday Worker*, 1 November 1925.

10 H. Carter, *The New Spirit in the Cinema*, New York, Arno Press,

1970, first published 1930, pp. 285–91.

11 R. Bond, 'Workers' Films: Past and Future', *Labour Monthly*, January 1976.

12 See M. Seton, *Serge M. Eisenstein*, London, Dobson, 1978, pp. 141–4, 482–5.

13 E. Barnouw, *Documentary. A History of the Non-Fiction Film*, New York, Oxford University Press, 1974, p. 87.

14 *Sunday Worker*, 20 October 1929.

15 *The Worker*, 1 November 1929.

16 R. Bond, 'Cinema in the Thirties: Documentary Film and the Labour Movement', in J. Clark et al. (eds), *Culture and Crisis in Britain in the Thirties*, London, Lawrence & Wishart, 1979, p. 247.

17 *Daily Worker*, 4 February 1930.

18 *Daily Worker*, 15 October 1930.

19 *Daily Worker*, 12 February 1930.

20 *Daily Worker*, 4 February and 14 April 1930.

21 *The Worker*, 22 November 1929.

22 *Daily Worker*, 17 February 1930.

23 *Daily Worker*, 15 May 1931. For further details of the Newcastle Society, founded in March 1931, see B. Hogenkamp, *Film and the Labour Movement in the North East – exhibition purposes*, Trade Films/Northern Film and Television Archive, 1985, pp. 3–6.

24 G.A. Atkinson, 'Propaganda Behind Soviet Film Show', *Daily Telegraph*, 24 February 1931.

25 T. Ryan, '"The New Road To Progress": the Use and Production of Films by the Labour Movement, 1929–39', in J. Curran and V. Porter (eds), *British Cinema History*, London, Weidenfeld & Nicolson, 1983, pp. 123–4.

26 'Benn', 'Why Not a Socialist Newsreel?', *New Leader*, 31 May 1929. For a detailed study of the commercial newsreel, see A. Aldgate, *Cinema and History. British Newsreels and the Spanish Civil War*, London, Scolar Press, 1979.

27 Bond, 'Cinema in the Thirties', op. cit., p. 248.

28 For further details, see P. Marris, 'Politics and "Independent" Film in the Decade of Defeat', in D. Macpherson (ed.), *British Cinema: Traditions of Independence*, London, BFI, 1980, pp. 72–3.
   B. Hogenkamp, 'Workers' Newsreels in the 1920's and 1930's', *Our History*, no. 68, n.d., pp. 12–4.

29 *Daily Worker*, 10 March and 3 May 1930.

30 Hogenkamp, op. cit., p. 13. *The Worker*, 9 May 1931.

31 *The Worker*, 6 June and 8 August 1931. *Daily Worker*, 7 and 29 July 1931.

32 *Daily Worker*, 4 November 1931.

33 *Daily Worker*, 25 and 30 November 1931.

34 *Daily Worker*, 27 January 1932.

35 Ryan, op. cit., p. 115.

36 R. Bond, 'Labour and the Cinema: A reply to Huntley Carter', *The Plebs*, August 1931.

37 *New Red Stage*, September 1932.

38 See R. Bond, 'Acts under the Acts', *Close Up*, April 1930. Idem, 'Dirty Work', *Close Up*, August 1930.

39 *Daily Worker*, 7 December 1931.

40 See *Young Worker*, 17 August 1929. *Sunday Worker*, 4 August 1929. *Daily Worker*, 12 June 1930. *The Worker*, 16 May 1931. Communist party Archives (CPA), George Sinfield Papers, BWSF National Sub-Committee Minutes, 16 November 1928; 13 December 1929. Interestingly, Kino's workers' newsreel of 1934 included several shots of workers' sport.

41 CPA, George Sinfield Papers, BWSF National Sub-Committee Minutes, 14 February 1930.

42 *The Worker*, 13 June 1931.

43 *The Worker*, 16 May 1931.

44 *Daily Worker*, 7 October 1931.

45 *Daily Worker*, 10 April 1934; 8 October and 8 November 1935.

46 Manchester and Salford Film Society, *Twenty One Years: 1930–1951*, Manchester, The Society, n.d., p. 1. There is a file on the Society in the North West Film Archive, Manchester Polytechnic.

47 Working Class Movement Library (WCML), F28 Box 4, Manchester and Salford Workers' Film Society, *Report*, 1930–1.

48 *Daily Worker*, 25 November 1930.

49 A. Williams interviewed by S. Robertson, 19 January 1978, North West Film Archive, Manchester Polytechnic.

50 *Ibid.*

51 Manchester and Salford Workers' Film Society, *Report*, 1930–1. Cf *Daily Worker*, 6 March 1931.

52 *Manchester Guardian*, 26 January 1931.

53 *Manchester Guardian*, 20 April 1931. Interestingly enough, Alistair Cooke, who in later years was to become one of the nation's most well-known journalists, was a member of the Society.

54 Manchester and Salford Film Society, op. cit., pp. 7–8.

55 WCML, F27 Box 6, Hyde Socialist Church, *Lecture Syllabus 1932–33*, p. 12.

56 Details from the *Kinematograph Year Book*, 1935, p. 522. Manchester and Salford Workers' Film Society, *Prospectus 1936–37*.

57 *Red Stage*, April-May 1932. *Manchester Guardian*, 10 April 1933.

58 WCML, F28 Box 4, Manchester and Salford Film Society, *Points from Financial Statements*. Manchester Central Reference Library Theatre Collection, Manchester and Salford Workers' Film Society, *Financial*

Statement, 1934; *Notice of Extra Special Meeting*, 15 September 1935.

59 R. Cordwell, interviewed by S. Robertson, 21 July 1977, North West Film Archive, Manchester Polytechnic. *Manchester Guardian*, 4 February 1936.

60 Manchester and Salford Film Society, op. cit., p. 4.

61 R. and E. Frow, *The Communist Party in Manchester 1920–1926*, Manchester, North West Group of the CP, n.d.

62 Williams interview, op. cit.

63 *Manchester Guardian*, 3 May 1937.

64 M. Jenkins, interview with the author, 7 September 1981.

65 *Manchester Guardian*, 2 March 1931.

66 *Manchester Guardian*, 7 May 1937. Cf B. Hogenkamp, *Deadly Parallels: Film and the Left in Britain 1929–1939*, London, Lawrence & Wishart, 1986, pp. 53–66.

67 *Daily Worker*, 3 August 1933.

68 Marris, op. cit., pp. 84–5.

69 *Daily Worker*, 17 December 1932.

70 Cited in T. Dennett, 'England: The (Workers') Film and Photo League', in T. Dennett and J. Spence (eds), *Photography/Politics: One*, London, Photography Workshop, 1979, p. 103. See also Hogenkamp, *Deadly Parallels*, op. cit., pp. 116–35, 159–65, 203–4.

71 Ryan, op. cit., p. 116. See also Hogenkamp, *Deadly Parallels*, op. cit., ch. 6.

72 *Daily Worker*, 27 April 1936. Cf Ryan, op. cit., pp. 124–5.

73 WCML, F52 Box 1, *Kino Presents*, n.d.

74 See *Reynolds' News*, 3 October 1937.

75 Bond, 'Cinema in the Thirties', op. cit., p. 249. Hogenkamp, 'Workers' Newsreels', op. cit., p. 19.

76 *The Times*, 20 April 1939. For a discussion of the film, see B. Hogenkamp, 'Film and the Workers' Movement in Britain, 1929–39', *Sight and Sound*, vol. 45, 1976, p. 76.

77 See E. Trory, *Between the Wars: Recollections of a Communist Organiser*, Brighton, Crabtree Press, 1974, *passim*.

78 V. Wegg-Prosser, 'The Archive of the Film and Photo League', *Sight and Sound*, vol. 46, 1977, p. 246.

79 *Daily Worker*, 27 April 1936. *Kino News*, Spring 1936.

80 Bond, 'Workers Films: Past and Future', op. cit., p. 29. EP Microform Collection, Colne Valley Divisional Labour party Executive Committee Minutes, 9 February 1935.

81 F. Jackson, 'A People's Cinema Grows', *Daily Worker*, 9 August 1938.

82 *New Leader*, 27 September 1935. *Daily Worker*, 8 October 1935.

83 *Left Film Front*, July 1937.

84 For discussion of Unity Theatre, see for example, M. Page, 'The Early Years at Unity', *Theatre Quarterly*, vol. 1, 1971, pp. 60–6. J. Clark,

'Agitprop and Unity Theatre: Socialist Theatre in the Thirties', in Clark, op. cit., pp. 224–35. R. Travis, 'The Unity Theatre of Great Britain 1936–1946: A Decade of Production', unpublished MA thesis, University of Southern Illinois, 1968 – there is a copy of this in the Marx Memorial Library.

85 *Left Review*, November 1936; September 1937.

86 *Left Review*, March 1938.

87 Aldgate, op. cit., p. 50.

88 J. Lewis, *The Left Book Club: An Historical Record*, London, Victor Gollancz, 1970, pp. 28, 66.

89 *Left News*, February 1938.

90 *Daily Worker*, 9 August 1938. For further details of this widely publicized and exhibited film, see *Daily Worker*, 28 December 1936. *New Leader*, 1 January 1937. *Challenge*, 2 January 1937. *Tribune*, 15 January 1937. *World Film News*, January 1937.

91 *Daily Worker*, 23 January 1937.

92 *Report of the Central Committee to the 14th National Congress of the CPGB*, 1937, p. 18.

93 K. Zygulski, 'Popular Culture and Socialism', *Cultures*, vol. 1, no. 2, 1973, p. 104.

94 I. MacDougall (ed.), *Militant Miners: Recollections of John McArthur, Buckhaven; and letters, 1924–26, of David Proudfoot, Methil, to G. Allen Hutt*, Edinburgh, Polygon Books, 1981, p. 141.

95 *Ibid.*, p. 195.

96 The best treatment is S. Macintyre, *A Proletarian Science: Marxism in Britain 1917–1933*, Cambridge, Cambridge University Press, 1980, pp. 66–90.

97 'The Workers' Theatre Movement: an interview with Philip Poole by Jon Clark and David Margolies', *Red Letters*, no. 10, 1980, p. 9. M. Henery, 'The Y.C.L. and the 1930s', *Scottish Marxist*, no. 21, 1981, p. 18. H. Goorney, *The Theatre Workshop Story*, London, Eyre Methuen, 1981, p. 10.

98 MacDougall, op. cit., p. 307.

99 Ryan, op. cit., p. 113.

100 *Daily Worker*, 31 March 1930; 7 December 1931. *Salford City Reporter*, 30 January 1931. *The Worker*, 9 May 1931.

101 Bond, 'Workers' Films: Past and Future', op. cit., p. 28.

102 H. Carter, 'Labour and the Cinema', *The Plebs*, November 1930. It should be noted that Carter was rather critical of the FWFS and the MSFG.

103 J. Coombes, 'British Intellectuals and the Popular Front', in Glover-smith, op. cit., pp. 76–7.

104 *Kino Presents*, op. cit.

105 D. Allen, '"Culture" and the Scottish Labour Movement', *Scottish Labour History Society Journal*, no. 14, May 1980, p. 34.

Conclusion

1 J. Richards, *The Age of the Dream Palace: Cinema and Society in Britain 1930–1939*, London, Routledge & Kegan Paul, 1984, p. 323.
2 R. Bond, 'Cinema in the Thirties: Documentary Film and the Labour Movement', in J. Clark et al. (eds), *Culture and Crisis in Britain in the Thirties*, London, Lawrence & Wishart, 1979, p. 255.

Select Bibliography

This bibliography is composed of material used in this study.

Archives

*Broadcasting and Entertainment Trades Alliance Archives (BETA),
London*, National Association of Theatrical Employees: Committee
Minute Books; Correspondence; Journals; Leaflets.
Communist Party Archives, London, George Sinfield Papers.
EP Microform Collection, The development of the Labour party at local
level.
Greater London Record Office, London County Council: Minutes of
Proceedings.
Labour Party Archives, London, Labour party: Committee Minutes and
related papers.
London School of Economics Library, Beatrice Webb Diaries.
North West Film Archive, Manchester Polytechnic, File on Manchester and
Salford Workers' Film Society; taped interviews.
Public Record Office (PRO) London, Board of Trade, Cabinet Office, Home
Office and Ministry of Labour Papers.
Stockport Public Library Archives Department, Stockport Labour
Fellowship: Minutes.
Tameside Local History Library, Ashton and District Trades Council:
Minutes.
Trades Union Congress (TUC) Archives, London, TUC General Council:
Minutes.
University of Warwick Modern Records Centre (MRC), Federation of
British Industries: Records; Union of Post Office Workers: Records.
Working Class Movement Library, Manchester, Manchester and Salford
Workers' Film Society: Records; Numerous Labour Records.

Official Publications

Board of Trade, *Minutes of Evidence Taken Before the Departmental
Committee on Cinematograph Films*, London, HMSO, 1936.

Census of England and Wales 1931, London, HMSO, 1934.
Census of Production 1935, London, HMSO, 1940.
Hansard (Commons).
Minutes of Evidence Taken Before the Committee on Holidays with Pay,
    1937–8, London, HMSO.
*Minutes of Evidence Taken Before the Royal Commission on Licensing
    (England and Wales)*, 1930–32, London, HMSO.
*Report of a Committee appointed by the Board of Trade to consider the
    Position of British Films*, cmd. 5320, London, HMSO, 1936.
*Report of the Departmental Committee of Inquiry into the Miners' Welfare
    Fund*, cmd. 4236, London, HMSO, 1932.

Newspapers, Journals and Reports

ACT, *Annual Report*
AEU *Monthly Journal*
The *Amusement Workers' News*
Ashton-Under-Lyne Reporter
The *Bioscope*
The *Blackshirt*
The *British Worker*
Challenge
The *Cine-Technician*
Close-Up
Communist Party, *Reports*
The *Co-operative News*
Co-operative Party, *Annual Conference Report*
Co-operative Union, *Annual Congress Report*
Cotton Factory Times
Daily Express
Daily Herald
Daily News
Daily Telegraph
Daily Worker
The Economist
Electrical Trades Journal
The *Era*
Financial News
General Council Circular
Gloucester Labour News
Hyde Reporter
ILP, *Annual Conference Report*
Industrial Welfare

International Labour Review
The *Journal*
The *Kinematograph Year Book*
Kino News
Labour
The *Labour Magazine*
Labour Monthly
Labour Party, *Annual Conference Report*
The *Labour Pioneer*
The *Labour Woman*
Labour Year Book
Labour's Northern Voice
Leeds Weekly Citizen
Left Film Front
Left Review
The *Listener*
Manchester Evening News
Manchester Guardian
The *Millgate*
The *Miner*
Ministry of Labour Gazette
The *Monthly Circular of the Labour Research Department*
Morning Post
The *Musicians Journal*
National Federation of Building Trade Operatives, *Annual Conference
    Report*
NATKE, *Annual Report*
The *New Leader*
New Red Stage
The *New Statesman and Nation*
News Chronicle
Oldham Chronicle
Oldham Evening Chronicle
Oldham Labour Gazette
The *Plebs*
The *Post*
The *Railway Review*
The *Record*
Red Letters
Red Stage
Reynolds' News
Russia To-day
Salford City Reporter
Scottish Co-operator

Scottish Marxist
Scottish TUC, *Annual Report*
The *Shop Assistant*
Socialist Review
Sunday Worker
The Times
Town Crier
Tribune
TUC, *Annual Report*
The *Worker*
Workers' Film Association, *Annual Report*
Workers' Life
World Film News
Young Worker

Books and Articles

ACTT, *Action: Fifty Years in the Life of a Union*, London, Pear
   Publications, 1983.
Aldcroft, D.H. *The British Economy. volume 1 The Years of Turmoil
   1920–1951*, Brighton, Wheatsheaf, 1986.
Aldcroft, D.H. *The Inter-War Economy: Britain 1919–1939*, London,
   Batsford, 1970.
Aldgate, A. *Cinema and History: British Newsreels and the Spanish Civil
   War*, London, Scolar Press, 1979.
Aldgate, T. 'Comedy, Class and Containment: The British Domestic
   Cinema of the 1930s', in J. Curran and V. Porter (eds), *British Cinema
   History*, London, Weidenfield & Nicolson, 1983, pp. 257–71.
Aldgate, T. 'The British Cinema in the 1930s', in *The Historical
   Development of Popular Culture in Britain 2*, Milton Keynes, Open
   University, 1981.
Allen, D. '"Culture" and the Scottish Labour Movement', *Scottish Labour
   History Society Journal*, no. 14, 1980, pp. 30–9.
Althusser, L. 'Ideology and Ideological State Apparatuses (Notes towards
   an Investigation)', in *Lenin and Philosophy and other Essays*, London,
   New Left Books, 1971, pp. 121–73.
Attfield, J. *With Light of Knowledge: A Hundred Years of Education in the
   Royal Arsenal Co-operative Society, 1877–1977*, London, RACS and
   Journeyman Press, 1981.
Balcon, M. 'The Film Industry', in H. Schofield (ed.), *The Book of British
   Industries*, London, Denis Archer, 1933, pp. 151–7.
Barnouw, E. *Documentary. A History of the Non-Fiction Film*, New York,
   Oxford University Press, 1974.

Barr, C. *Ealing Studios*, London, Cameron & Tayleur, 1977.

Barratt Brown, A. *The Machine and the Worker*, London, Nicolson & Watson, 1934.

Barsam, R.M. *Nonfiction Film*, London, Allen & Unwin, 1974.

Benewick, R. *The Fascist Movement in Britain*, London, Allen Lane, 1972.

Bergonzi, B. *Reading the Thirties: Texts and Contexts*, London, Macmillan, 1978.

Betts, E. *The Film Business: A History of British Cinema 1896–1972*, London, Allen & Unwin, 1973.

Bigsby, C.W.E. 'The Politics of Popular Culture', *Cultures*, vol. 1, no. 2, 1973, pp. 15–35.

Bond, R. 'Cinema in the Thirties: Documentary Film and the Labour Movement', in J. Clark *et al.* (eds), *Culture and Crisis in Britain in the Thirties*, London, Lawrence & Wishart, 1979, pp. 241–56.

Booth, A. 'Essays in Bibliography: The Labour Party and Economics Between the Wars', *Bulletin of the Society for the Study of Labour History*, no. 47, 1983, pp. 36–42.

Booth A. and Pack, M. *Employment, Capital and Economic Policy: Great Britain 1918–1939*, Oxford, Basil Blackwell, 1985.

Bourchier, A. *Art and Culture in Relation to Socialism*, London, ILP Publications, 1926.

Branson, N. *History of the Communist Party of Great Britain 1927–1941*, London, Lawrence & Wishart, 1985.

Braverman, H. *Labor and Monopoly Capital*, New York, Monthly Review Press, 1974.

Britain, I. *Fabianism and Culture: A Study in British Socialism and the arts c. 1884–1918*, Cambridge, Cambridge University Press, 1982.

Brockway, A.F. *Hungry England*, London, Gollancz, 1932.

Brown, K.D. *The English Labour Movement 1700–1951*, Dublin, Gill & Macmillan, 1982.

Burgess, K. *The Challenge of Labour*, London, Croom Helm, 1980.

Burns, C.D. *Leisure in the Modern World*, London, Allen & Unwin, 1932.

Burns, R. and van der Will, W. 'Working-Class Organisation and the Importance of Cultural Struggle: A critique of James Wickham', *Capital and Class*, vol. 10, 1980, pp. 166–81.

Buscombe, E. 'Bread and Circuses: Economics and the Cinema', in P. Mellencamp and P. Rosen (eds), *Cinema Histories Cinema Practices*, Los Angeles, University Publications of America, 1984, pp. 3–16.

Carder, G.H. *The Man in the Box: Memoirs of a Cinema Projectionist*, Cornwall, United Writers, 1984.

Carter, H. *The New Spirit in the Cinema*, New York, Arno Press, 1970, first published 1930.

Chanan, M. 'The Emergence of an Industry', in J. Curran and V. Porter (eds), *British Cinema History*, London, Weidenfeld & Nicolson, 1983, pp. 39–58.

Chanan, M. *The Dream That Kicks: The Prehistory and Early Years of Cinema in Britain*, London, Routledge & Kegan Paul, 1980.

Chanan, M. *Labour Power in the British Film Industry*, London, BFI, 1976.

Chapman, A.L. and Knight, R. *Wages and Salaries in the United Kingdom 1920–1938*, Cambridge, Cambridge University Press, 1953.

Clark, J. 'Agitprop and Unity Theatre: Socialist Theatre in the Thirties', in Clark J. *et al.* (eds), *Culture and Crisis in Britain in the Thirties*, London, Lawrence & Wishart, 1979, pp. 219–35.

Clarke J. and Critcher, C. *The Devil Makes Work: Leisure in Capitalist Britain*, London, Macmillan, 1985.

Clegg, H.A. *A History of British Trade Unions since 1889 vol. II: 1911–1933*, Oxford, Oxford University Press, 1985.

Clegg, H.A. 'Employers', in A. Flanders and H.A. Clegg (eds), *The System of Industrial Relations in Great Britain: Its History, Law and Institutions*, Oxford, Basil Blackwell, 1954, pp. 197–251.

Clegg, H.A. 'Some Consequences of the General Strike', *Transactions of the Manchester Statistical Society*, 1953–4.

Clinton, A. *Post Office Workers: A Trade Union and Social History*, London, Allen & Unwin, 1984.

Clinton, A. *The Trade Union Rank and File: Trades Councils in Britain 1900–40*, Manchester, Manchester University Press, 1977.

Cole, G.D.H. *History of the Labour Party from 1914*, London, Routledge & Kegan Paul, 1948.

Cole, G.D.H. *A Century of Co-operation*, London, Allen & Unwin, 1944.

Coombes, J. 'British Intellectuals and the Popular Front', in F. Gloversmith (ed.), *Class, Culture and Social Change: A New View of the 1930s*, Brighton, Harvester, 1980, pp. 70–100.

Corrigan, P. 'Film Entertainment as Ideology and Pleasure: A Preliminary Approach to a History of Audiences', in J. Curran and V. Porter (eds), *British Cinema History*, London, Weidenfeld & Nicolson, 1983, pp. 24–35.

Cowell, F.R. *Culture: In Private and Public Life*, London, Thames & Hudson, 1959.

Cronin, J.E. 'Coping with Labour, 1918–1926', in J.E. Cronin and J. Schneer (eds), *Social Conflict and the Political Order in Modern Britain*, London, Croom Helm, 1982, pp. 113–45.

Cronin, J.E. *Labour and Society in Britain 1918–1979*, London, Batsford, 1984.

Dennett, T. 'England: The (Workers') Film and Photo League', in T. Dennett and J. Spence (eds), *Photography/Politics: One*, London, Photography Workshop, 1979, pp. 100–17.

Dickinson, M. and Street, S. *Cinema and State: The Film Industry and the*

British Government 1927–84, London, BFI, 1985.

Durbin, E. *New Jerusalems, The Labour Party and the Economics of Democratic Socialism*, London, Routledge & Kegan Paul, 1985.

Ehrlich, C. *The Music Profession in Britain Since the Eighteenth Century. A Social History*, Oxford, Clarendon Press, 1985.

ETU, *The Story of the ETU: The Official history of the Electrical Trades Union*, Bromley, ETU, 1952.

Evans, R.J. 'Introduction: The Sociological Interpretation of German Labour History', in R.J. Evans (ed.), *The German Working Class 1888–1933*, London, Croom Helm, 1982, pp. 15–53.

Field, S. *The First Thirty Years – a record of the first thirty years of the NATKE*, Glasgow, Civic Press, 1973.

Frow, R. and E. *The Communist Party in Manchester 1920–1926*, Manchester, North West Group of the CP, n.d.

Gallacher, W. and Campbell, J.R. *Direct Action: An Outline of Workshop and Social Organisation*, London, Pluto, 1972, first published 1919.

Goorney, H. *The Theatre Workshop Story*, London, Methuen, 1981.

Gosling, H. *Up and Down Stream*, London, Methuen, 1927.

Gramsci, A. 'Socialism and Culture', in Q. Hoare (ed.), *Antonio Gramsci, Selections from Political Writings (1910–1920)*, London, Lawrence & Wishart, 1977, pp. 10–3.

Hall, S. 'Notes on Deconstructing the Popular', in R. Samuel (ed.), *People's History and Socialist Theory*, London, Routledge & Kegan Paul, 1981, pp. 227–39.

Halliwell, L. *Seats in all Parts: Half a Lifetime at the Movies*, London, Granada, 1985.

Hammond, J.L. *The Growth of Common Enjoyment*, London, Oxford University Press, 1933.

Harris, C. *The Use of Leisure in Bethnal Green: A Survey of Social Conditions in the Borough 1925 to 1926*, London, Lindsey Press, 1927.

Harris, J.S. *Government Patronage of the Arts in Great Britain*, Chicago, University of Chicago Press, 1970.

Harrison, B. 'Remembering the Sabbath Day', *Times Literary Supplement*, 26 December 1980.

Hartog, S. 'State Protection of a Beleaguered Industry', in J. Curran and V. Porter (eds), *British Cinema History*, London, Weidenfeld & Nicolson, 1983, pp. 59–73.

Hicks, G. *Give New Life and Purpose to the Labour Clubs!*, London, Federation of Trade Union, Labour, Socialist, and Co-operative Clubs, 1928.

Hoare, Q. and Nowell Smith G. (eds), *Selections from the Prison Notebooks of Antonio Gramsci*, London, Lawrence & Wishart, 1971.

Hobsbawm, E. 'The Formation of British Working-Class Culture', in *Worlds of Labour: Further Studies in the History of Labour*, London,

Weidenfeld & Nicolson, 1984, pp. 176–93.

Hobsbawm, E. *Industry and Empire*, London, Pelican, 1972.

Hogenkamp, B. *Deadly Parallels: Film and the Left in Britain 1929–1939*, London, Lawrence & Wishart, 1986.

Hogenkamp, B. *Film and the Labour Movement in the North East – exhibition purposes*, Trade Films/Northern Film and Television Archive, 1985.

Hogenkamp, B. 'Miners' Cinemas in South Wales in the 1920's and 1930's', *Llafur*, vol. 4, no. 2, 1985, pp. 64–76.

Hogenkamp, B. 'Making Films with a Purpose: Film-making and the Working Class', in J. Clark et al. (eds), *Culture and Crisis in Britain in the Thirties*, London, Lawrence & Wishart, 1979, pp. 257–69.

Hogenkamp, B. 'Film and the Workers' Movement in Great Britain, 1929–1939', *Sight and Sound*, vol. 45, no. 2, 1976, pp. 68–76.

Hogenkamp, B. 'Workers' Newsreels of the 1920's and 1930's', *Our History*, no. 68, n.d.

Hoggart, R. *The Uses of Literacy*, Harmondsworth, Penguin, 1977.

Hollins, T.J. 'The Conservative Party and Film Propaganda between the Wars', *English Historical Review*, vol. 96, no. 379, 1981, pp. 359–69.

Howell, D. *British Social Democracy: A Study in Development and Decay*, London, Croom Helm, 1980.

Howkins, A. 'Leisure in the Inter-War Years: an auto-critique', in A. Tomlinson (ed.), *Leisure and Social Control*, Brighton, Brighton Polytechnic, 1981.

Howkins, A. 'Class Against Class: The Political Culture of the Communist Party of Great Britain 1930–35', in F. Gloversmith (ed.), *Class, Culture and Social Change: A New View of the 1930s*, Brighton, Harvester, 1980, pp. 240–57.

Howkins A. and Saville, J. 'The 1930s: A revisionist history', *Socialist Register* 1979, pp. 274–84.

Hutt, A. *The Condition of the Working Class in Britain*, London, Martin Lawrence, 1933.

Joad, C.E.M. *Diogenes or The Future of Leisure*, London, Kegan Paul, Trench and Trubner, n.d.

Joll, J. *Gramsci*, London, Pluto, 1977.

Jones D.C. (ed.), *The Social Survey of Merseyside*, vol. 3, Liverpool, Liverpool University Press, 1934.

Jones, G.S. *Languages of Class: Studies in English Working Class History 1832–1982*, Cambridge, Cambridge University Press, 1983.

Jones, J. *My Lively Life*, London, John Long, 1929.

Jones, S.G. 'Trade Union Policy Between the Wars: The Case of Holidays with Pay in Britain', *International Review of Social History*, vol. 31, part 1, 1986, pp. 40–67.

Jones, S.G. *Workers at Play: A Social and Economic History of Leisure*

1918–1939, London, Routledge & Kegan Paul, 1986.

Jones, S.G. 'Sport, Politics and the Labour Movement: The British Workers' Sports Federation, 1923–1935', *British Journal of Sports History*, vol. 2, no. 2, 1985, pp. 154–78.

Klingender F.D. and Legg, S. *Money Behind the Screen*, London, Lawrence & Wishart, 1937.

Klugmann, J. *History of the Communist Party of Great Britain*, 2 vols, London, Lawrence & Wishart, 1969.

Leavis, F.R. 'Mass Civilisation and Minority Culture', in *For Continuity*, Cambridge, Minority Press, 1933, pp. 13–46.

Lewis, J. *The Left Book Club: An Historical Record*, London, Victor Gollancz, 1970.

Littler, C.R. *The Development of the Labour Process in Capitalist Societies*, London, Heinemann, 1982.

Low, R. *The History of the British Film*, 7 vols, London, Allen & Unwin, 1948–85.

Lowerson, J. 'Sport and the Victorian Sunday: The Beginnings of Middle-Class Apostasy', *British Journal of Sports History*, vol. 1, no. 2, 1984, pp. 202–20.

Lowerson, J. 'Scottish Croquet: The English Golf Boom', 1880–1914, *History Today*, no. 33, 1983.

Lowerson, J. 'Joint stock companies, capital formation and suburban leisure in England, 1880–1914', in Vamplew W. (ed.), *The Economic History of Leisure*, papers presented at the Eighth International Economic History Congress, Budapest, 1982, pp. 61–71.

Lyman, R. 'The British Labour Party: The Conflict between Socialist Ideals and Practical Politics between the Wars', *Journal of British Studies*, vol. 5, no. 2, 1965, pp. 140–52.

McDonnell K. and Robins, K. 'Marxist Cultural Theory: the Althusserian Smokescreen', in Clarke S. et al. *One Dimensional Marxism: Althusser and the Politics of Culture*, London, Allison & Busby, 1980.

MacDougall I. (ed.), *Militant Miners: Recollections of John McArthur, Buckhaven; and letters, 1924–26, of David Proudfoot, Methil, to Allen Hutt, G.* Edinburgh, Polygon Books, 1981.

Macfarlane, L.J. *The British Communist Party. Its Origins and Development Until 1929*, London, Macgibbon & Kee, 1966.

Macintyre, S. *A Proletarian Science: Marxism in Britain 1917–1933*, Cambridge, Cambridge University Press, 1980.

Macintyre, S. 'British Labour, Marxism and Working Class Apathy in the Nineteen Twenties', *Historical Journal*, vol. 20, no. 2, 1977, pp. 479–96.

Mackerness, E. D. *A Social History of English Music*, London, Routledge & Kegan Paul, 1964.

Manchester and Salford Film Society, *Twenty One Years: 1930–1951*, Manchester, The Society, n.d.

Marcuse, H. *One-Dimensional Man*, London, Routledge & Kegan Paul, 1964.

Marris, P. 'Politics and "Independent Film", in the Decade of Defeat', in Macpherson D. (ed.), *British Cinema: Traditions of Independence*, London, BFI, 1980, pp. 70–95.

Marsh A. and Ryan, V. *Historical Directory of Trade Unions, vol. 1 Non-manual unions*, Farnborough, Gower, 1980.

Martin, R.M. *TUC: The Growth of a Pressure Group 1868–1976*, Oxford, Oxford University Press, 1980.

Marwick, A. 'The Labour Party and the Welfare State in Britain 1900–48', *American Historical Review*, vol. 73, no. 2, 1967–68, pp. 380–403.

Marx K. and Engels, F. *Manifesto of the Communist Party*, Moscow, Progress Publishers, 1977, first published 1848.

Mayer, J.P. *British Cinema and their Audiences*, London, Dobson, 1948.

Mayor, S. *The Churches and the Labour Movement*, London, Independent Press, 1967.

Middlemas, K. *Politics in Industrial Society: The British Experience of the System Since 1911*, London, Andre Deutsch, 1979.

Middleton, R. *Towards the Managed Economy: Keynes, the Treasury and the Fiscal Policy Debate of the 1930s*, London, Methuen, 1985.

Minney, R.J. *Puffin Asquith: The Biography of the Honourable Anthony Asquith. Aristocrat, Aesthete, Prime Minister's Son and Brilliant Film Maker*, London, Leslie Frewin, 1973.

Moorehead, C. *Sidney Bernstein: A Biography*, London, Cape, 1983.

Mowat, C.L. *Britain Between the Wars 1918–1940*, London, Methuen, 1955.

Murphy, R. 'Coming of Sound to the Cinema in Britain', *Historical Journal of Film, Radio and Television*, vol. 4, no. 2, 1984, pp. 143–60.

Murphy, R. 'A Brief Studio History', in S. Aspinall and R. Murphy (eds), *Gainsborough Melodrama*, London, BFI, 1983, pp. 3–13.

Murphy, R. 'Fantasy Worlds: British Cinemas Between the Wars', *Screen*, vol. 26, no. 1, 1985, pp. 10–20.

Orwell, G. *The Road to Wigan Pier*, Harmondsworth, Penguin, 1979, first published 1937.

Page, M. 'The Early Years at Unity', *Theatre Quarterley*, vol. 1, 1971, pp. 60–6.

Paul, E. and C. *Proletcult (Proletarian Culture)*, London, Leonard Parsons, 1921.

Peden, G.C. *British Economic and Social Policy: Lloyd George to Margaret Thatcher*, Oxford, Philip Allan, 1985.

Pelling, H. *A Short History of the Labour Party*, London, Macmillan, 1978.

Perry, G. *The Great British Picture Show*, London, Pavilion, 1985.

Perry, G. *Forever Ealing, A Celebration of the Great British Film Studio*, London, Pavilion, 1981.

Phillips, G.A. *The General Strike: The Politics of Industrial Conflict*, London, Weidenfeld & Nicolson, 1976.

Pierson, S. *British Socialists: The Journey from Fantasy to Politics*, Cambridge, Massachusetts, Harvard University Press, 1979.

Pimlott, B. 'The Labour Left', in Cook C. and Taylor I. (eds), *The Labour Party: An Introduction to its History, Structure and Politics*, London, Longman, 1980, pp. 163–88.

Pimlott, B. *Labour and the Left in the 1930s*, Cambridge, Cambridge University Press, 1977.

Pimlott, J.A.R. *Recreations*, Studio Vista, 1968.

Political and Economic Planning, *The British Film Industry*, London, PEP, 1952.

Pollard, S. 'Trade Union reactions to the economic crisis', *Journal of Contemporary History*, vol. 4, no. 4, 1969, pp. 101–15.

Porter, V. *On Cinema*, London, Pluto, 1985.

Priestley, J.B. *English Journey*, Harmondsworth, Penguin, 1979, first published 1934.

Pronay, N. 'The First Reality: Film Censorship in Liberal England', in K.R.M. Short (ed.), *Feature Films as History*, London, Croom Helm, 1981, pp. 113–37.

Pronay, N. 'British Newsreels in the 1930s 1. Audience and Producers', *History*, vol. 56, 1971, pp. 411–8.

Redfern, P. *The New History of the CWS*, London, Dent & CES, 1938.

Reeves, J. *The Film and Education*, National Association of Co-operative Education Committees, 1936.

Richards, J. *The Age of the Dream Palace: Cinema and Society in Britain 1930–1939*, London, Routledge & Kegan Paul, 1984.

Richards, J. 'Boy's Own Empire: Feature Films and Imperialism in the 1930s', in MacKenzie J.M. (ed.), *Imperialism and Popular Culture*, Manchester, Manchester University Press, 1986, pp. 140–64.

Richards, J. 'The Cinema and Cinema-going in Birmingham in the 1930s', in J.K. Walton and J. Walvin (eds), *Leisure in Britain 1780–1939*, Manchester, Manchester University Press, 1983, pp. 31–52.

Richards J. and Aldgate A, *Best of British: Cinema and Society 1930–1970*, Oxford, Basil Blackwell, 1984.

Rickwood, E. *War and Culture: The Decline of Culture Under Capitalism*, London, CP, n.d.

Robertson, J. *The British Board of Film Censors: Film Censorship in Britain, 1896–1950*, London, Croom Helm, 1985.

Rosenzweig, R. *Eight hours for what we will: Workers and leisure in an industrial city, 1870–1920*, Cambridge, Cambridge University Press, 1983.

Rowntree, B.S. *Poverty and Progress: A Second Social Survey of York*, London, Longmans, 1942.

Rowson, S. 'A Statistical Survey of the Cinema Industry in Great Britain in 1934', *Journal of the Royal Statistical Society*, no. 99, 1936, pp. 67–129.

Ryan, T. '"The New Road To Progress": the Use and Production of Films by the Labour Movement, 1929–39', in Curran J. and Porter V. (eds), *British Cinema History*, London, Weidenfeld & Nicolson, 1983 pp. 113–28.

Ryan, T. 'Film and Political Organisations in Britain 1929–39', in Macpherson D. (ed.), *Traditions of Independence: British Cinema in the Thirties*, London, BFI, 1980, pp. 51–69.

Samuel, R., MacColl E. and Cosgrove, S. *Theatres of the Left: Workers' Theatre Movements in Britain and America 1880–1935*, London, Routledge & Kegan Paul, 1985.

Sanderson, M. *From Irving to Olivier: A Social History of the Acting Profession 1880–1983*, London, Athlone Press, 1984.

Seton, M. *Serge M. Eisenstein*, London, Dobson, 1978.

Showstack Sassoon, A. *Gramsci's Politics*, London, Croom Helm, 1980.

Smith H.L. (ed.), *The New Survey of London Life and Labour*, vol. 9, *Life and Leisure*, London, King, P.S. 1935.

Stead, P. 'Essays in Bibliography: British Society and British Films', *Bulletin of the Society for the Study of Labour History*, no. 48, 1984, pp. 72–5.

Stead, P. 'The people and the pictures. The British working class and film in the 1930s', in Pronay N. and Spring D.W. (eds), *Propaganda, Politics and Film, 1918–45*, London, Macmillan, 1982, pp. 77–97.

Stead, P. 'Hollywood's Message for the World: the British response in the nineteen thirties', *Historical Journal of Film, Radio and Television*, vol. 1, no. 1, 1981, pp. 19–32.

Stevenson, J. *Social Conditions in Britain Between the Wars*, Harmondsworth, Penguin, 1977.

Stevenson J. and Cook, C. *The Slump: Society and Politics During the Depression*, London, Quartet, 1979.

Stone R. and Rowe, D.A. *The Measurement of Consumers' Expenditure and Behaviour in the United Kingdom 1920–1938*, vol. II, Cambridge, Cambridge University Press, 1966.

Street, S, 'Alexander Korda, Prudential Assurance and British Film Finance in the 1930s', *Historical Journal of Film, Radio and Television*, vol. 6, no. 2, 1986, pp. 161–79.

Street, S, 'The Hays Office and the Defence of the British Market in the 1930s', *Historical Journal of Film, Radio and Television*, vol. 5, no. 1, 1985, pp. 37–55.

Suthers, R.B. *Let the People Decide – What?: The Labour Programme and the Liquor Problem*, London, reprinted from the *Railway Review*, n.d.

Symons, J. *The Thirties: A Dream Revolved*, London, Faber & Faber, 1975.

Tawney, R.H. 'Introduction', in Boyd W. and Ogilvie V. (eds), *The Challenge of Leisure*, London, New Education Fellowship, 1936, pp. ix-xvi.

Taylor, A.J.P. *English History 1914–1945*, London, Book Club Associates, 1977.

Taylor, P.M. 'Propaganda in International Politics, 1919–1938', in K.R.M. Short (ed.), *Film and Radio Propaganda in World War II*, London, Croom Helm, 1983, pp. 17–47.

Thompson, E.P. 'The Peculiarities of the English', in *The Poverty of Theory*, London, Merlin Press, 1978, pp. 35–91.

Trory, E. *Between the Wars: Recollections of a Communist Organiser*, Brighton, Crabtree Press, 1974.

Vamplew, W. *The Turf: A Social and Economic History of Horse Racing*, London, Allen Lane, 1976.

Walvin, J. *Leisure and Society 1830–1950*, London, Longman, 1978.

Waters, C. 'Social Reformers, Socialists, and the opposition to the commercialisation of leisure in late Victorian England', in W. Vamplew (ed.), *The Economic History of Leisure*, papers presented at the Eighth International Economic History Congress, Budapest, 1982, pp. 106–24.

Webb, S. and B. *The History of Trade Unionism*, London, Longmans, 1920.

Wegg-Prosser, V. 'The Archive of the Film and Photo League', *Sight and Sound*, vol. 46, 1977, pp. 245–7.

Wigley, J. *The Rise and Fall of the Victorian Sunday*, Manchester, Manchester University Press, 1980.

Williams, G. 'From Grand Slam to Great Slump: Economy, Society and Rugby Football in Wales During the Depression', *Welsh History Review*, vol. 11, no. 3, 1983, pp. 338–57.

Williams, R. 'Ideas and the labour movement', *New Socialist*, no. 2, 1981, pp. 28–33.

Williams, R. 'Base and Superstructure in Marxist Cultural Theory', *New Left Review*, no. 82, 1973, pp. 3–16.

Williams, R. 'Minority and popular culture', in Smith, M.A. Parker S. and Smith, C.S. (eds), *Leisure and Society in Britain*, London, Allen Lane, 1973, pp. 22–7.

Willis, T. *Whatever Happened to Tom Mix? The Story of One of My Lives*, London, Cassell, 1970.

Wright, I. 'F.R. Leavis and the Scrutiny Movement and the Crisis', in Clark J. et al. (eds), *Culture and Crisis in Britain in the Thirties*, London, Lawrence & Wishart, 1979, pp. 37–65.

Yeo, E. 'Culture and Constraint in Working-Class Movements, 1830–1850', in E. and S. Yeo (eds), *Popular Culture and Class Conflict 1590–1914: Explorations in the History of Labour and Leisure*, Brighton, Harvester, 1981, pp. 155–86.

Zygulski, K. 'Popular Culture and Socialism', *Cultures*, vol. 1, no. 2, 1973, pp. 101–20.

Unpublished Work

Ford, C. '"One Man's Town?" – the life and struggles of Wilcockson of Farnworth, a remarkable figure in the labour movement who dominated a town', paper presented to the Spring Conference of the North West Labour History Group, 1983.

Hollins, T.J. 'The Presentation of Politics: The Place of Party Publicity, Broadcasting and Film in British Politics, 1918–1939', unpublished PhD thesis, University of Leeds, 1981.

Jackson, W.G. 'An Historical Study of the Provision of Facilities for Play and Recreation in Manchester', unpublished MEd thesis, University of Manchester, 1940.

Jacques, M. 'The Emergence of "Responsible" Trade Unionism, A Study of the "New Direction" in T.U.C. Policy 1926–1935', unpublished PhD thesis, University of Cambridge, 1976.

Jones, S.G. 'The British Labour Movement and Working Class Leisure 1918–1939', unpublished PhD thesis, University of Manchester, 1983.

Power, J. 'Aspects of Working Class Leisure During the Depression Years: Bolton in the 1930s', unpublished MA thesis, University of Warwick, 1980.

Richards, J. 'The Secret Diaries of the Film Censors', Channel 4 television, 31 March 1986.

Shafer, S. '"Enter the Dream House": The British Film Industry and the Working Classes in Depression England, 1929–1939', unpublished PhD thesis, University of Illinois at Urbana-Champaign, 1982.

Street, S. 'Financial and Political Aspects of State Intervention in the British Film Industry, 1925–1937', unpublished DPhil thesis, University of Oxford, 1985.

Swann, P. 'The British Documentary Film Movement, 1926–1946', unpublished PhD thesis, University of Leeds, 1979.

Travis, R. 'The Unity Theatre of Great Britain, 1936–1946: A Decade of Production', unpublished MA thesis, University of Southern Illinois, 1968.

Index